Acclaim for Sweet!

"Here at last is a sweet treatise on the heartbeat ingredient of every baker's kitchen: the sweetener. But not just white or brown sugar—here are the full spectrum of sugars, examined at close range. In prose that is as engaging as it is informative, professional pastry chef and baker extraordinaire Mani Niall corrals over thirty natural—and readily available—sugars, sweeteners, and syrups and matches them up with original and totally creative recipes that sing with flavor."

—Marcy Goldman, pastry chef, author of *A Passion for Baking*, and host of www.betterbaking.com

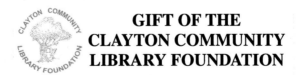

Sweet!

Also by Mani Niall

Sweet & Natural Baking: Sugar-Free, Flavorful Desserts from Mani's Bakery

Covered in Honey: The Amazing Flavors of Varietal Honey

Sweet!

From Agave to Turbinado,
Home Baking with Every Kind of
Natural Sugar and Sweetener

with More Than 100 Recipes

Mani Niall

Da Capo
LIFE

A Member of the Perseus Books Group

Text design by Trish Wilkinson
Set in 12 point Goudy by the Perseus Books Group

Library of Congress Cataloging-in-Publication Data

Niall, Mäni.
    Sweet! : from agave to turbinado, home baking with every
kind of natural sugar and sweetener—with more than 100 recipes /
Mani Niall. — 1st Da Capo Press ed.
        p.   cm.
    Includes bibliographical references and index.
    ISBN 978-1-60094-004-0 (alk. paper)
    1. Baking. 2. Desserts. 3. Sweeteners. 4. Sugar. I. Title.
TX765.N48 2008
641.8'15—dc22   2008033065

First Da Capo Press edition 2008
ISBN: 978-1-60094-004-0

Published by Da Capo Press
A Member of the Perseus Books Group
www.dacapopress.com

Da Capo Press books are available at special discounts for bulk purchases in the United States by corporations, institutions, and other organizations. For more information, please contact the Special Markets Department at the Perseus Books Group, 2300 Chestnut Street, Suite 200, Philadelphia, PA 19103, or call (800) 810-4145, extension 5000, or e-mail special.markets @perseusbooks.com.

1 2 3 4 5 6 7 8 9

This book is dedicated to my mother,
Barbara Case Nial.

Contents

Chapter 7 • Spoon Desserts 157

Chapter 8 • Candy 177

Preface

MORE THAN A few years ago, I spent a summer in England as a private chef for a family with five children. Those kids could eat a lot of cookies, so I did a lot of baking. The family's big Aga oven was on every day, for one or another freshly baked treat. But first, I had to get used to the family referring to cookies by their British name, "biscuits," and brewing a pot of tea every two hours. The next order of business had to do with the cooking ingredients. Rather than using as the primary sweetener in these treats the standard American sweetening agent, granulated white sugar, I had to familiarize myself with a whole new roster of sweeteners—demerara, muscovado, treacle (also called golden syrup), and many others with which I had only slight or, up to that point, no familiarity or first-hand experience.

I very soon discovered that a familiar American cookie recipe, when I made it with a substitute sugar, revealed an entirely different personality. Flavors were deeper, textures were sometimes crumbly, and other times softer or crisper. Some baked goods browned more quickly than I would have liked, but nothing was a total failure. And if I was truly desperate, I could just cover the questionable dessert with whipped cream and turn it into a trifle—a widely beloved English "pudding," or dessert.

After that stint ended and I returned to Los Angeles, I expanded my sugar palate by using more brown sugar, honey, and molasses in an attempt to replicate the British sugars. I was not entirely incorrect to assume that darker color meant richer flavor. But, in those days, sugar choices were limited, even for the most dedicated baker. To obtain golden syrup, for example, one had to fly to London to get a can or persuade visiting British friends to bring some over with them.

Eventually, after various projects as a personal chef and catering events all over Los Angeles, I opened Mäni's Bakery. At its two locations, I concentrated on wholesome baked goods made with all-natural ingredients. We were known for our tasty desserts for people with dietary restrictions, including gluten-free, low-fat, and, of course, sugar-free. This led me to appreciate even more sweeteners, such as concentrated fruit juices, agave syrup, and honey. (My first book, *Sweet & Natural Baking: Sugar-Free, Flavorful Desserts from Mani's Bakery*, features recipes for many of the bakery's most popular treats.)

Meanwhile, the culinary world exploded, and many of the sweeteners I had discovered in Britain finally traveled over the ocean to America. And other sugars from around the world showed up, too—Indian jaggery and Thai palm sugar, South American *panela* and Mexican *piloncillo*, and more. For many years, both in my professional life and home baking, I experimented with these newly arrived sweeteners. In savory foods, I began to notice how sugar played a role in balancing and rounding out flavors. The collective American palate noticed, too, as more and more "sweet and spicy" snacks were produced. Phrases like "glazed" and "sweet-and-sour" became commonplace on restaurant menus. Of the four primary flavors—sweet, sour, bitter, and salty—only the first could be relatively acknowledged as being universally loved. (Some experts believe that there is a fifth flavor, umami, which is more of a flavor enhancer than a taste that can be defined.)

Although I am no longer involved with Mäni's Bakery, I still work in the commerical bakery business, as executive chef for Just Desserts in the San Francisco Bay Area, where we bake thousands of pastries, cakes, cookies, and other sweets every day for retail sale and wholesale distribution. As a professional baker, I must have extensive, hands-on knowledge of the essential role sugar plays in many sweet-oriented recipes. Why is sugar creamed with butter to create the base for so many cakes? How does sugar contribute to the tenderness and color of baked goods? Why is sugar cooked to certain temperatures to create different candies? Can cooks substitute one sweetener for another, and if so, what should they expect?

In this cookbook, I will answer these questions, and many others. Together we will explore the vast range of sweeteners available to the home cook. (I will not address artificial sweeteners, because each main variety and brand, especially when heated, reacts in ways very different from the sugars and other sweeteners I discuss here.) White granulated sugar has long been popular for many reasons—including its versatility, the relative ease of working with it, and its relatively low cost—but in this book, I hope to expose you to new sugars, especially the minimally processed varieties that I love.

A good baker should have more than just one or two sweeteners at his or her disposal. You are likely to have white granulated and brown sugar (either light or dark, but probably not both) in your kitchen. They are a good place to start, but you may be using these sugars only because they are the ones that you were taught to bake with. Now that there are so many options for sweetening, *Sweet!* will help you to expand your knowledge. The richness and moisture of gingerbread can only be acquired when molasses is in the recipe; ethnic cooking tastes all that much more authentic when you use jaggery or *panela* instead of the commonplace brown sugar; your crème brûlée will never be better than when you use turbinado to make its glassy surface.

In addition, I will be sure that you learn where to purchase these sweeteners. Although most are easy to find at your local natural food store and supermarket (a few may require a trip to a specialty food store or ethnic market), I also provide mail-order sources at the end of the book.

We will travel together all over the world to discover new flavors, and not all of them particularily sweet, as sugar can also work as a harmonizer to bring together disparate ingredients. This is a trip that started a couple of millennia ago in New Guinea, moved to Arabia, then the Caribbean, and ends up in your kitchen, where I hope to inspire you to continue the journey with sweeteners, both familiar and new.

Mani Niall
Oakland, California
March, 2008

Sugar and Your Kitchen

SUGAR HAS THE power to transform. The right amount of sugar can balance such sour ingredients as the tart juice in lemonade or vinegar in sweet-and-sour sauce. It can tame the bitterness of cocoa or coffee. It can provide contrast for saltiness—many snacks, from beer nuts to caramel corn, take advantage of this combination.

But sugar really takes off when used specifically in desserts. Sugar solutions can be cooked and manipulated to make candies that are smooth, slightly grainy, or chewy. When mixed with fruit, sugar draws out juices and softens bitter peels. Sugar also is an essential ingredient in jellies, jams, and preserves, as it combines with fruit (and even vegetable) juices to maintain desirable color and texture, and acts as a preservative. In baked goods, sugar not only sweetens and adds bulk to doughs and batters, it is also a tenderizer. As the food bakes, its sugar deepens in flavor and changes color to help it brown. Coarse sugar decorates cookies and tops cupcakes. Confectioners' sugar is often used to make frosting. Add sugar to egg whites and beat them together, and the sugar strengthens the whites so they can inflate with air and eventually become meringue.

Granulated sugar (refined and crystallized sugarcane juice) is the most popular sweetener among home bakers. It is such a workhorse because it often does things that no other sweetener can do as well. But it isn't the only sweetener on the block. Many other plants, including the agave cactus, maple trees, date and coconut palms, and sugar beets (as well as countless blossoms on trees, bushes, cultivated fields, wildflowers, and even weeds as their nectar passes through bees to become honey) all yield sweet juices that are processed into crystallized sugars and liquid syrups. And, unlike granulated sugar, certainly not all of them are refined until they are as white as the driven snow.

When I bake (and I know this is true of my friends who are also professional chefs, whether they specialize in baking or not), I choose the right sweetener for the job, and it may or may not be granulated sugar. If I want a moist, chewy texture, I might add molasses or maple syrup. For deeper, richer flavor, I may experiment with a brown sugar. Or I might use a sugar specific to an ethnic cuisine—*piloncillo* in a Mexican-inspired dish, for example. My selection boils down to which sweetener will taste best and provide the various characteristics that I want for the recipe.

However, the various colors, textures, sources, and flavors (beyond mere sweetness) of the different sweeteners mean that they are not always interchangeable. In this book, the recipes were chosen specifically to show you how certain sugars work. By tasting a traditional chai made with Indian jaggery (a pale brown raw sugar derived from palm tree sap, not the ubiquitous brown cane sugar in Western kitchens), you may think of other ways to bring its earthy flavor into your cooking.

Your kitchen would be a very different place without sugar. Understanding its secrets is one of the signs of a great cook.

A (Short) Explanation of Sugar in Nutrition

What makes sugar—and by association, other foods that supply sweet flavor, such as agave syrup and Sucanat—so versatile? And why is it so pleasurable to eat? What is the difference between sucrose, glucose, and fructose, three sugars that you may find in institutional recipes or listed on ingredient labels? To understand this, one has to take a quick peek into sugar's place in nutrition.

All food is composed of three major nutritional components (often referred to as macronutrients): carbohydrates, protein, and fat. We need these macronutrients in our diet to support various body processes. Among other functions, carbohydrates supply energy. So, obviously our body needs a certain amount of carbs. In fact, they play such an important role that most medical experts say that about 60 percent of our calories (which are units of energy) should come from carbohydrates.

All sugars are carbohydrates—starches and fiber are carbohydrates, too. The presence of sweetness in food is an indicator that it has lots of calories. (I am speaking of sweeteners from natural sources, not artificial sweeteners, which are not addressed in this book.) When you taste something sweet, the sweetness receptors on your tongue set off a pleasurable alarm in your brain, letting your body know that this calorie-rich food will give you the energy you require.

Carbohydrates are so called because of their molecular structure, wherein carbon atoms are attached to groups of hydrogen and oxygen atoms to create chains. Simple carbohydrates (the most basic sugars) are easy for the body to digest, while complex carbohydrates (starches and fiber) take longer for us to process. The chemical formula for the simple sugar, glucose, is $C_6(H_{12}O_6)$. That means six atoms of carbon, twelve atoms of hydrogen, and six of oxygen. As the carbohydrate becomes more complex, the value of the small numbers increases.

There are basically three kinds of sugar: monosaccharides, disaccharides, and polysaccharides (*saccharide* is just another word for "sugar"). Monosaccharides (literally, "one sugar") are also called simple carbohydrates, as they are formed of one sugar molecule. Examples are glucose (the simple sugar that our body prefers for converting food into energy, as it is an important component in blood plasma), fructose (found in fruits and vegetables), and galactose (a factor of mother's milk).

These simple sugar molecules can be linked in pairs to form disaccharides ("two sugars"). Sucrose, otherwise known as white sugar (the very same kitchen workhorse I spoke of before), is formed from a combination of glucose and fructose. Other disaccharides include maltose (which occurs when grains are sprouted, roasted, and ground to create malt) and lactose (made of glucose and galactose, which make milk naturally sweet).

Polysaccharides ("many sugars") are complex carbohydrates. These are the ones with the most numbers in their formulas. Starches and fibers, from whole-grain flour to oats and potatoes to corn, are all complex carbohydrates with many sugars.

A (Brief) History of Sugar

Much like a visualization of the long molecule chains that make up complex carbohydrates, the history of sugar is a complicated series of events. Entire books have been written on the subject, which takes place over many centuries all over the world, from India to the Caribbean to the capitals of Europe. Sugar's social and political history can hardly be called sweet as, for many years, sugar harvesting fueled the African slave trade. It is with an awareness of the more disturbing aspects of sugar's history that many of today's sugar manufacturers are producing sweeteners that are both ecologically viable and produced under guidelines that guarantee a fair wage.

What follows is an overview, not a detailed discussion, and I encourage you to read one of the books in the bibliography for the full picture.

The first sweetener was honey, which nature supplied via wild bees. For eons, outside of eating fruit, honey was the most uncomplicated way for humans to get the sweetness that their bodies craved. Then, probably in what is now New Guinea, around 6000 BCE, people started cultivating sugarcane (*Saccharum officinarum*), a tropical, bamboolike grass that contained an irresistably sweet juice. To get to the juice, the plant's stalk was cut down and the cane was chewed (you may have encountered sugarcane in some modern-day Southeast Asian dishes, such as Vietnamese *chao tom*).

From there, the sugarcane plant traveled to India, where it took to the hot climate. The Indians developed a process to extract, boil, and crystalize sugarcane juice. Sugar established itself in Indian cuisine and culture. It was said that Buddha was born in Gur (today's Bengal), known as "the land of sugar," and *gur* is still used as a word for sugar in Bengalese and other Indian languages. These mounds of hard sugar remained a local product until Persians invaded India in 510 BCE, when King Darius wrote of a new find: "the reed which gives honey without bees." Persians were now the guardians of sugar production, and they closely held these secrets for over nine hundred years.

Control over the sugar industry changed again in 642 CE, when the Arabs invaded Persia. The Arabs traveled far and wide to expand their empire and, in doing so, brought sugar to Spain and North Africa, neither of which had any Western influence to note.

Sugar remained locked in Eastern culture until the Crusades and wasn't mentioned in English until 1099. Until then, honey was Western civilization's only sweetener. (To this day, honey-rich gingerbreads and cookies remain European favorites.) The Crusaders came across the "sweet salt" in their efforts to bring the Holy Land, which was Arab territory, under their control. Sugar crystals were similar to the rare spices that were so important to European cooking and Europe's economy—expensive, and for the rich. As was the case with spices, obtaining them necessitated trade with the Eastern nations. Much of the sugar passed through the markets of Venice, and the Venetian wholesalers were notoriously tough. To help lighten the financial burden, sugarcane crops were established in the warmest European regions, such as Portugal and Spain, and then in their colonies off the African coast. To this day, very sweet desserts are intristic to these areas' cuisines, as sugar was a local product that could be used with relative abandon (not to mention their being part of the Arabic influence in Spain).

Sugar production and trade went through a monumental change with the discovery of the New World and its abundance of warm locales that would support the growth of tropical sugarcane. During his second voyage to Hispaniola (the island that today is Haiti and the Dominican Republic), Christopher Columbus stopped off in the Canary Islands for provisions and acquired sugarcane stalks. These were duly planted back home and the resulting crop flourished.

Sugar was just one reason why the European powers strove to establish colonies in warm regions where it would thrive (the desire for tobacco and cotton, and the quest for gold also played their parts), but it was a very important reason. Sugarcane does not cut, refine, pack, and ship itself, and the industry required workers—by the hundreds of thousands. When the Native Americans proved to be very susceptible to diseases carried by the Europeans, millions of Africans were enslaved and brought to work on sugar plantations.

The New World products created what historians call "the triangle trade." A boat would travel from a European port to Africa, laden with manufactured products to sell. Once the boat was emptied of its goods, African humans were bought as slaves. The boat sailed across the Atlantic to the next stop on the triangle, South and Central America, where the slaves were put to work on sugar plantations. Finally, the boats were loaded again, this time with sugar and other New World goods to close the triangle with a voyage back to Europe (often with a stop in Boston), where those goods were sold to eager buyers.

The Portuguese were the first to establish sugar plantations in the New World, in Brazil. When the Dutch invested in sugar plantations in the Caribbean Islands, sugar (and its by-products, molasses and rum) flowed into Europe. France considered the tiny island of Guadeloupe, which had fallen under British rule, so important to its economy that they traded the whole of Canada for its return. (Voltaire dissed Canada as "a few acres of snow.") Canada wasn't the only colony that was considered of little value to the Old World. When given a choice of where to spend their efforts and money, the Dutch chose the South American island of Suriname over New Amsterdam (now New York).

While Europe clamored for more sugar, the Caribbean, especially San Domingue (today's Haiti), Barbados, and the various islands in the British West Indies, supplied it through the suffering of slaves. Over the years, mechanization improved to the point where less human power was needed, and the British government could afford to abolish slavery in 1838.

The British upper classes were especially enamored of sugar. Most of it was stirred into tea, but when the industrial revolution mechanized sugar production and made sugar less expensive, jams, jellies, and candies could be produced cheaply, and this satisfied the sweet tooth of the masses, rich and poor.

FOR CENTURIES, white sugar was available to home cooks in blocks or cones that tediously needed to be nipped and shaved with special implements to obtain small quantities. Sir Henry Tate, originally a sugar refinery worker, made his fortune by creating and patenting a device that cut blocks of sugar into what was marketed as "Tate's Cube Sugar." (A philanthropic art collector who became a millionaire from his firm's success, he built the Tate Gallery of London and filled it initially with his own collection of contemporary paintings.) Sugar cubes are still available as an elegant teatime alternative to bowls of sugar or single-teaspoon packets, and the tide has turned to make even brown sugar cubes fashionable. (And to think that, as a kid, I thought sugar cubes were only good to build igloos!)

The next revolution in the sweet world took some time to take hold. In 1747, a German chemist isolated sucrose in a sweet white tuber, the sugar beet (*Beta vulgarus*). It took awhile to take hold, but eventually sugar beet factories sprang up in Europe to extract their sweet juice. The home-grown sugar was particularly useful to France during the Napoleonic Wars, when the British embargoed their Caribbean product. Today, beet sugar provides about 30 percent of world production of granulated sugar.

Cane sugar is still king, but public interest in alternative sweeteners, from honey to agave, is strong. Also gaining momentum is the natural sugars movement, with sugars that are grown according to fair trade guidelines or are minimally processed. Now the world of sugar encompasses many varieties of sweeteners available in your local markets, and so you don't have to restrict yourself to white granulated sugar unless you want to.

How Sugarcane Becomes Sugar

Sugarcane is a tropical and subtropical grass that strongly resembles bamboo. The five- to twenty-foot-tall stalks thrive with regular, strong sunlight and abundant water. It is currently grown in over two hundred countries, with Brazil the industry leader. In the United States, it is cultivated in warm states such as Louisiana and Texas. The once-mighty Hawaiian sugar industry has been reduced to a handful of artisan producers, as it lost ground to sugar produced in third-world countries.

The transformation of sugarcane to crystallized sugar occurs in two stages, milling and refining. Milling the sugarcane into raw sugar takes place at the location of the sugarcane plantation. In some cases, the sugar is not processed further and is sold in its raw state, in varying degrees of moistness and crystallization. But to remove impurities and make white granulated sugar and molasses, sugar needs to be refined. For this to be accomplished, the sugar is usually transported to a refinery closer to its sales point—there are sugar refineries all over America, even though very little sugarcane is grown and milled here.

The cane harvest starts with burning the crop to remove leaves and chase vermin, snakes, and other unwanted creature-tenants out of the field. The sucrose-rich canes are so juicy that they are not harmed by the intense heat. Some producers do not burn the crop, as they consider the practice ecologically unsound. They merely chop the stalks down, leaving the residual leaves to act as mulch for the next crop.

The stalks are now harvested by hand or mechanization. It is said that a skilled human worker, using a machete, can chop about a half ton of cane in an hour. On the other hand, a mechanized combine harvests one hundred tons in the same period. In either case, care is taken to cut the stalks just above the roots, leaving them intact, so the cane can grow again for next year's harvest.

The harvested sugarcane must be quickly milled in the next twenty-four hours, or the juices will begin to ferment and decompose from sucrose into its two components, fructose and glucose. The cane is cleaned, washed, and chopped into bits, then makes four passes through a large roller-type mill to extract the juice from the unwanted fiber This pulpy material, called *bagasse*, is not discarded, as it can be burned to fuel the mill or sold as a product that can be processed into a paperlike material to make biodegradable plates and the like. Fresh sugarcane juice, *guarapo*, is a very popular drink in Latin America and is available canned as a soft drink at Latino markets.

The mineral lime is added to the juice to separate the solids and some of the other impurities, leaving behind a sweet liquid. This substance is then boiled in large tanks to evaporate much of its water. The resulting syrup is concentrated under pressure. To get the syrup to crystallize, sugar dust is added to "seed" the syrup. (The small particles of sugar act as a catalyst to attract and encourage the sucrose molecules to harden around it.) Although it has been cooked a number of times, the coarsely crystallized, yellow to pale brown product is called *raw sugar*. Rustic, full-flavored sugars, such as Mexican *piloncillo* and Indian jaggery, belong to this category of sugars. These sugars are usually sold in loaf shapes that must be crumbled or crushed before using. At this stage, sugar contains some of its source's vitamins and minerals.

At the next stage of milling, the raw sugar can be spun in a centrifuge to separate the liquid from the crystalline sugar. The liquid that is thrown off, molasses, is almost as familiar to an American baker as is the sugar itself and in its darker forms is particularly rich in iron, potassium, and magnesium. There are a number of subsequent spinnings, and each time more molasses is extracted. Some sugars are only lightly processed at this stage, to retain various amounts of molasses, such as full-flavored, rich muscovado and demerara sugars.

Cane Sugar Versus Beet Sugar

SUCROSE IS SUCROSE, regardless of its source. When sugarcane juice is refined to the ultimate stage, it is virtually pure sucrose with the barest traces of minerals, vitamins, and impurities. When the extracted juice of the sugar beet is refined, the result is also pure sucrose with those trace ingredients. In theory, they should be identical. However, in cooking applications, the two sugars don't always behave the same way. Beet sugar can be more difficult to melt and has a tendency to foam up in candy making. The infinitesimal amount of trace ingredients may be causing the problems, but no one has yet pinpointed the precise culprit.

It is not required to label the source of the sugar on packaging. Especially in the Midwest where beet sugar production is centered, it may be difficult to find cane sugar. And beet sugar is creeping up on cane sugar, now accounting for 30 percent of world production. So, if it matters to you, look carefully at the ingredients on the label for "pure cane sugar" to be sure that you are buying what you want.

If a pure white, finely crystallized sugar is desired, refining must take place. For this final stage, the sugar is shipped to a refinery, which is very often near the point of final sale. The sugar goes through a number of processes to remove the remaining impurities, such as calcium and magnesium salts, ending up as finely crystallized, pure white sugar. The sugar's vitamins and minerals are removed along with the impurities, and only the sucrose and calories remain, which is why sugar is sometimes referred to as having "empty calories." (However, as sugar is often mixed with other ingredients, the individual cook can return some nutrients back to the food, but more on that later.) To keep the fine crystals from sticking together, they are dried with hot air for several days.

A Compendium of Sweeteners from Agave to Yacón

In case you need to borrow a cup from your neighbor, the word for sugar sounds remarkably similar wherever you go, as they are all derived from the Sanskrit *shakkara:* French *sucre*, Spanish *azúcar*, Danish *sukker*, Turkish *eker*, Italian *zucchero*, and Russian, *sakhar*.

Sugar professionals often define sugarcane-derived sugar by its level of processing and refining—raw or minimally processed sugars are first-stage sugars; brown sugars are second-stage sugars, and refined sugars are third stage. But you won't see these categories on the sugar you buy at the store, and what happens if you want to buy a non-sugarcane-based sweetener? The following glossary lists the sweeteners that you are most likely to find at your supermarkets, natural food stores, and specialty food shops, grouped in categories that the home baker will recognize.

Ethnic Sugars

I start with these sugars because they are the least processed, and virtually raw. They are similar to the ones common in the premechanized era. Sugar would be formed into blocks or cones for shipping, then transported to the final destination country, where it had to be chipped from the block to use. Virtually all cane sugars go through this stage before further refining to the forms of sugar we are more familiar with.

In India, Southeast Asia, and all over Latin America, sugarcane juice is concentrated by a process of evaporation to produce a type of raw sugar, with varying amounts of molasses suspended in the sugar. These are the firm brown sugars that add authentic flavor to Mexican and Asian recipes. They are often sold in solid chunks, cones, or disks, occasionally wrapped in dried banana leaves, and may be so hard that they are grated or crushed before using. Some producers make ground sugar that is much easier to use. Like granulated sugars, their shelf life is indefinite but they are subject to both drying out or absorbing moisture. For best results, store at room temperature in airtight containers for up to two years.

Jaggery. This traditional Indian sugar is cane sugar boiled in large, uncovered vats in the open air by artisan methods, then shaped into golden yellow to dark brown cones. The color, texture, and cone size changes very much from manufacturer to manufacturer. If necessary, grate the jaggery on the large holes of a box grater.

This is the sugar to use in your Indian cooking. It is an essential component of chai, with a full, earthy sweetness to balance the strong spices. It is also used in chutneys and sauces or made into caramels, toffee, and other sweets. If you can't find it, use light brown sugar.

Panela (Also Called Piloncillo, Penuche, and Panocha).   This first-stage sugar is often made on family farms in Mexico and South America. The cones vary in size, although they rarely weigh more than one pound. The smallest ones, which are easiest to handle, are called *panocha*. You will find that these dark brown, hard, squat cones must be grated on the small holes of a box grater. Or, prepare it for cooking the Mexican way, by chipping off chunks, and grinding them in a stone mortar and pestle called a *molcajete*. Well-stocked Latino markets carry pulverized *panela* (*panela en polvo*), which is an excellent time- (and knuckle) saver. Labeling can be confusing because *panela* goes by different names, including *piloncillo* and *penuche* (not to be confused with the brown-sugar-based fudge also called *penuche*), in different Spanish-speaking countries, but if it looks like a dark brown cone of sugar, and starts with a *p*, you have what you want.

Because of its density, *panela* is often melted in hot liquid. It is found in many desserts and sweet sauces and is added to meat marinades to balance sour ingredients. Any of the moist dark brown sugars would be a good substitute.

Chinese Rock Sugar.   This yellow-beige, relatively clear sugar looks like an elementary school science experiment on how to make rock sugar. It is not exactly a raw sugar, as the evaporated cane juice is not formed into a block or loaf but allowed to crystallize around a string. Hard as glass, the chunky crystals must be crushed in a heavy-duty plastic bag, using a hammer, until small enough to measure. Don't worry about getting them so small that they fit into your measuring spoon—you can add more or less to taste.

Rock sugar adds character to Chinese "red cooking," soy sauce–braised dishes that take on a reddish color from the combination of the brown soy sauce and yellowish sugar. Use it in any Chinese recipe that calls for sugar, or substitute turbinado or light brown sugar.

Raw Sugars

Raw sugars are in fact boiled a few times to remove impurities, so the name is a little confusing—if it is cooked, how can it be raw? However, the relatively lesser amount of processing used allows these sugars to retain molasses, which includes the minerals and vitamins that are refined out of white granulated sugar.

Fair Trade Sugar

MANY FOODS (coffee, sugar, and tea, among others) are produced in third-world countries with inexpensive labor, and unfortunately, all too often, the workers do not sufficiently benefit from the profits. Some producers are working under fair trade guidelines, whereby the labor force is paid fairly for its work in an effort to alleviate poverty and improve quality of life. Efforts are also made to keep the product sustainable.

Wholesome Sweeteners is such a company. I love cooking with their third party–certified organic and fair trade sugars, for their high quality and for the company's commitment to their production team. They work with plantations in Costa Rica and Mauritius, but nowhere has there been such a direct and tangible difference in the lives of their team as in the African Republic of Malawi. According to company spokesperson Pauline McKee, "The impact of the quarterly premium they receive from our sugar sales go directly to funding community projects. They now have a freshwater well for both residential and irrigational use, land set aside from cane growing for their own farming, and a health clinic. Working with the Malawians is a joy and an honor, and it really puts life into perspective."

Evaporated Cane Juice and Organic Sugar.   This term *evaporated cane juice* was approved by the Federal Drug Authority to clarify the difference between this sugar and white granulated sugar, which it resembles in appearance and sweetness level. Evaporated cane juice is crystallized sugar, minus the final refining stages, which allows it to retain a small amount of molasses and gives the crystals their light tan color. Most organic sugar

(sugar raised under organic agricultural guidelines without pesticides) is evaporated cane juice, and vice versa. You can substitute evaporated cane juice (or organic sugar) for granulated sugar in your recipes without any changes. It is commonly used in the natural foods industry to manufacture baked goods.

Sucanat.   Because it has its own proprietary manufacturing process, Sucanat (its name created from the words *sugarcane natural*) belongs in its own category, but I include it here because it is the least processed of all sugars. Its proprietary processing method of dehydration and aeration was developed by Dr. Max-Henri Béguin in the 1950s. Sucanat, processed from organic Costa Rican sugarcane, is the least processed of dry sugars, maintaining trace amounts of potassium, calcium, and magnesium and other vitamins and minerals, but that doesn't make it a nutritional superfood.

Sucanat is granular, not crystallized. Sucanat does not dissolve as readily as crystallized sugar, so a butter-Sucanat mixture will stay gritty and the resultant baked good will be speckled in recipes that call for such creaming. This may be a small tradeoff for some bakers. Many sources say that it can be used as a substitute for brown sugar, but Sucanat is much drier, so in most recipes I don't recommend swapping it for brown sugar.

Sucanat lends its molasses-rich flavor to cookies, bars, fruit crisps, and cobblers.

Turbinado.   A light brown sugar with detectably coarse crystals and a light toffee flavor, turbinado is "turbinated" from steaming evaporated cane juice. It is considered a raw sugar, and one brand is named Sugar in the Raw, which is made in Maui and is a vestige of the once-booming Hawaiian sugarcane economy.

Turbinado is versatile and accommodating in all manner of cooking and baking. In butter-based doughs and batters, it creams more smoothly than demerara. But it stays crunchy when sprinkled as a topping for cookies, cobblers, and crisps. For its toffee flavor and ease of melting (its moderate-size crystals melt into larger pools than does granulated sugar), it is the best sugar for topping crème brûlée.

THE HAWAIIAN Commercial & Sugar Company on Maui produces a variety of raw sugars, including turbinado. Their Premium Hawaiian Turbinado is the result of slow boiling, producing a crunchy crystal of deep amber-colored sugar, rich with molasses flavors. Asked about further details about their turbinado, they demurred, referring to such matters as being proprietary secrets.

Annually, about 500,000 tons of bagasse (discarded cane fiber) is used to generate steam for electricity. This supplies all the power necessary to run the plant; the surplus energy provides up to 10 percent of the power for the entire island.

Moist Brown Sugars

In the second stage of sugar processing, a centrifuge is used to remove as much, or as little, molasses as the manufacturer chooses. In brown sugars made by the traditional methods, such as demerara and muscovado, the molasses is left in, and then the sugar is crystallized via dehydration. During this process, the molasses remains intact, as in first-stage sugars, yet these sugars become fairly dry. These brown sugars are less sweet than white sugar, because the molasses is somewhat bitter.

Demerara.   A crunchy, sparkly, caramel-hued crystal sugar, demerara is renowned for its textural and visual qualities. It is named for the Demerara River in today's Guyana, a former British (and Dutch) colony, but most of today's demerara comes from Mauritius, in the Indian Ocean. If you are presented with a sugar bowl in a fine restaurant in Europe, chances are that it will be filled with demerara. Stirred into hot coffee or tea, its caramel flavor is released.

Demerara sugar is ideal for decorating baked goods, as it will not melt in the heat of the oven. It adds a delicious crunch to the surface of muffins, cookies, scones, and other pastries.

Muscovado.   Rich, dark, and aromatic, muscovado sugar is available in both light and dark varieties. This moist, flavorful sugar has a hint of butterscotch. It is also known as Barbados sugar and dark molasses sugar.

Use muscovado sugar whenever you want to upgrade your recipes that call for standard light or dark brown sugar—try it on your morning oatmeal, and you may never use anything else. It is incomparable in gingerbread.

ON THE SHELVES of the best specialty food shops, you are likely to find sugar products under the India Tree label—amber-colored light and seriously dark muscovado, rough-textured demerara, and golden baker's sugar that is as pale as tropical sand. India Tree owner Gretchen Goehrend credits professional chefs for unleashing the unrivaled flavors of these sweeteners in their cooking.

Goehrend says, "Both Nancy Silverton and Alice Medrich told me these sugars are elegant just as they are—much like any ingredient they scour the globe for. With something this good, there is no need for other flavors or spices, not even vanilla. They couldn't believe they ignored these sugars for years and now find them indispensable in their baking."

Light and Dark Brown Sugars. Supermarket light and dark brown sugars can be made by a highly mechanized variation on the traditional method, which is how muscovado sugar is still made, whereby raw sugar is centrifuged to remove the molasses and attain the desired sugar color. However, many brands, especially beet sugars, make their brown sugars by another process. The sugar is completely refined to the white granulated stage, then molasses is sprayed back on in amounts to create either light or dark sugar. The molasses used for this is always the cane sugar variety, as beet sugar molasses is considered unfit for human consumption. Choose a brand that you like (look at the label for "pure cane sugar," if you prefer it) and stick with it.

Brown sugar is called for in many all-American baked goods. Light and dark are interchangeable, depending on the desired amount of molasses flavor. Brown sugar must be packed firmly into a metal measuring cup to get a level measure.

White Sugars

When the final stage of molasses removal and refining is complete, the result is white sugar, the most versatile of all the sugars. It melts easily into a syrup, creams seamlessly into batters, recrystalizes after baking, and lends a crisp texture to cookies. In large enough amounts, it can be a preservative for some foods. The fact that it provides a clean, single note of sweet flavor and neutral color is a plus to some bakers and a minus to others.

White sugar is processed in a number of crystalline forms, and each one acts differently in cooking. But they are all white sugar. Here are the most common white sugars available to the home cook, starting with the coarsest and ending with the finest crystals:

Large-Grained Sugars.   With crystal sizes of 1 to 2 millimeters (mm), these sugars are used to decorate baked goods. They are made of highly re-fined sucrose to be especially shiny. *Coarse* and *sanding sugar* are crystalline, and sometimes colored for added effect, whereas *pearl sugar* is round.

Granulated Sugar.   Standard *granulated sugar* has crystals that are about 0.3 to 0.5 mm across, a size that makes it suitable for many cooking appli-cations. Just as all-purpose flour is considered a "one size fits all" product, granulated sugar plays the same role in the sugar industry.

Fine Granulated Sugars.   *Superfine sugar* is a very fine sugar that has two very useful properties to the home cook. First, it dissolves very easily in liquids (it is sometimes called *bar sugar*, as it is used to make cocktails that won't be gritty with undissolved sugar). It also can help the baker create fine-crumbed, meltingly tender baked goods. Comparing a creamed butter-and-sugar mixture made with standard granulated sugar to one with superfine, the increased number of superfine crystals allows more air bub-bles to form, and these extra bubbles will translate into baked goods with a more delicate texture. Usually sold in one-pound boxes, superfine sugar is sold at most supermarkets.

In some U.S. markets, particularly on the West Coast, *baker's sugar*, de-signed specifically for baked goods but very similar to superfine sugar, is available. Many bakers love (and count me in their number) *golden baker's sugar*, which has the butterscotch flavor profile of a demerara or turbinado and the baking properties of white baker's sugar. British and Australian recipes often call for *caster (or castor) sugar*, which for all in-tents and purposes, is superfine sugar.

In a pinch, you can make your own superfine sugar by grinding granulated sugar in a food processor fitted with the metal chopping blade or in a blender, until it is very fine. It will take a few minutes for it to reach this texture, so be patient. Because factory-manufactured superfine sugar has a uniform crystal size, it is a better choice than homemade.

Superfine sugar performs very well, producing delicate cookies, cakes, and soufflés. They make especially tender meringues, as they dissolve better in the egg whites than does granulated sugar.

Storing Sugar

ALL WHITE SUGAR will keep indefinitely if stored in an airtight container in a cool, dark place. Once opened, remove from the original packaging and store in an airtight container. For easy measuring, the container should be wide enough to fit your hand and a measuring cup. If clumping occurs, it can often simply be stirred or broken up with a fork. Powdered sugar can be sifted or whisked when using, which typically renders it smooth and creamy. Never refrigerate sugar, as it could pick up moisture from the refrigerator. Unopened liquid sugars (with the exception of maple syrup, which should be refrigerated) will keep for a year or two in their original containers in a cool, dark place.

Brown sugar tends to solidify in its original packaging over time. It is imperative to remove it from its packaging and transfer it to an airtight container (a zippered plastic bag works fine) to reduce evaporation that can lead to dry sugar. If the sugar hardens, place a moistened paper towel or a couple of apple slices in the covered container with the brown sugar and let stand overnight, and the sugar will rehydrate from the introduced moisture.

Powdered Sugars

Made by pulverizing white sugar, these sugars have minute crystals that are barely perceptible as such. They have very specific attributes and are most useful in making icings and frostings and the creamy candy center called *fondant*. Still-warm cookies can be rolled in powdered sugar to add a delectably sweet layer, or sift powdered sugar over finished cakes and bars as a decorative element.

The most readily available powdered sugar is *confectioners' sugar*. It often carries a designation of 10X, being the smallest mesh that a sugar crystal can pass through. Powdered sugars of 6X and 4X are sometimes available at cake or candy supply shops. A very small amount of neutral cornstarch is added to powdered sugar to keep it from absorbing too much humidity. *Fondant* and *icing sugar* are specialty sugars that behave much in the same way as confectioners' sugar, although you may reserve them for their specific use and may or may not include cornstarch.

Liquid Sugars

These viscous syrups can add flavor to desserts and savory foods, but they are often poured directly on food as a flavoring. Some syrups are hygroscopic, which means they attract the moisture from the atmosphere, a talent that contributes to the chewiness of baked goods and helps keeps them moist.

Cane Syrup. This is simply evaporated sugarcane juice, prior to crystallization. Used in both traditional Southern and Caribbean cooking, it can be light or dark brown, and the molasses-like flavor intensifies with the color. Cane sugar is still produced in small batches regionally throughout Louisiana, parts of Alabama, Georgia, and Florida. Try cane syrup Southern style, poured over biscuits or corn bread. Keep a bottle handy to use in any cocktail that calls for *simple syrup*, keeping in mind that it will color the drink. It makes the best mojito imaginable.

Golden Syrup. England, Australia, and New Zealand all have minor variations of this clear, light brown syrup with flavor notes of buttered toast. It is made from raw sugar that has been filtered to concentrate the glucose and fructose components, both of which prevent crystal formation. Ersatz golden syrup is on the market, concocted of molasses, invert sugar, and corn syrup, so look for pure cane syrup and nothing else on the ingredient label. Lyle's Golden Syrup is a very reliable cane-based product, available regular and "black" (see "Treacle," page 19; do not use this extra-dark kind unless specifically called for in a recipe).

Golden syrup is becoming increasingly available in the United States and can be found at well-stocked supermarkets. The original container was a pry-top metal tin that is still broadly available, but now it also comes in a clear plastic squeeze bottle. If you can't find it, use dark corn syrup.

Molasses.   Molasses is the thick, dark, slightly bitter syrup that was traditionally made from the liquid thrown off the dry sugar crystals during the centrifugal stage of sugar refinement. (Some manufacturers now simply boil sugar cane juice until it is dark and syrupy and do not use the centrifuge process.) I use it as much for its hearty flavor as for its ability to attract the moisture from the atmosphere, which helps to make chewy, moist baked goods. Of course, it is a must in gingerbread, and essential in many spice cookies.

Molasses from the first round of centrifuge is relatively sweet and often labeled "mild." The second round is less sweet and somewhat more bitter; it can be called "robust" or "full flavor." Blackstrap is molasses from the final spinning; while it has little sweetness, it has the highest amount (although still just trace amounts) of minerals and vitamins. You will find blackstrap molasses at natural food stores, as it does have a variety of homeopathic uses. Do not use blackstrap unless specifically called for in a recipe.

Molasses is sometimes labeled "sulfured" or "unsulfured." During the centrifuge process, the sugar mass can be treated with sulfur dioxide, which helps release more molasses from the sugar crystals and also acts as a preservative. As sulfur contributes to the bitterness in molasses, unsulfured molasses will have the sweetest flavor.

Molasses is an acidic ingredient, and like other acids used in baking, it is usually neutralized with an alkaline ingredient like baking soda. Many gingerbread recipes use both baking soda (to neutralize the molasses and/or brown sugar and give the batter an initial rise from the resulting carbon dioxide) and baking powder (to supply the bulk of the rising power).

Treacle.   Treacle is a dark, sticky syrup made during the refining process and is essentially molasses under a different name. It is very bitter, and the flavor is more akin to blackstrap than the mild or robust molasses. Confusion exists because the British use the term *treacle* to describe both clear, sweet golden syrup and the robust dark syrup (which Lyle markets as "black treacle"). Moreover, in the United Kingdom, the consistency of any sticky sweet syrup is called "treacly." Use true treacle in place of molasses and combine small amounts of it with sugar in cookies to impart a dark color and a chewy texture, but take care not to casually substitute it for golden syrup.

Cooking with Rum

RUM IS THE most common sugar spirit, originating from Barbados in the seventeenth century. Most rum is distilled molasses. As sugar cane is vital to its production, the Caribbean is a natural source for most of the world's rum. The liquor quickly became a part of sugar's history, and therefore, the history of shipping throughout the colonial period. It was so common among sailors that by Christmas, 1768, Captain Cook's ship log reports (punctuation corrected), "Christmas day; all good Christians, that is to say all hands, get abominably drunk, so that at night there was scarce a sober man on the ship. Wind, thank God very moderate or the Lord knows what would become of us."

Cuba and Puerto Rico produce light, smooth tasting rums that are popular in the United States. Darker rums with more of the molasses flavor intact still hail from Barbados and Jamaica. Lighter, sugar cane–based rums come from Guadeloupe and Martinique. Brazil makes a rumlike liquor called *cachaca*, used to make the national drink, *caipirinha*, a mojito-like drink with muddled lime and sugar.

Of course, most people keep a bottle in their bar to make mojitos, rum and cola, and other heady cocktails. I keep my rum in the kitchen, as it can really enhance cooking.

Rum is not sweet, although it may have sweet undertones. Golden and dark rums have been colored with caramel and the best get their color from molasses in the distillation and long aging in charred barrels. Dark rums have the richest flavor, but they may color the batter or dough.

If rum doesn't have much flavor, then why cook with it? Alcohol is a great flavor fixative in cooking. Only some foods release their flavors in water, but alcohol unlocks flavors in virtually all foods. This may be one of the reasons why French and Italian food is so tasty—all of that wine in the cooking does make a difference.

Sweeteners from Non-Sugarcane Sources

Sugarcane provides the world with over 70 percent of its sweeteners, and beet sugar the remaining portion. Actually, I should say "almost all." Corn, maple, and agave are just a few plants that also give sweet juice for human consumption and enjoyment, and honey has long provided tasty pleasure.

Agave Syrup. Nectarlike agave syrup is one of the hottest of the new sweeteners, used in baked goods and drinks, and available in squeeze bottles in natural food stores. Revered since the Aztec empire, the blue agave plant produces a juice that can be fermented into tequila. When this same juice is evaporated, an enzymatic process takes place that results in a syrup with 90 percent fructose, making it an excellent liquid sweetener. (The exact percentage of fructose varies with the producer.) The syrup is minimally processed and popular with vegan cooks. (White sugar may be refined with animal by-products such as bone char, and honey is processed through bees' bodies, so neither is considered vegan.) Agave syrup is also reported to have a very low glycemic index. The glycemic index measures the blood sugar response to carbohydrates; foods low on the glycemic index are absorbed slowly without causing a spike in blood sugar. Using natural low-GI sweeteners such as agave allows people with certain types of diabetes or hypoglycemia to still enjoy sweet foods without playing havoc on their blood sugar and is far preferable to substituting artificial sweeteners or shunning sweets altogether. In fact, everyone would benefit from incorporating low-GI foods into their diet.

Since agave syrup is about the same consistency as maple syrup, it is easy to substitute one for the other in baking and even as pancake syrup. Agave syrup will not spoil or crystallize. It is hygroscopic and will help keep baked goods moist. It also works well as a ready-made simple syrup— I have one friend whose secret ingredient in sangria is agave syrup.

Corn Syrup. In manufactured foods, this light-colored syrup has muscled in on sugar cane syrups. Also known as high-fructose corn syrup, it is intensely sweet and inexpensive. Made by "inverting" the glucose in corn starches to fructose (which is why it is considered an invert sugar), corn syrup is a major source of sugar in processed foods. This increased use of high-fructose corn syrup is relatively recent and appears to be the result of the need to find a home for all the excess corn stored as surplus grain. Nutritionists claim high-fructose corn syrup as one of the main culprits in obesity. As a cook, I use it for very specific purposes, such as candy making.

Invert sugars will not crystallize, so they are often added to candy recipes to keep the larger-grained granulated sugar crystals from attaching to each other and becoming grainy (see box, below). Corn syrup also adds sheen and stability to frostings and ganache.

INVERT SUGAR is a boon to candy makers, yet the bane of sugar processors. Cane juice, which is pure sucrose, is only available from the cane for a short period after harvesting. The cane juice must be boiled within twenty-four hours of cutting, or the enzymes will break down (invert) into simple sugars of fructose and glucose, preventing crystallization. But even inverted sugar has its uses.

Bakers and candy makers often must cajole, coddle, and coax processed sugar to ensure a smooth texture. This is accomplished by stirring, temperature control, and choice of ingredients. For example, in fudge, the fat in butter coats the sugar crystals and slows crystallization. But the real secret to success is invert sugar, which is added in critical steps in the recipe to discourage crystallization. Corn syrup mimics invert sugar and replaces it in most home recipes, but professionals usually use glucose (which is easily found at crafts stores that carry cake and candy supplies).

Fruit Juice Concentrate. In the 1980s, fruit juice concentrates were one of the first alternate natural sweeteners to appear in the marketplace. Grapes, apples, and mixed fruit juices are reduced to a thick syrup and used to make beverages, cereals, cookies, yogurt, and snacks in the natural foods industry.

For home baking, I prefer to use thawed frozen apple juice, as it is easy to find at the local supermarket. I use amounts that do not require further evaporation into a syrup and deliver a natural sweet flavor to fruit fillings, jams, and muffins.

Palm Sugar. Palm sugar is a solid sugar processed from the sweet sap of the sugar palm. (Date palms and coconut palms are also cut for their sugary saps.) The sap is boiled down to a sticky syrup, then whipped and heaped in lumps to solidify. Palm sugar's appearance is very similar to jaggery, but it has a buttery flavor that jaggery lacks. Produced in open air on plantations throughout India (where it is sometimes called *gur* to differentiate it from jaggery) and Southeast Asia (especially Thailand), it varies greatly in quality, depending on the manufacturer. Some palm sugars are flavored with ginger or turmeric, and although they are tasty, look carefully at the label if you want plain, unflavored, sugar.

Use palm sugar in all Southeast Asian cooking, from rice pudding and caramelized banana desserts to beverages, and especially in savory recipes to balance salty and spicy flavors.

BEN AND BLAIR RIPPLE, founders of Big Tree Farms, have patched together a network of sustainable farms on Bali, working with farmers that had been marginalized by industrial agricultural methods. Island farmers climb high into the swaying palms to harvest palm flowers. According to Ben, "The palm sugar begins as a sweet nectar, oozing from the fragrant coconut palm flowers, [which is] boiled in kettles over an open hearth within an hour of harvest, in the same small batch process it has always been made. The subtly sweet paste is ladled into coconut shells to cool and set. The haunting aroma of smoke and caramel are unrivaled by any sugar I have ever tasted. These sugar loaves turned out to be a challenge for cooks to work with, so we perfected a technique to grind and dry the sugars for ease of use."

Honey. The color and flavor of honey is determined by the nectar of the plants visited by the bees that pollinated them. Dark, earthy, molasses-like buckwheat honey from Brittany was a required ingredient in gingerbread for members of the medieval French pastry bakers' guild. Herbaceous thyme honey from the slopes of Mount Hymettus was prized in Greece, especially when paired with cheese, fruit, and nuts. Mild and free-flowing tupelo honey was the first varietal to take hold in this country and may have been Elvis's favorite—fried peanut butter, honey, and banana sandwiches, anyone?

Many supermarket brands of this sweetener are blended from a variety of honeys, which helps keep the price stable. Varietal honey, which is any honey gathered from a single nectar source within a small, defined region, has a unique flavor, aroma, and other volatile elements inherent to that plant and season. Varietal honeys have their own terroir, like wine, if you will. Perfect for those trying to eat foods from closer to home, local honey is the only sweetener that comes from near where you live, unless you happen to live in maple country or the tropics. These honeys deserve to be savored so their flavor can be appreciated—serve them in small spoonfuls, much like caviar, or simply drizzled over cheese and simple desserts.

In my experience, multiple variables—starting with the obvious problem of swapping a liquid for a solid, and moving on to the different qualities of a particular honey such as viscosity, acidity, and flavor—make it difficult to provide an easy formula for substituting honey for sugar, or vice versa. Most guidelines for using honey in place of sugar call for reducing the amount of honey (honey is about a third sweeter than sugar) and reducing the overall volume of liquid in the recipe. But this is misleading; after all, cookies and pies generally do not call for any liquid as a specific ingredient. So the one-size-fits-all method of substitution is not truly applicable to all baking possibilities.

However, recipes designed specifically for the honey's moisture and sweetness can be very successful. I have used honey in everything from cookies, muffins, scones, cakes—even buttercreams—and fruit cobblers, at times in conjunction with sugar. Sugar may give structure to the batter while honey provides a deep, satisfying flavor and also holds moisture in the finished product. Seek out recipes and cookbooks that use honey exclusively to learn the best approaches to baking and cooking with this amazing and versatile sweetener.

Malt Syrup. Malting is a centuries-old tradition that converts grain (such as barley, corn, and rice) into sugars through a process of sprouting, roasting, cooking, and drying. Careful monitoring of the enzymatic process yields a full-flavored, mildly sweet, and extremely thick syrup. Malt syrup is not very sweet at all and consists of mainly maltose with a very small percentage of glucose, sucrose, and fructose. It is used for manufactured cook-

IN AN EFFORT to improve her garden, Kathy Cox sought bees for their ability to pollinate. "I was scared of the thought of all those bees on me, but then a beekeeper told me a woman could not be a beekeeper. [To prove him wrong] by the end of that summer, I had six hives and within three years I had eighty." Cox's company, Bloomfield Bees, in Sebastopol, California, whips their honey to make it light, creamy, and more semisolid than liquid honeys. As most raw honey crystallizes anyway, she stirs in a pound of the finest crystallized honey for every nine pounds of creamed honey to give it a unique texture that is smooth and rough on the palate at once. During the fall harvest, she will even add warm spices to the honey for another layer of flavor. She says that her favorite way to serve creamed honey is to heap a tower onto a platter, surrounded by fruit, nuts, and cheeses, and let guests help scoop out portions of the concentrated sweetness with a melon baller.

ies, candies, and other snacks, mainly as a humicidant (to soak up moisture from the air and help keep the food moist, increasing its shelf life).

Malt syrup is also a fairly common ingredient in bread, where it does more than just sweeten the dough. Sugar retards yeast growth, but malt encourages it. Gluten is the combination of proteins in wheat (and wheat flour) that allow dough to stretch and rise when yeast is added. Some grains, such as rye and corn, have low or no gluten, so when bread uses a high proportion of these flours, the dough needs an extra boost to get it to rise. Malt syrup often replaces sugar in these recipes to ensure strong yeast activity and give a better texture to the bread. Also, in old European bread recipes, especially those for rye bread, it was much easier to obtain malt (which was, and is, also used in beer making) than sugar.

Maple Syrup. The only sweetener native to North America, maple syrup is produced in small quantities throughout the Northeast and Canada. With the help of sunlight, the starch in the maple tree converts into a watery sap that can be tapped by drilling a spout into the trunk. The sap is easiest to tap when the nights fall below freezing and the daytime temperatures rise above freezing. Native Americans called this season "the sugar moon," running from midwinter to early spring. The collected sap is boiled to remove excess water: it takes about forty gallons of maple sap for one gallon of finished maple syrup.

The range of color and intensity of maple flavor depends on the time of processing. Early-season syrup is designated Light Amber or Grade A, lightest in color and mildest in taste. Grade A Medium Amber follows, then Grade A Dark Amber, and finally Grade B. The grades have absolutely no bearing on quality and are simply an attempted guide to color and flavor. There is a movement within the maple industry to establish terroir, defining the characteristics and taste benefits that vary from region, soil, shade, and other conditions that contribute to its taste. Canada has a slightly different grading system than the United States, and Vermont has its own rating system. It's best to try a variety of syrups and make your own choice. Taste is very personal; I prefer the darker flavors, and I know some cooks who search out Grade B to give their food the strongest maple taste. If the bottle is labeled "pancake syrup," then it is not pure maple syrup, but corn syrup doused with maple flavoring.

After opening, store maple syrup in the refrigerator. It should keep for about a year, but check for signs of mold before using. Frozen maple syrup keeps almost indefinitely. To make the cold syrups easier to measure (and to avoid pouring ice-cold syrup on hot pancakes or biscuits), warm it before using by standing the container in a bowl of very hot tap water. Because it can be difficult to determine whether a container is microwave-safe, do not microwave maple syrup in its container to reheat.

Use maple syrup over such breakfast treats as pancakes and waffles, and with meats as a marinade or glaze. Maple syrup may generally be substituted for honey on a one-to-one basis.

Sorghum. Sorghum is an important food crop in Africa and was brought by slaves to the Americas in the 1600s. Primarily grown as a cereal grain, a sweet juice can be squeezed from the grain and then boiled into a sweet, sticky syrup. During the preindustrial era, in many parts of the South, sorghum was the only available sweetener, sugar being too expensive for the average user. There, it is still considered to be the traditional topping for biscuits and hotcakes. Milder than molasses, it adds a roasted sweetness in cookies and quick breads.

Stevia.   The finely ground leaves of a wild shrub, *Stevia rebaudiana*, native to Paraguay, stevia is one of the sweetest foods on earth, 150 to 400 times sweeter than sugar. Stevia has struggled to get a foothold in the market and, since the 1980s, the FDA has been lobbied aggressively to maintain strict controls on its import and use. Currently, it is approved as a food supplement only and may not be listed or referred to as a sweetener.

Because of its intense sweetness and aftertaste, stevia is best used as an enhancement for the likes of oatmeal, stirred into sour beverages, or to add a dash of sweetness to salty and spicy preparations. Stevia has no ability to add texture, cream with butter, caramelize, or activate yeast, so it takes an intrepid cook to use it as a recipe's major sweetener.

Yacón.   The most recent sweetener to arrive on the market hails from the Andes. *Yacón* is a syrup pressed from tubers that resemble sugar beets. It is popular with advocates in the raw food movement because it is heated only to 104°F to kill enzymes that would cause fermentation during storage. Vegans like it, too, as it contains no animal products. The syrup has a light caramel color and viscosity, a very mild molasses taste with minimal bitterness, and surprisingly light, fruity notes. It is very expensive, so you probably won't be cooking with it casually. I like it poured over uncooked desserts, such as a fruit sorbet or raw fruit, mixed with raw cacao nibs or in salad dressing.

In the Baker's Kitchen

2

*L*IKE A PAINTER with a preferred palette of certain colors and mediums, I create a wide range of desserts from a group of core ingredients: eggs, flour, butter, and, of course, sugar. A fine dessert succeeds or fails on those first four components. Was the dessert too sweet? Did the wrong choice of flour give it an unpleasant texture? Did the baker use the freshest butter and eggs? From there, auxiliary flavors come into play—chocolate, fruit, nuts, vanilla, cinnamon, ginger, and a wide array of other spices.

It isn't enough to have an understanding of the ingredients in your kitchen. You actually must have relationship with them. I love discovering new foods to experiment with, and I have boxes full of sugar, grains, and chocolate to prove it—it is not unlike making new friends. As for the day-to-day staples, don't take them for granted, but do note when they were purchased and be sure that they are stored properly, so they will perform well when called into action.

Here are some of the other ingredients besides sweeteners that you will use again and again. I encourage you to get to know them well, as each one is a baker's friend.

Flour

Mix eggs and sugar without flour and bake it, and you might get something edible, but it won't resemble a cake, muffin, cookie, or almost anything recognizable as dessert, except in the case of meringues. Flour, a seemingly simple, ubiquitous ingredient, is indispensable in baking.

29

Just as only fairly recently can you now purchase a huge variety of sweeteners at your neighborhood market, it wasn't too long ago that only a couple of flours were available on supermarket shelves. Today, you have a wide choice of grains, and choosing among them can be confusing.

Wheat makes the flour that is, by far, the most useful to the baker. This is the only grain that contains a high proportion of gluten, a combination of proteins that, when moistened and mixed, produces an elastic microscopic network enclosing tiny air bubbles that expands in the heat of the oven, making the dough or batter stretch and rise. The heat also evaporates the liquids in the mixture, enabling what was once a wet glop to become tender or chewy.

The end texture of baked goods often depends on the amount of gluten in the recipe's flour. The hardness of the wheat kernel determines whether it is hard or soft. Hard flour has a large amount of gluten and is used to make whole wheat, unbleached, or bread flour. Flour made from soft wheat is used for cake flour and all-purpose flour (the latter of which is actually a blend of hard and soft flours). If you see a season (winter or spring) mentioned in conjunction with a flour, it merely indicates when the wheat was planted and isn't an indication of quality.

Whole wheat flour retains the germ and bran, and while it is nutritious, it can make heavier baked goods than some people like. Most flour has had the germ and bran removed. Once refined to that degree, flour may additionally be bleached, a process that increases its shelf life but also decreases its gluten content.

I use organic unbleached all-purpose flour as my usual baking flour and recommend its use in many of the recipes in this book. Compared with other organic products, and considering its excellent quality, organic flour is a very good value and guarantees the purity of the grain. I see no advantage to using bleached flour. I just don't understand why my flour has to be treated with gases to whiten it. I love the light beige color of unbleached flour . . . I don't need it to be pristine white. Yes, unbleached flour has more gluten than bleached, and in theory should make tougher baked goods. However, butter and sugar, two ingredients found in almost all desserts, are tenderizing agents that more than compensate for any extra gluten. And I think that unbleached flour has a rounder, nuttier, more distinctive taste than bleached flour does.

The Pros and Cons of Refining

HISTORICALLY, REFINED white sugar and white flour were much prized for their supposed purity and pristine color. It is true that, in their refined state, they both offer benefits for long-term storage. Plus, the sticky, unrefined sugar was more difficult to transport than dry, granulated sugar, and the germ and bran in whole-grain flour were prone to spoilage. We now know, however, that whole-grain flours have more nutritional value and the dark, moist, and lumpy sugars have trace minerals such as potassium. In contrast with our ancestors, today's chefs and home cooks alike seek whole grains and less-processed sugars, for their taste, interesting textures, and nutritional value.

I now make my own cake flour from organic all-purpose flour, rather than use the hyperrefined commercial variety. To make 1 cup of cake flour, sift together 15 tablespoons of unbleached all-purpose flour (1 cup minus 1 tablespoon) with 1 tablespoon of cornstarch.

I do have a caveat, should you be baking with recipes from other sources than this book: always use the type of flour called for in a recipe, as each kind absorbs liquid at a different rate. Recently, I made an old recipe that called for cake flour instead of unbleached flour. Cake flour is famous for its ability to absorb liquids and for this reason is used in commercial baking, as you can use less flour in proportion to the liquid ingredients, and often save money that way. When I swapped unbleached flour for the cake flour in the recipe, the liquid-to-dry ingredients ratio was thrown off, and my batter was too heavy and baked into a doorstop of a cake. When I made it again with my "homemade" cake flour, things went better.

Whole-grain flours add nutrition to baking, and I do recommend having a pound or two of whole wheat flour and whole wheat pastry flour (a lower-gluten flour made from soft, not hard, wheat) on hand. I also like to bake with spelt flour and yellow stone-ground cornmeal.

Unbleached flour can be stored in an airtight container at room temperature for up to one year. As the bran and germ in whole-grain flours and cornmeal can go rancid, store them in zippered plastic bags in the freezer for up to six months. Be sure to bring to room temperature before using, as it is difficult to mix ice-cold flour with room-temperature ingredients into a well-made batter.

Butter

Remove the cream from milk, and it is still a liquid. But if the cream is manipulated to incorporate air, you get butter, a semisolid, malleable fat that forms the indispensable backbone for many baked goods. Its flavor cannot be matched by another fat—please don't ask if you can substitute margarine. Butter plays many parts in a recipe, besides the simple act of providing flavor. It can be creamed with sugar to create millions of tiny bubbles that expand in the oven, directly affecting the texture of the crumb. And butter acts as a tenderizer, coating the individual strands of gluten so they can't toughen.

Always bake with unsalted butter, which allows you to more accurately control the amount of salt in a recipe. Unsalted butter is also fresher than salted, as salt was originally added to mask rancidity, but it is now used merely as a matter of taste—it can be argued that bread that is slathered with salted butter is "better" and more flavorful than unsalted. The words "sweet cream," which appears on some butter packaging, does not mean that the butter is unsalted; rather, the phrase is pure marketing, meant to convey something old-timey. The color of butter changes throughout the year according to the cow's feed, and butter can be colored with annatto to maintain a consistent hue. In my opinion, this is needless, and I pass over butter that is labeled "color added seasonally."

Since butter freezes well, stock up when your favorite brand is on sale, to have a pound or two on hand for when the baking bug strikes. Thoroughly wrap the entire pound in plastic wrap to help keep out unwanted freezer flavors.

When a recipe calls for room-temperature butter, resist the temptation to warm it in a microwave oven, which will only melt it. Room temperature is actually a misleading term, because what you want is malleable butter that has lost its chill, regardless of the exact temperature. If you slice the butter thinly, spread the slices in the mixing bowl, and place the bowl near a preheating oven, your butter will reach the right consistency in about fifteen minutes—probably the amount of time you need to make other preparations for the recipe, anyway.

Heavy Cream

With its satisfyingly unctuous body, cream can be a major component of a dessert, or act as the finishing touch. Cream is always pasteurized to increase its shelf life, but pass over ultrapasteurized cream, which has been processed at such high temperatures that its flavor is compromised.

Heavy cream has a butterfat content of 36 to 40 percent. With this amount of fat, the cream whips readily and holds its shape. It is sometimes labeled "whipping cream" or "heavy whipping cream," terms that are interchangeable. Do not confuse heavy cream with light cream or half-and-half, both of which have much lower butterfat content and will not whip nearly as well. Also, check the label well to be sure that you are not buying presweetened cream for whipping, a product that is popular on the West Coast.

Before whipping cream, chill the bowl and beaters (just place in the fridge or freezer for a few minutes). This helps the butterfat firm up and speeds the whipping process.

Eggs

When I shop for eggs, I look for two words: *organic* and *local*. I feel confident that organic birds have been fed wholesome vegetarian feed, and that translates into better flavor. Also, because I live in an area with nearby farms, I choose eggs from a local source, as there is no need to buy a brand that takes extra gasoline to deliver. I choose the carton with the most distant sell-by date, check for cracked shells, and that's it.

I use large eggs. If you use a different size, say, medium or jumbo, the liquid in the recipe will be thrown off. This isn't so much of an issue if you are using a single egg in a recipe, but if you are making custard with many eggs, there is quite a bit of difference between the volumes of six medium eggs compared with six large ones.

To kill potentially harmful bacteria (such as salmonella) that can be found in raw or undercooked eggs, the eggs must be cooked to at least 170°F.

A few recipes in this book call for raw or undercooked eggs. Although the risk of salmonella poisoning is low, do not serve these desserts to people who are infirm, the elderly or very young, or anyone whose immune system is compromised.

Store eggs in the refrigerator but not (if your refrigerator has one) in the egg holder on the door, where the temperature tends to be warmer than the shelves.

Baking Soda and Baking Powder

These two leavenings are not interchangeable, even if they both have the word *baking* in their names. When a batter is mixed and heated, many chemical reactions take place, but how one or the other of these two leavening agents react with other ingredients is crucial to the success of a baked good.

Mix an alkali and an acid, moisten them, and you will get carbon dioxide, a gas that helps make baked goods rise. Baking soda (bicarbonate of soda) is alkali. When it is combined with an acidic ingredient such as molasses, sour milk, honey, yogurt, buttermilk, brown sugar, or lemon juice, the reaction will produce carbon dioxide. But what happens if you don't have acids in your recipe? In such a case, you will need baking powder to do the job.

Baking powder is a mixture of alkali baking soda and acidic salts (often, sodium aluminum sulfate). When moistened, the reaction between the alkali and acids creates carbon dioxide, regardless of the other ingredients in the recipe. Some bakers can detect a metallic aftertaste in baked goods made with baking powder. To avoid this, use a brand made without aluminum products, such as Rumford's.

Chocolate and Cocoa

Chocolate is a familiar flavor, and Americans love it in their cakes, candies, cookies, and other sweets. It may seem to be a friendly, even innocuous, ingredient, but the ugly truth is . . . chocolate, and its cousin cocoa, can be temperamental. And chocolate and sugar have a very special relationship. If you have ever nibbled on unsweetened chocolate or tasted plain cocoa, you know that it doesn't begin to reach its full expression of flavor until it is sweetened.

Chocolate is made from cacao beans that are fermented, roasted, and ground. The beans are pressed to remove some of the cocoa butter, a naturally occurring nondairy fat that gives the chocolate its silky smoothness and cocoa its richness. To make chocolate for cooking and eating, the ground cacao mass is mixed with varying amounts of sugar.

Many chocolate brands now list the amount of cacao on the label. The range is very large, going from very bittersweet (about 70 percent cacao) to semisweet (50 to 60 percent). Cacao percentages are kind of a slippery slope, because the USDA puts all dark chocolates with 35 to 88 percent cacao in the same category and doesn't differentiate between semisweet and bittersweet. As the amount of cacao changes, so does the amount of cocoa butter, a fat that contributes a lot to a dessert's texture.

I love to eat very bittersweet chocolate, but it isn't always the most versatile choice for baking. For the most reliable results, use a chocolate with 55 to 60 percent cacao, otherwise you may have trouble with the recipe, thanks to the increased amount of cacao solids and decrease in cocoa butter.

There are a few ways to melt chocolate. Chocolate hates two things: moisture and heat. The tiniest bit of water can make melted chocolate seize into a thick clump. When chocolate is overheated, it becomes gritty.

Start by chopping the chocolate with a heavy knife. Do not use a food processor, as the friction generated by the turning chopping blade could melt the chocolate. The finer the chocolate is chopped, the more quickly it will melt, but just go for pieces that are about 1/2 inch square.

To melt the chocolate in a double boiler, bring water just to a simmer in the bottom part of a double boiler. Turn the heat to very low so the water stays hot but does not boil. (If steam escapes and condenses on the upper part of the double boiler, water could form and ruin the melted chocolate.) Place the chocolate in the top part of the double boiler and let stand, stirring occasionally with a rubber spatula, until the chocolate is smooth and melted. Do not overheat the chocolate.

You can also melt the chocolate in a heatproof bowl placed in 1/2 inch or so of very hot water in a skillet, if you take extra care not to splash any of the water. Because of the increased surface of chocolate, this method is quicker than using a double boiler.

Chocolate can be melted in a microwave-safe bowl in a microwave oven, but it can be easy to overheat the chocolate. Use medium (50 percent) power, and check the chocolate at thirty-second intervals. When you take it out, you may find that the chocolate does not look melted, but brief stirring will push it to the melted stage, or most of it. If not all the chocolate has melted, return it to the microwave oven for fifteen or so more seconds at medium power (because of the wide variability in the power put off by microwave ovens, you will likely soon develop a sense for how quickly your microwave melts chocolate).

Cocoa powder is pulverized cacao beans. Different brands contain more or less cocoa butter (which is one of the reasons why one may be more expensive than another). But the most important distinction is between Dutch-processed and natural cocoa.

Chocolate, and therefore cocoa, is a very acidic ingredient and can be troublesome in baking, as a batter with too much acid won't rise properly. In the 1830s, a Dutch chocolate manufacturer developed a process to treat the acidic cocoa powder with alkali to make it more neutral and easier to work. This is *Dutch-processed or alkalized cocoa*. The alkalization process gives it a reddish hue, and baked goods made with it will be a richer shade of brown. *Natural cocoa* is the familiar, light brown cocoa powder, and while desserts made with it may be a little less deeply colored than if Dutch-processed, it has a slightly more rounded flavor. It has not been processed with alkali, so it is acidic, and most recipes that use it include baking soda (which is alkaline) to act as a neutralizer. It is important to use the cocoa designated in the recipe, to ensure that the correct chemical reaction between the recipe's leavening and the cocoa take place. So, serious bakers have both kinds of cocoa in the pantry.

As a rule of thumb, you can be guaranteed that all imported European cocoas (such as Dröste and Valhrona) will be alkalized; Ghirardelli, one of my local cocoa producers and a popular supermarket brand, is also made by the Dutch process. For natural cocoa, you can't go wrong with Hershey's, in the dark brown container. If you have any doubts about your cocoa's alkalized status, look at the ingredient listing, where alkali products will be listed.

Nonhydrogenated Shortening

Although vegetable shortening has been a staple ingredient in baking for generations, the processing involved in hydrogenation (treating vegetable oil with hydrogen to solidify it at room temperature) has come under scrutiny for its high amount of trans fats and its potential contribution to obesity.

Most nonhydrogenated shortening is 100 percent palm or coconut oil, which remain solid at room temperature without hydrogenation. These tropical oils were once vilified as being unhealthy. However, they have recently been shown to be free of both trans fats and cholesterol and are a good source of heart-healthy monounsaturated fat. Nonhydrogenated shortening does tend to set up a little too firmly after baking and cooling. To solve this problem, most of my recipes that call for nonhydrogenated shortening include some vegetable oil, as well, to add needed moisture to the dough.

Spices

Get in the habit of buying smaller amounts of spices than you think you need. I buy mine at a spice shop, an ethnic market (Indian and Asian markets have spices at good prices), or online. Most commercial spices are sold in containers much larger than you need, and with no sell-by date. If you buy spices in jars, write the date of purchase on the label so you can keep track of its age. Stored in airtight containers in a cool, dark place, most spices will last for six months.

Spices begin to lose flavor as soon as they are ground, so buy whole spice seeds or pods and grind them yourself, as you need them. Freshly grated nutmeg is easy to prepare; freshly ground cinnamon, which is difficult to process into a fine powder at home, less so. Have a mortar and pestle (a mortar with a ridged interior bowl grinds hard spices best) or reserve an inexpensive, electric, blade-operated coffee grinder for spice-grinding.

Sugar and Your Well-Balanced Diet

UNFORTUNATELY, I SEE too many recipes for supposedly delicious desserts that make no sense to me. Just because a recipe has three ingredients (usually highly processed "convenience" foods) or takes five minutes to make, doesn't make it good. To me, a recipe, above all, has to taste great. It may take a little effort to make, but in the final analysis, it should be so delicious that you feel that you have made a good investment of your valuable time. I've already talked about the psychological effect that an enjoyable dessert can have. But we also have to consider the physical effect.

There is room for sugar in a healthful lifestyle. Yes, it is true that refined white sugar doesn't have any nutritive value, and that too much sugar can lead to health problems. Too much of *anything* can be bad for you.

When I bake, I look for ways to balance the various ingredients to enhance a dessert's flavor while making it more healthful. Here are some of my most reliable, essential suggestions and tips:

- Replace some of the all-purpose flour in the recipe with whole wheat pastry flour, which is much higher in protein and fiber than all-purpose flour. Substitute up to half of the all-purpose flour with whole wheat pastry flour. Regular whole wheat flour is coarser than the pastry flour, and I don't recommend it for dessert baking.
- Add flaked whole grains, such as old-fashioned rolled oats or rolled quinoa, to quick breads, cobbler toppings, and bar cookies.
- For a slight increase in nutrients and vitamins, use natural sugars instead of highly refined ones.
- Use highly nutritious "superfoods," such as pumpkin and flaxseeds, to increase the healthful profile of your baked goods.
- Replace heavy cream in ice cream with soy milk.
- Nuts and dried fruits add nutrients and fiber to your baked goods, so use them liberally in recipes where their flavor and texture would be an asset.
- Serve rich desserts with a helping of vitamin- and fiber-packed fresh fruit. Serve the dessert in small portions, but be generous with the fruit.

3

Breakfast Treats

$\mathcal{A}$T BREAKFAST TIME, sugar and its relatives are front and center, probably because of the quick energy they provide to jump-start the day. Think of a steaming tower of pancakes or French toast, topped with a stream of maple syrup. Or a platter of sticky buns, shining with gooey caramel or maple crowns. A mundane bowl of hot oatmeal is much improved with a generous sprinkle of molasses-y brown sugar or a pool of fragrant honey.

When I ran Mäni's Bakery in Los Angeles, the morning hours were always our busiest. From as early as seven A.M. on, we had a steady stream of customers who often ended up in a line that snaked outside the front door. These people didn't just come for their morning cup of coffee or tea—they rarely left the premises without a paper bag containing a fresh-from-the-oven muffin, warm scone, or chunk of coffee cake. One of my best sellers was a faux doughnut that was baked, not fried. While there should be room in one's life for indulgences, I do not endorse a steady diet of pastries that are nothing more than sugary empty calories—especially at the beginning of a day where one hopes to eat well throughout. My favorites always include nutritional whole grains, fruits, and/or nuts, such as the Fig and Orange Spelt Muffins and Cranberry-Almond Breakfast Bars.

Of course, the sweet breakfast experience is only half baked until you include a cup of a hot beverage to go with your pastry. You can drink coffee and tea black, but chai and hot chocolate are nothing without sweetening. For a special treat, make the Wallah's Vanilla-Spice Chai or Spicy Hot Chocolate—and dunk if you wish.

Mom's Classic Granola

Makes about 10 cups

. . . .

DURING THE 1970s, my mother, like many others, embraced the health food movement. I remember coming home to a house filled with the aroma of freshly baked granola. Homemade granola is very much worth the minimal effort required to make it, as you get to adjust the recipe to your taste. For example, I've added rolled quinoa, available in natural food stores, to pump up the protein profile. (If you can't find it, use more oats or substitute wheat germ.) And, for a deeper, more rounded sweetness, I have bolstered the honey with turbinado sugar.

6 cups old-fashioned rolled oats

2 cups rolled quinoa

3/4 cup desiccated or unsweetened flaked coconut

3/4 cup sliced natural almonds or shelled pumpkin seeds

1/3 cup turbinado sugar

1/4 cup sesame or sunflower seeds

1/2 teaspoon ground cinnamon

1/2 teaspoon fine sea salt

1/2 cup canola oil

1/3 cup honey

1 1/2 teaspoons vanilla extract

Raisins or dried cranberries, cherries, or dried blueberries for serving (optional)

- Position oven racks in the center and top third of the oven and preheat to 325°F. Spread the oats on two baking sheets. Bake, stirring occasionally, until the oats are toasted, about 10 minutes.

- Meanwhile, stir together the rolled quinoa, coconut, almonds, sugar, sesame seeds, cinnamon, and salt in a large bowl. In a separate bowl, whisk together the oil, honey, and vanilla until well blended.

- Stir the toasted oats into the quinoa mixture. Drizzle with the honey mixture and stir well to combine. Spread evenly on the sheets.

- Bake, stirring every 10 minutes or so, until nicely browned, about 30 minutes. Cool completely. (The granola can be stored in an airtight container at room temperature for up to 1 month.) Serve in bowls, adding your favorite dried fruit, if desired.

NOTE: Do not add dried fruit (cranberries, cherries, raisins, and the like) to granola until serving. If mixed into the granola and stored together, the fruit could give off moisture that will soften the cereal.

Wild Berry Pancakes

Makes 4 to 6 servings

· ·

PANCAKES, WITHOUT SYRUP, aren't much to write home about. But pour on a stream of your favorite liquid sweetener, and they rock. I have spent a lot of time in Idaho, where there is a profusion of huckleberries, so I prefer them in my hotcakes. If you live in the Northeast and can get small wild blueberries, use them, or even the larger standard blueberries. As for the choice of topping, why not serve a variety so everyone can pick his or her own favorite?

1 cup unbleached all-purpose flour, preferably organic

1/2 cup whole wheat flour

2 tablespoons granulated sugar

1 teaspoon baking powder

1/2 teaspoon baking soda

1 teaspoon fine sea salt

2 cups buttermilk

2 large eggs, separated

4 tablespoons (1/2 stick) unsalted butter, melted

2 cups huckleberries, fresh or frozen (do not thaw)

Vegetable oil, for brushing the griddle

Unsalted butter, for serving

Maple syrup, agave nectar, or honey, for serving

- Whisk together the flours, sugar, baking powder, baking soda, and salt in a large bowl. Whisk together the buttermilk and egg whites in another bowl. Whisk together the egg yolks and melted butter in a small bowl, then whisk into the buttermilk mixture. Make a well in the center of the dry ingredients and pour in the liquids. Whisk briefly, just until combined. Stir in the berries.

- Preheat the oven to 200°F. Line a baking sheet with a clean kitchen towel that has been folded in half. Heat a griddle or large skillet over high heat until a splash of water splashed across the surface forms skittering droplets. Using 1/4 cup for each, pour the batter onto the griddle, leaving plenty of space around the pancakes. Cook until bubbles form on tops of the pancakes, about 2 minutes. Turn and cook until the other sides are browned, about 1 minute. Nestle the pancakes between the folds of the kitchen towel on the baking sheet and warm in the oven while making the remaining pancakes.

- Serve hot, with butter and pitchers of syrup passed at the table.

TIP FROM A PRO

Even when they are stored in a warm oven between batches, pancakes can cool too quickly. However, there is a way to avoid cold hotcakes. As they come off the grill, slip the hot pancakes between the folds of a clean kitchen towel on a baking sheet, then keep warm in a very low (200°F) oven. The cloth insulates the pancakes to maintain their warmth and also absorbs the steam that could make them soggy. Just be sure that the towel is free of perfumes from detergents or fabric softeners, as those aromas can be easily transferred to the pancakes.

Pumpkin Waffles with Muscovado Syrup

Makes six 6½-inch waffles

• •

THE PUMPKIN in this recipe is a good example of how I like to use healthful ingredients whenever I can to pump up the nutritional value of sweets. Pumpkin is considered a "superfood" by many nutrition experts, as it is packed with antioxidant carotenoids that have been shown to prevent some kinds of cancer. Muscovado sugar makes a thick, dark syrup rivaled only by maple syrup in richness and taste. Use either light or dark sugar, depending on whether you prefer a mild or robust flavor. The muscovado is the perfect match for the slightly savory notes in these pumpkin waffles. Be sure to use the syrup the same day as it is made, as it will recrystallize if held longer.

Syrup

1½ cups light or dark muscovado
    sugar, packed

Waffles

1⅓ cups unbleached all-purpose flour,
    preferably organic

2 teaspoons baking powder

¼ teaspoon salt

1 cup solid-pack pumpkin

¾ cup plus 2 tablespoons milk

2 large eggs, separated

3 tablespoons muscovado sugar, light
    or dark, packed

3 tablespoons unsalted butter, melted

Grated zest of 1 orange

Unsalted butter, at room temperature,
    for serving

• To make the syrup, bring the muscovado sugar and ½ cup of water to a boil in a medium-size saucepan over medium heat, stirring to dissolve the sugar. Stop stirring and lower the heat to low. Simmer for 3 minutes. Keep warm.

- To make the pancakes, whisk together the flour, baking powder, and salt in a medium-size bowl, and make a well in the center. Whisk together the pumpkin, milk, egg yolks, muscovado sugar, melted butter, and orange zest. Pour into the well in the dry ingredients, and stir just until combined.

- In a separate bowl, beat the egg whites with an electric mixer on high speed until they form soft peaks. Stir one-fourth of the whites into the pumpkin batter to lighten it, then fold in the remaining whites.

- Bake in a waffle iron according to the manufacturer's instructions. Remove from the iron and serve hot, with the syrup and butter passed on the side.

Banana Upside-Down Muffins

Makes 12 muffins

· ·

Every Brazilian cook seems to have a recipe for *bolo de banana*, an irresistible banana upside-down cake. I've turned it into an easy muffin that is just the thing to serve for breakfast or brunch. For the richest caramelized layer, make these with dark muscovado, which is about the most flavorful sugar you can get.

Nonstick cooking spray, for the muffin pan

4 tablespoons (½ stick) unsalted butter

½ cup dark muscovado or brown sugar, packed

4 ripe bananas

Muffins

1 cup unbleached all-purpose flour, preferably organic

2 teaspoons baking powder

½ teaspoon freshly grated nutmeg

½ cup dark muscovado brown sugar, packed

⅓ cup canola oil

2 large eggs, at room temperature

3 tablespoons whole milk

3 tablespoons dark rum

1 teaspoon vanilla extract

- Position a rack in the center of the oven and preheat to 375°F. Lightly spray a 12-cup muffin pan with the cooking spray.

- To prepare the pans, place 2 teaspoons of the butter and 2 teaspoons of the brown sugar in each muffin cup. Bake until the mixture in each cup is melted and bubbly, about 10 minutes. Remove the pan from the oven and cool for a few minutes. Peel the bananas and cut them on a diagonal into 48 thin slices. In each muffin cup, place two banana slices on the bottom and two banana slices along the sides.

- To make the muffins, sift together the flour, baking powder, nutmeg, and salt into a medium-size bowl. In a separate bowl, whisk together the brown sugar, oil, eggs, milk, rum, and vanilla. Make a well in the center of the dry ingredients, add the egg mixture, and stir just until blended. Do not overbeat. Divide evenly among the prepared muffin cups, filling them as full as possible.

- Bake until the center of a muffin springs back when pressed gently with your finger, about 18 minutes. Immediately invert and unmold the muffins onto a wire cake rack. Cool briefly and serve. The muffins are best the day they are made.

Orange and Fig Spelt Muffins

Makes 12 muffins

· ·

WITH ITS HEALTHFUL makeup and hearty flavor, spelt flour is one of my favorite baking ingredients. It is higher in protein and B vitamins than modern wheat flour is and may be acceptable for people on a low-gluten diet, but it deserves to be better appreciated than as just a wheat substitute. In Italy, where it is called *farro*, cooks have used it for thousands of years, usually simmered as a whole grain in soups in the same way that Americans cook with wheat berries or barley, and only very rarely as a flour. These muffins, which use olive oil, figs, and orange zest, have a Mediterranean sensibility. Although, granted, agave syrup is not Italian, it does make these muffins particularly moist. Therefore, don't line the muffin cups with paper liners, or they will stick mercilessly. As dough with agave syrup will not brown as readily as one with processed sugar, to promote quicker browning, bake the muffins in the top third of the oven, where the heat rises and gathers to form a hot zone.

Nonstick cooking spray, for the pan

2¼ cups whole spelt flour (see Note)

1 teaspoon baking powder

½ teaspoon baking soda

½ teaspoon salt

1 cup low-fat buttermilk

⅔ cup agave syrup

⅓ cup plus 1 tablespoon extra-virgin olive oil

2 large eggs

¾ cup (¼-inch dice) dried figs

Grated zest of 1 orange

- Position a rack in the upper third of the oven and preheat to 350°F. Spray a 12-cup muffin pan with the cooking spray.

- Whisk together the flour, baking powder, baking soda, and salt in a large bowl. Make a well in the center. Whisk together the buttermilk, agave syrup, oil, and eggs in another bowl, pour into the well, and stir just until blended. Fold in the figs and orange zest, being careful not to overmix the batter. Divide the batter among the muffin cups, filling them as full as possible.

- Bake until the muffins spring back when pressed gently, about 20 minutes. Cool in the pan for 5 minutes. Remove from the pan and serve hot or warm. (The muffins can be cooled and stored in an airtight container for up to 2 days.)

MIX IT UP

Cranberry and Pecan Spelt Muffins: Omit the figs. Mix together 1/2 cup of fresh or frozen cranberries and 1/2 cup (2 ounces) of coarsely chopped pecans. Reserve 1/3 cup of the mixed cranberries and pecans. Stir the remaining 2/3 cup of cranberries and pecans into the batter. Spoon into the pan and sprinkle the tops with the reserved mixture.

NOTE: Spelt flour is available at natural food stores and some supermarkets. This recipe was tested made with organic whole-grain spelt flour. White or light spelt flour has had much of the bran and germ removed and is similar to unbleached white flour. If you want to use white spelt or unbleached wheat flour, use 3 1/4 cups, as it absorbs the liquid at a different rate than does whole-grain spelt.

Sunflower and Fresh Berry Whole-Grain Muffins

Makes 12 muffins

· ·

Don't think that just because you see the words "whole grain" in the name of a sweet pastry or other treat, it will be heavy and dense. I'm highly partial to baking with whole wheat pastry flour made from soft wheat, which I described in chapter 2. It has a lower gluten content than does regular whole wheat flour and keeps these muffins nice and light. Wheat germ, with more nutrients per ounce than any other grain, is another powerhouse ingredient that you easily add to your baking to give it a more healthful profile. Sucanat provides a rounded sweetness with a hint of molasses flavor. And, the muffins have lots of additional vitamins from the apple juice and berries.

Nonstick cooking spray, for the pan

2½ cups whole wheat pastry flour

1 cup old-fashioned rolled oats

¼ cup wheat germ

1½ teaspoons baking soda

1 teaspoon baking powder

½ teaspoon fine sea salt

2 large eggs

1 cup fresh apple cider or apple juice

⅔ cup Sucanat

½ cup canola oil

1½ cups berries, such as blueberries, cranberries, raspberries, or a combination

½ cup sunflower seeds

- Position a rack in the center of the oven and preheat to 375°F. Lightly spray a 12-cup muffin pan with the cooking spray.

- Whisk together the whole wheat pastry flour, rolled oats, wheat germ, baking soda, baking powder, and salt in a large bowl. In another separate bowl, lightly whisk the eggs, then whisk in the apple cider, Sucanat, and oil. Make a well in the center of the dry ingredients, pour in the egg mixture, and stir just until combined. Fold in the berries and sunflower seeds.

- Divide the batter among the cups, filling them about three-fourths full. Bake until the tops spring back when pressed with a forefinger, about 20 minutes. Cool in the pan for 10 minutes. Remove the muffins from the cups. Serve warm or cool to room temperature. (The muffins can be cooled and stored in an airtight container for up to 2 days.)

MIX IT UP

Fresh Berry Muffins with Flaxseed: Omit the wheat germ and substitute 1/4 cup of flaxseeds, ground in a mini food processor or electric spice grinder. Be sure to grind the flaxseeds first before using, or the muffins will be too crunchy.

Cinnamon "Doughnuts"

Makes 12 baked doughnuts

• •

DURING MY HOLLYWOOD period, one day I got an interesting phone call. A certain star had to eat a lot of doughnuts in a movie, but he didn't want to eat fried foods. Could I create baked doughnuts that would resemble the real thing? I could, and did, and it made my reputation as "Baker to the Stars." Over the years, the recipe has evolved into these mini tube cakes. Bake them in miniature molds that come six to a pan, available at kitchenware shops. Superfine sugar gives them an especially fine crumb.

"Doughnuts"

Nonstick cooking spray, for the pan

4 cups unbleached all-purpose flour, preferably organic

1 tablespoon plus $\frac{1}{2}$ teaspoon baking powder

$1\frac{1}{4}$ teaspoons fine sea salt

1 teaspoon freshly grated nutmeg

$\frac{1}{2}$ teaspoon baking soda

16 tablespoons (2 sticks) unsalted butter, at room temperature

1 cup plus 2 tablespoons superfine or granulated sugar

3 large eggs, at room temperature

$1\frac{1}{4}$ cups whole milk

Cinnamon-Sugar Coating

12 tablespoons ($1\frac{1}{2}$ sticks) unsalted butter, melted

$1\frac{1}{2}$ cups granulated sugar

$1\frac{1}{2}$ tablespoons ground cinnamon

- Position a rack in the center of the oven and preheat to 350°F. Spray a 6-mold individual Bundt pan with the cooking spray.

- Sift together the flour, baking powder, salt, nutmeg, and baking soda. Using an electric mixer at high speed, beat the butter and sugar in a large bowl until the mixture is light in color and texture, about 3 minutes. One at a time, beat in the eggs. Reduce the mixer speed to low. Beat in four additions of the dry ingredients, alternating with three additions of the milk, scraping down the sides of the bowl as needed, to make a smooth batter. Do not overmix. Divide the batter evenly among the molds, filling them only about one-third full, no more, or the cakes may overflow during baking.

- Bake until the tops spring back when pressed gently with a finger, about 18 minutes. Cool in the pan on a wire cake rack for about 10 minutes. Invert the pan, hold it at an angle and give it a firm whack on the counter, repeating until all the "doughnuts" pop out. Repeat with the remaining batter, being sure to cool the pans and respray them before filling and baking.

- While the second batch is baking, prepare the cinnamon-sugar coating. Melt the butter in a saucepan over low heat, taking care that it does not boil. Whisk together the sugar and cinnamon. Brush the first batch of "doughnuts" all over with the melted butter, and then roll them in the cinnamon-sugar. Transfer to a wire rack and cool completely. (You will have leftover cinnamon-sugar, which can be stored in an airtight container to sprinkle on breakfast cereal, make cinnamon toast, or stir into hot beverages. Do not try to use less cinnamon sugar, as you need the full amount to completely coat the "doughnuts.") Repeat with the remaining "doughnuts," butter, and cinnamon sugar.

Cranberry–Almond Breakfast Bars

Makes 12 bars

· ·

EVERYONE KNOWS THE benefits of a good breakfast, but most of us don't seem to find the time to make one. In this easy recipe, you will bake twelve bars that are good for quite a few breakfasts on the run. Each bar is packed with fiber from whole wheat flour, oats, and flaxseeds, along with protein from almonds, and antioxidant-rich cranberries. If you freeze the bars, thaw them overnight so they are ready to enjoy the next morning. The moist brown sugar gives these an appealing chewy texture.

Nonstick cooking spray, for the pan

1 cup whole wheat flour

1 cup old-fashioned rolled oats

1/4 cup flaxseeds

1/2 teaspoon baking powder

1/2 teaspoon baking soda

1/4 teaspoon fine sea salt

1/2 cup orange juice, preferably freshly squeezed

1/2 cup light brown sugar, packed

1 large egg

2 tablespoons canola oil

1 cup (4 ounces) chopped natural almonds

1/2 cup dried cranberries

- Position a rack in the center of the oven and preheat to 350°F. Spray an 8-inch square baking pan with the cooking spray.

- Whisk together the flour, oats, flaxseeds, baking powder, baking soda, and salt in a large bowl to combine them. Make a well in the center, add the orange juice, brown sugar, egg, and oil, and whisk just until combined. Stir in the almonds and cranberries.

- Spread the batter evenly in the pan. Using a knife, cut the moist dough into thirds. Turn the pan and cut the dough into fourths to make twelve bars. (Precutting will make it easier to cut through and separate the bars after baking.)

- Bake until the top of the pastry is lightly browned, 24 to 28 minutes. Cool in the pan on a wire cake rack. Invert onto a cutting board. Following the previously cut divisions, use a large, sharp knife to cut the pastry into bars. (The bars can be stored in an airtight container for up to 5 days. To store longer, individually wrap each bar in plastic wrap and then aluminum foil and freeze for up to 3 months. Thaw at room temperature overnight.)

MIX IT UP

Cherry-Hazelnut Breakfast Bars: Substitute toasted, peeled, and coarsely chopped hazelnuts for the almonds, and dried cherries for the cranberries.

Crystallized Ginger Scones

Makes 8 scones

● ●

TEA AND SCONES have a long-standing relationship that dates back to the Victorian age. Scones weren't well-known in London until Queen Victoria established residence at Balmoral in Scotland. The original scones were quite heavy, made from oats and cooked on a griddle, and their triangular shape was reminiscent of the Scone (Stone) of Destiny, the chunky rock-hewn throne where the Kings of Scotland were crowned. London's bakers refined them into round, flour-based baked goods that could be served at the new teatime ritual, popularized by members of Victoria's court. The crystallized ginger in these deliver a delicious jolt of spicy flavor—and make these an especially welcome accompaniment to your cup of afternoon tea. In addition to the ginger, these benefit from two sugars: golden baker's sugar, which ensures a light crumb, and pearl sugar, for a bit of textural interest.

2 cups unbleached all-purpose flour, preferably organic

1/3 cup golden baker's, superfine, or granulated sugar

2 teaspoons baking powder

1/4 teaspoon ground cinnamon

1/2 teaspoon fine sea salt

8 tablespoons (1 stick) unsalted butter, cut into 1/2-inch dice, chilled

1/2 cup (1/4-inch dice) crystallized ginger (see Note)

1 cup half-and-half, plus more for glazing the scones

1 tablespoon pearl or decorating sugar

- Position a rack in the center of the oven and preheat to 425°F. Line a baking sheet with parchment paper or a silicone baking mat.

- Sift the flour, sugar, baking powder, cinnamon, and salt into a large bowl. Add the butter. Using a pastry blender, cut the butter into the dry ingredients until the mixture resembles coarse crumbs. Stir in the crystallized ginger. Make a well in the center and pour in the half-and-half. Stir just until combined—the dough will look rough. Knead a few times in the bowl to smooth out the dough a little. Do not overwork the dough.

- Turn the dough onto a very lightly floured board. Pat into an $8\frac{1}{2}$-inch diameter round about $\frac{3}{4}$-inch thick. Using a sharp knife, cut into eight equal wedges. Lightly brush the top of the round with half-and-half and sprinkle with the pearl sugar. Gently lift each scone onto the baking sheet, placing them about 1 inch apart.

- Bake until golden brown, 12 to 15 minutes. Cool for a few minutes on the baking sheet, then serve warm.

NOTE: For the best price, buy cubes of sugar-coated crystallized ginger in bulk, available at Asian grocers, health food stores, or large supermarkets. They need to be cut into smaller dice before using in baking, and as they tend to stick to the knife (don't even think of using a food processor), lightly oil the knife and chop them methodically. You can also buy ready-to-use diced crystallized ginger at specialty markets, which is a very good product, but pricey.

MIX IT UP

Berry-Ginger Scones: Stir $\frac{3}{4}$ cup of fresh or frozen blueberries or raspberries into the dough after adding the half-and-half. If you use frozen berries, they will chill the dough, so allow an extra few minutes of baking time.

Demerara Currant Scones

Makes 8 scones

. . . .

WITH FLAX- AND sunflower seeds, wheat germ, and dried fruit in every bite, as well as the caramelized notes of demerara sugar, these muffins remind me of granola. A little extra sugar sprinkled on top finishes them off with a light crunch. As usual with baking, there is room for experimentation here. Use rolled oats or rolled barley flakes instead of wheat germ, substitute your favorite dried fruit for the currants, or swap chopped nuts for one of the seeds.

1½ cups unbleached all-purpose flour, preferably organic

6 tablespoons demerara sugar

¼ cup flaxseeds

¼ cup sunflower seeds

¼ cup wheat germ

2 teaspoons baking powder

½ teaspoon fine sea salt

6 tablespoons (¾ stick) unsalted butter, cut into ¼-inch dice, chilled

½ cup low-fat buttermilk, plus more for glazing the scones

½ cup dried currants

- Position a rack in the center of the oven and preheat to 425°F. Line a baking sheet with parchment paper or a silicone baking mat.

- Whisk together the flour, 3 tablespoons of the demerara sugar, and the flaxseeds, sunflower seeds, wheat germ, baking powder, and salt in a large bowl. Add the butter. Using a pastry blender, cut in the butter until the mixture resembles coarse crumbs. Make a well in the center, pour in the buttermilk and currants, and stir just until the dough comes together—it will look rough. Knead a few times in the bowl to smooth out the dough a little. Do not overwork the dough.

- Turn the dough onto a very lightly floured board. Pat into an 8½-inch diameter round about ¾-inch thick. Using a sharp knife, cut into eight equal wedges. Lightly brush the top with a little buttermilk and sprinkle with the remaining 3 tablespoons of demerara sugar. Gently lift each scone onto the baking sheet, placing them about 1 inch apart.

- Bake until golden brown, 15 to 18 minutes. Cool for a few minutes on the baking sheet, then serve warm.

Mexican Breakfast Bread Pudding

Makes 4 to 6 servings

. . . .

CAPIROTADA, THE MEXICAN national bread pudding, is usually served for dessert, but as it is quite substantial, it also makes a fine brunch dish. Instead of the custard in other bread puddings, the bread is mixed with a spiced *panela* syrup. The best bread to use is a standard, soft (if not pillowy) French or Italian bread. Don't use a rustic sourdough with a thick crust and a lot of interior air holes, as it won't soak up the custard properly. To cut the sweetness, the pudding is served with sharp Manchego cheese and tangy sour cream. For other savory flavor notes to balance the sugar, offer scrambled eggs and bacon or sausage alongside, too.

6 tablespoons (¾ stick) unsalted butter

12 (1-inch-thick) slices French or Italian bread

2 cups grated *panela* or packed dark brown sugar

3 (3-inch) cinnamon sticks, or ¾ teaspoon ground cinnamon

1½ teaspoons anise seeds

⅔ cup (about 3 ounces) slivered almonds

½ cup dried cherries or cranberries

4 ounces Manchego or mild Cheddar cheese, sliced thinly, for serving

Crema Mexicana (see Note), crème fraîche, or sour cream, for serving

- Position a rack in the center of the oven and preheat to 350°F. Melt the butter in small saucepan. Lightly brush the interior of a 9 by 13-inch glass baking dish with some of the butter.

- Brush the melted butter over the bread, reserving any remaining butter. Place the buttered bread on a large baking sheet. Bake for 10 minutes. Turn the bread slices over and bake until golden and crisp, about 5 minutes longer. Arrange the slices, overlapping as needed, in the baking dish.

- Meanwhile, bring the *panela*, 1½ cups of water, the cinnamon sticks, aniseeds, and reserved butter to a boil in medium-size saucepan, stirring just until the sugar dissolves. Boil, uncovered, stirring occasionally, until reduced to 2 cups, about 15 minutes.

- Gradually strain the warm syrup through a wire sieve over the bread slices, turning the bread over and allowing some of syrup to be absorbed before adding more. Sprinkle with the dried fruit and almonds. Cover the dish with aluminum foil, Bake until the syrup is bubbling, about 25 minutes.

- Spoon the pudding into bowls and top each with a slice or two of Manchego and a dollop of crema. Serve hot.

NOTE: Crema Mexicana is a dairy product similar to crème fraîche. Both are buttery, thick, and pourable, but not as tart as sour cream, and can be added to boiling hot foods without danger of curdling. The best brands are cultured cream without unnecessary preservatives, thickeners, or other additives. You'll find crema Mexicana in tall jars in the dairy section of Latino grocers and many supermarkets.

MIX IT UP

Mexican Bread Pudding with Sautéed Apples: Omit the dried cranberries. Peel and core 3 Golden Delicious apples, and cut them into ½-inch wedges. Melt 2 tablespoons of unsalted butter in a large skillet over medium-high heat. Add the apples and cook, turning them occasionally, until they are lightly browned and barely tender, about 5 minutes. Transfer to a serving bowl and serve warm with the bread pudding, cheese, and sour cream.

Pear-Raspberry Coffee Cake

Makes 12 servings

• •

QUITE OFTEN, THE easiest recipes are the most satisfying. I appreciate this fruit-studded coffee cake, not only for its old-fashioned goodness, but because the batter and streusel can be made ahead, covered, and refrigerated overnight. That way, serving a warm coffee cake to morning guests is a snap. Turbinado sugar gives the cake crumb a layer of butterscotch flavor.

Cake

2 cups unbleached all-purpose flour,
   preferably organic

1 teaspoon baking powder

½ teaspoon baking soda

½ teaspoon fine sea salt

8 tablespoons (1 stick) unsalted butter,
   at room temperature, plus more for
   the pan

1 cup turbinado sugar

2 large eggs, lightly beaten

1 cup plain whole-milk yogurt

1 cup fresh or frozen raspberries

2 firm, ripe Bosc or Bartlett pears,
   peeled, cored, and cut into
   ½-inch dice

Streusel

1¼ cups old-fashioned rolled oats

¼ cup turbinado sugar

¼ cup unbleached all-purpose flour,
   preferably organic

Grated zest of 1 large orange

¼ teaspoon fine sea salt

5 tablespoons (½ stick plus
   1 tablespoon) unsalted butter,
   cut into ½-inch cubes, chilled

• Position a rack in the center of the oven and preheat to 350°F. Lightly butter a 9 by 13-inch baking pan.

• Sift together the flour, baking powder, baking soda, and salt. Using an electric mixer at high speed, beat the butter and sugar until light in color and texture, about 3 minutes. Gradually beat in the beaten eggs. Reduce the mixer speed to low and mix in half of the flour mixture. Add the yogurt and mix well, followed by the remaining flour, scraping down the sides of the bowl as needed. When the batter is just smooth, return the speed to high and beat until the batter is very smooth and glossy, about 30 seconds. (The batter can be made up to 10 hours ahead, without the fruit covered and refrigerated. Remove from the refrigerator and let stand for 30 minutes to 1 hour before baking.) Using a rubber spatula, fold in the raspberries and pears.

- For the streusel, combine the oats, sugar, flour, orange zest, and salt. Add the butter. Use your fingertips to work the butter into the dry ingredients until the mixture is combined and crumbly. (The streusel can be made up to 10 hours ahead, covered and stored at room temperature.)

- Spread the batter evenly in the pan and sprinkle with the streusel. Bake until a wooden toothpick inserted in the center comes out clean, 35 to 40 minutes.

- Transfer to a wire cake rack and cool in the pan for 30 minutes. Cut into 12 pieces and serve warm or cool completely.

Pineapple Gingerbread Turnovers

Makes 8 turnovers

. . . .

FRESH SWEET-TART pineapple chunks are tucked into a spicy gingerbread crust. I devised these turnovers to be tropical Pop-Tarts for grown-ups, but they are much more than something to eat for breakfast on the run. Freeze any leftovers to reheat in a toaster oven, or serve warm as a dinner dessert with vanilla ice cream. Molasses, one of the flavors in gingerbread, is supplied by the muscovado sugar.

Gingerbread Dough

2$1/2$ cups unbleached all-purpose flour, preferably organic

2 teaspoons baking powder

$1/2$ teaspoon salt

8 tablespoons (1 stick) unsalted butter, at room temperature

$1/2$ cup light muscovado or light brown sugar, packed

3 large eggs

1 teaspoon vanilla extract

2 tablespoons peeled and shredded fresh ginger (use a box grater)

Granulated sugar, for glazing the turnovers

Pineapple Filling

$1/3$ cup light muscovado or brown sugar, packed

1 tablespoon unbleached all-purpose flour, preferably organic

Grated zest of 1 lemon

$1/4$ pineapple, peeled and cored

- Make the dough at least 2 hours before baking the turnovers. Whisk together the flour, baking powder, and salt in a large bowl. Using a an electric mixer (preferably a heavy-duty standing mixer fitted with the paddle attachment) at high speed, beat the butter and sugar until light in color and texture, about 3 minutes. One at a time, beat in two of the eggs, then the vanilla and ginger. Reduce the mixer speed to low. Add the flour mixture and mix until thoroughly combined. (If using a hand mixer, use a wooden spoon to stir in the flour.) Gather up the dough and divide in half. Flatten each portion into a thick disk. Wrap each in plastic wrap and refrigerate until chilled and firm, at least 2 hours or overnight.

- Position a rack in the center of the oven and preheat to 400°F. Line two baking sheets with parchment paper or a silicone baking mat. Whisk the remaining egg with 2 teaspoons of water.

- Lightly flour a work surface. Working with one disk of dough at a time, roll out the dough into a 12-inch square. Cut into four 6-inch squares.

- To make the filling, whisk together the brown sugar, flour, and lemon zest in a bowl. (To discourage the pineapple from giving off too many juices, chop it just before making the filling, and mix the pineapple with the flour mixture in two batches.) Chop the pineapple into 1/2-inch dice. You should have 2 cups of chopped pineapple. In another bowl, mix half of the flour mixture with half of the pineapple.

- Brush the edges of a gingerbread square with the egg mixture. Place about 1/4 cup of the pineapple mixture in the center of the square. Fold the edges together to meet, forming a triangle, and press gently but firmly. Dip the tines of a fork in flour, then press and seal the edges with the fork. Place the turnovers on the baking sheet and poke air holes in the dough with the tines of the fork. Repeat with the remaining three squares of one batch of dough and the filling. (This should not be done until ready to bake, as the fruit gives off its juices quickly.) Brush the turnovers with the egg mixture and sprinkle with granulated sugar.

- Place one sheet of turnovers in the oven. Bake until the turnovers are golden brown, 15 to 18 minutes. Transfer to a wire cake rack to cool. While the first tray is baking, roll out the second portion of dough, and fill with the second batch of the pineapple filling. Repeat the egg glaze and sugar topping with the second sheet.

- Serve warm.

MIX IT UP

Apple Gingerbread Turnovers: Omit the pineapple, and substitute 2 Golden Delicious or Cortland apples, peeled, cored, and cut into 1/2-inch dice.

Maple-Pecan Sticky Buns

Serves 9

. . . .

THE AROMA OF sticky buns baking is enough to rouse an entire household of people. The sticky part of most sweet buns is made of sugar alone, but I much prefer the deeper, more interesting flavor of maple syrup. Here, both maple sugar and maple syrup work in tandem to make these sticky buns perfect. The maple sugar, combined with butter, clings to the inner layers of each bun, while the maple syrup ensures a gooey, shiny glaze.

Sticky Bun Dough

1 cup whole milk

2 tablespoons maple syrup

4 tablespoons ($1/2$ stick) unsalted butter, cut into small pieces, plus more for the bowl

1 ($1/4$-ounce) envelope active dry yeast ($2^1/4$ teaspoons)

$2^1/2$ cups unbleached all-purpose flour, preferably organic

$1/2$ teaspoon fine sea salt

Filling

8 tablespoons (1 stick) unsalted butter, at room temperature

1 cup (4 ounces) chopped pecans

$2/3$ cup maple syrup

$1/2$ cup maple sugar

1 tablespoon ground cinnamon

1 cup raisins

- To make the dough, heat the milk in a medium-size saucepan over medium heat until small bubbles appear around the edge of the pan. Remove from the heat and stir in the maple syrup and butter. Cool until tepid (100 to 110°F). Sprinkle in the yeast. Let stand 5 minutes, then stir to dissolve the yeast.

- Stir together the flour and salt in a large bowl. Make a well in the center, add the milk mixture, and stir to form a soft, sticky dough. Turn out on a floured work surface and knead, adding additional flour as needed, until the dough is supple and elastic, about 8 minutes.

- Generously butter a medium-size bowl. Place the dough in the bowl and turn to coat the dough. Cover the bowl with a moistened kitchen towel. Let stand in a warm spot until the dough has doubled in volume and a finger pressed $1/2$ inch into the dough leaves an impression, about 1 hour.

- Butter a 9-inch square glass baking dish with 1 tablespoon of the butter. Sprinkle the pecans in the bottom of the dish. Pour the maple syrup evenly over the pecans. Stir together the maple sugar and cinnamon, add the 6 tablespoons of butter, and mash with a rubber spatula to make a spreadable paste.

- Punch down the dough. Roll out the dough on an unfloured work surface into a 12 by 15-inch rectangle. Drop spoonfuls of the maple-butter mixture over the dough, then spread evenly with the spatula, leaving a 1-inch-wide border at the bottom. Sprinkle the raisins over the maple butter. Starting at the long end at the top of the rectangle, roll up the dough into a thick cylinder, pinching the seam closed. Using a sharp knife, cut the dough crosswise into nine slices, each about $1^3/4$ inches wide. Arrange in the pan, cut side down.

- Cover the dish with a moist kitchen towel and place in a warm spot. Let stand until the dough has almost doubled, about 45 minutes.

- Position a rack in the center of the oven and preheat to 375°F. Melt the remaining 1 tablespoon of butter in a small saucepan over low heat. Cool slightly, then brush the melted butter over the tops of the buns. Bake until the tops are browned and the sauce is bubbling up in the center, 30 to 35 minutes.

- *Immediately* invert and unmold the buns onto a serving platter. Scrape any nuts and syrup clinging to the bottom of the pan onto the buns. Cool for about 20 minutes, then serve warm.

The Wallah's Vanilla-Spice Chai

Makes 6 servings

• •

In India, a chai wallah is the tea seller by the side of the road or in train stations, hawking freshly brewed milky tea. What makes chai so special is the seesawing of spicy and sweet flavors. For the most authentic chai, use an unrefined sweetener, such as jaggery or *gur*. Chai is easy to make and keeps fresh in the refrigerator for days.

2 whole star anise, or ½ teaspoon aniseeds

16 black peppercorns

15 whole cloves

10 green cardamom pods, crushed

5 (3-inch) cinnamon sticks

½ vanilla bean, split lengthwise

3 tablespoons black tea leaves, such as Darjeeling

1½ cups whole milk

⅓–½ cup crushed jaggery or *gur*

• Bring 5 cups of water to a boil in a large saucepan. Add the star anise, peppercorns, cloves, cardamom pods, cinnamon sticks, and vanilla bean. Lower the heat to medium-low. Cook at the barest simmer to infuse the water with the spices, about 25 minutes.

• Remove from the heat and stir in the tea leaves. Cover and let stand for 5 minutes. Add the milk and jaggery. Return to medium-low heat and heat, stirring constantly to dissolve the jaggery, just until the chai is almost simmering. Strain through a wire sieve into mugs and serve hot. (The chai can be cooled, covered, and refrigerated for up to 5 days. Surprisingly, and delightfully, the flavors intensify even after the spices have been strained and removed. Reheat over low heat or serve iced.)

MIX IT UP

Ginger Chai: Omit the star anise. Thinly slice a 2-inch knob of peeled fresh ginger, and add to the water along with the spices.

Spicy Hot Chocolate

Makes 6 cups

· ·

MOLE IS A SPICY Mexican sauce with a hint of chocolate. This is hot chocolate with a hint of spices. For the strongest chocolate flavor that allows the *panela* to assert itself, use a bittersweet chocolate with a high cacao content of around 70 percent.

6 cups whole milk

1 cup grated *panela*

4 (3-inch) cinnamon sticks

1/8 teaspoon crushed hot red
    chile flakes

4 ounces bittersweet chocolate
    (preferably 70% cacao),
    finely chopped

- Combine the milk, *panela*, cinnamon sticks, and chiles in a medium-size saucepan. Cook over low heat, stirring occasionally, until bubbles form around the edges of the pan. Remove from the heat, cover, and let stand for 20 minutes.

- Reheat over low until very hot. Remove from the heat. Add the chocolate and let stand for a few minutes. Whisk until the chocolate is smooth. Strain through a wire sieve into cups and serve immediately.

4

Cakes

*W*HENEVER I BAKE a cake, I get a good lesson on how sugar is truly a chameleon in the kitchen. Sugar creamed with butter in the batter adds structure to the cake, as well as flavor. (This role is even more important in cakes that have no butter to provide bulk, such as angel food or chiffon cakes.) Confectioners' sugar can be blended with butter and flavored to create a quick frosting, or granulated sugar can be melted into a caramel, hardened, and crushed to decorate my sweet creation. In some cases, sugar is boiled with water to make syrup to moisten the cake layers, or the syrup can be cooked longer to the proper temperature and whipped into egg whites as a base for a classic buttercream frosting. And these are just a few examples that come to mind.

Of course, there are countless styles of cake, literally one for every occasion. In general, cakes fall into two categories: butter based and foam based. In either case, regardless of the ingredients themselves, an invisible force has a big effect on the final result.

This element is air, which must be beaten into the batters to create millions of tiny bubbles that will expand in the heat of the oven, making the cake rise. In a butter-based cake, the butter and sugar are creamed together. The sugar crystals are solid enough to form a web that traps the air bubbles. When the creamed mixture is pale in color and light and fluffy in texture, enough air has been beaten in. This can take three minutes with an electric mixer, so don't skimp on time. The temperature of the butter is crucial, as the butter must have a somewhat plastic consistency to accept and hold the air that will be beaten in. You will often see "at room temperature" as an indicator. As long as the temperature is about

70°F, then that is true. But check the texture of the butter. It should be malleable with a matte surface, and not squishy and shiny. In butter-based cakes, chemical leaveners, such as baking powder and baking soda, are used to help the air bubbles expand, but they can't do the job on their own—the butter needs to be the right temperature and texture for the batter to rise.

In foam-based cakes (such as the genoise cake for the Mint Julep Cake on page 86), eggs or egg whites are beaten to incorporate air. For the eggs to accept the maximum amount of air, they must be at room temperature—just take them out of the refrigerator for about 45 minutes before using them. If you forget, there is an easy solution: place the uncracked eggs in a bowl of warm tap water, and let them stand for 5 minutes, then drain and use them.

And now . . . what cake to make? Layer cakes, of course, are a must at birthday parties, and you'll find a good selection here, from an agave-sweetened banana cake with milk chocolate ganache, to a light-as-a-feather mint julep cake. For a casual party dessert, or for snacking, a simple cake is in order, such as the cranberry gingerbread sheet cake inspired by my grandmother's baking (although I use agave and whole wheat pastry flour for my version). Or bake up a tube cake—the Orange-Walnut Cake with Brown Sugar–Rum Syrup is easy enough for everyday nibbling but attractive enough to serve to company. Chocolate cakes, a perennial favorite, are represented by a single-layer Argentinean cake served with a gooey drizzle of *dulce de leche*, and of course, the all-American icon, a deep, dark chocolate cake with fudgy frosting.

A special cake deserves an extra-special presentation. A cake stand will literally raise your cake above the other foods being served (which in my opinion, is the proper place). A stand with a cake dome is especially useful to help keep the cake moist and fresh. (Once the cake is cut, press a piece of plastic wrap directly on the cut surfaces to keep out air and further discourage drying out during storage.) If you like to serve cupcakes, a cupcake stand is also a good investment.

Cranberry Gingerbread

Makes 12 servings

• •

MY GRANDMOTHER, who had a sweet tooth and whose kitchen was always well-stocked with freshly baked treats, liked to have a version of this gingerbread on hand to serve to friends who stopped by. I've updated her recipe slightly, primarily by working in agave syrup, which mellows the bold molasses flavor. Also, I use whole wheat pastry flour to give the cake a more complex, almost nutty flavor, and a more nutritious profile. The cranberries will sink to the bottom to create a gooey, fruity layer that I find irresistible.

2 1/2 cups whole wheat pastry flour

2 teaspoons baking soda

1 1/2 teaspoons ground cinnamon

1 teaspoon ground ginger

1/2 teaspoon baking powder

1/2 teaspoon ground cloves

1/2 teaspoon freshly grated nutmeg

1/2 teaspoon fine sea salt

3/4 cup agave syrup

1/2 cup canola oil

3/4 cup mild or robust molasses

2 large eggs, at room temperature

1 cup boiling water

1/2 cup finely diced crystallized ginger

Grated zest of 1 lemon

2 cups fresh or frozen cranberries

- Preheat the oven to 350°F. Spray a 9 by 13-inch baking pan with cooking spray or brush with vegetable oil.

- Sift together the flour, baking soda, cinnamon, ground ginger, baking powder, cloves, nutmeg, and salt. Whisk together the agave, oil, molasses, and eggs. Make a well in the center of the flour mixture and add the egg mixture. Whisk, gradually adding the boiling water. Stir in crystallized ginger and the zest, but do not overmix. Spread the berries in the pan, pour in the batter, and smooth the top.

- Bake until the center springs back when pressed lightly with your finger, 35 to 40 minutes.

Caramel Applesauce Cake

Makes 12 servings

• •

THE ORIGINAL VERSION of this cake dates to the early 1970s, when my mom would have a sheet cake on hand for after-school snacking and quick desserts—an all-purpose cake, if you will. I, for one, would be happy to see such days again. Made with whole-grain spelt flour and applesauce for increased nutritional value, this is a good example of how you can make more healthful desserts with very little effort. (Although, admittedly, the caramel topping is over the top, and you could serve the cake without it—but live a little!)

Applesauce Cake

Nonstick cooking spray, for the pan

3 cups whole spelt flour
  (see Note, page 49)

2 teaspoons baking powder

1 teaspoon baking soda

2 teaspoons ground cinnamon

2 teaspoons ground ginger

1/2 teaspoon freshly grated nutmeg

1/2 teaspoon fine sea salt

4 large eggs, at room temperature,
  beaten

1 1/4 cups granulated sugar

1 1/2 cups unsweetened applesauce

3/4 cup canola oil

1 cup raisins

Caramel Topping

1 1/4 cups coarsely chopped walnuts

1 cup light or dark brown sugar,
  packed

8 tablespoons (1 stick) unsalted
  butter, cut up

1/4 cup whole milk

- Position a rack in the upper third of the oven and preheat to 350°F. Lightly spray a 9 by 13-inch baking pan with the cooking spray.

- To make the cake, sift together the flour, baking powder, baking soda, cinnamon, ginger, nutmeg, and salt. In another bowl, whisk together the eggs and sugar, then add the applesauce and oil, and whisk well. Make a well in the center of the dry ingredients and pour in the applesauce mixture. Stir just until combined. Fold in the raisins. Spread the batter in the pan.

- Bake until the cake springs back when pressed gently, 45 to 50 minutes. Set on a wire cake rack and let cool slightly.

- Meanwhile, make the caramel topping. Bring the walnuts, brown sugar, butter, and milk to boil in a medium-size saucepan over medium heat, stirring often to help dissolve the sugar. Boil, stirring constantly, until the topping is bubbling and thickened, about $2^{1}/2$ minutes.

- Poke the warm cake all over with a fork. Pour the hot caramel topping evenly over the cake. Let cool until the cake is warm or cool completely. Cut into twelve pieces and serve. (The cake can be stored at room temperature, covered with plastic wrap, for up to 2 days. If desired, reheat individual slices in a toaster oven.)

Orange-Walnut Cake with Brown Sugar–Rum Syrup

Makes 12 servings

• •

THANKS TO THEIR classic pan, Bundt cakes deservedly score high marks in the appearance category. Now that Nordic Ware, maker of Bundt pans, makes what seems like dozens of different decorative pans, including a wide variety of smaller and mini sizes beyond the original tube shape, a baker can hardly have too many recipes. Walnut lovers will thank you for making this, loaded as it is with two and a half cups of protein-rich nuts, not to mention that walnut oil is high in omega–3, which helps to balance cholesterol. The caramel notes in the brown sugar glaze accents the toasted nut flavor.

Orange-Walnut Cake

2¹/₂ cups toasted walnuts (see page 129)

1 cup granulated sugar

Grated zest of 1 large orange

2 large eggs, at room temperature

³/₄ cup walnut oil

¹/₄ cup honey

2¹/₂ cups unbleached all-purpose flour, preferably organic

1 teaspoon baking powder

1 teaspoon baking soda

1¹/₂ teaspoons ground cinnamon

¹/₂ teaspoon freshly grated nutmeg

¹/₂ teaspoon fine sea salt

1¹/₂ cups boiling water

Brown Sugar–Rum Syrup

²/₃ cup light brown sugar, packed

¹/₃ cup dark rum

¹/₃ cup fresh orange juice

- Position an oven rack in the lower third of the oven and preheat to 350°F. Butter and flour a 10- to 12-cup fluted tube pan and tap out the flour.

- To make the cake, combine the walnuts, ¹/₄ cup of the granulated sugar, and the orange zest in a food processor fitted with the metal chopping blade. Pulse about six times until the walnuts are very finely chopped, but not a powder.

- Whisk the remaining ³/₄ cup of granulated sugar with the eggs, oil, and honey in a bowl until combined. Sift together the flour, baking powder, baking soda, cinnamon, nutmeg, and salt into a large bowl and make a well in the center. Pour in the egg mixture and whisk, adding the boiling water as you whisk. (Do not pour the boiling water directly onto the egg mixture, or the eggs may curdle.) Stir in 2 cups of the chopped walnut mixture, reserving the remaining chopped walnuts. Spread in the pan.

- Bake until a wooden toothpick inserted in the cake comes out clean, about 50 minutes. (If using a cast-iron cake pan with a dark surface, bake for 5 minutes, then lower the oven temperature to 325°F, and start testing for doneness after 40 minutes of total baking time.) Let cool on a wire cake rack for 20 minutes. Invert and unmold onto the cake rack.

- Meanwhile, make the brown sugar rum syrup. Bring the brown sugar, rum, and orange juice just to a boil in a small saucepan over medium-low heat, stirring often to help the sugar dissolve. Cook at a low boil until slightly reduced, about 8 minutes.

- Place the warm cake on the cake rack over a rimmed baking sheet. In three applications, allowing about 5 minutes between each for the cake to absorb the syrup, brush the warm cake with the syrup. Pour any glaze in the baking sheet back into the saucepan, and brush over the cake. Place the cake on the rack over a clean plate, and press handfuls of the reserved chopped walnut mixture evenly over the top and sides of the cake. Gather up any walnuts that fall onto the plate, and press onto the cake. Let cool completely. Cut into wedges and serve. (The cake can be stored in an airtight container, or wrapped in plastic wrap, at room temperature for up to 5 days.)

TIP FROM A PRO

Decorative tube pans, in shapes of everything from roses to castles, are an easy way to make simple unfrosted cakes (which can be on the plain side) more attractive. But take note of your pan's construction. Pans that are made from cast iron with dark surfaces soak up the oven heat more efficiently than do thin metal pans with shiny surfaces, and it is easy to overbake the cake at the average oven temperature of 350°F. (An overbaked cake will be dry with a bitter, overly browned exterior.) If you have such a heavy, dark pan, bake the cake for 5 minutes at 350°F to help warm the batter and activate the baking powder, then turn the oven heat down to 325°F. Continue baking until a wooden toothpick inserted in the center of the cake comes out clean, but start testing for doneness about 10 minutes before the estimated baking time of the original recipe.

Mocha Toffee Crunch Cake

Makes 12 servings

· ·

THIS OLD-FASHIONED cake may remind you of something you might see at a bake sale . . . and I mean that as the highest compliment. The cake doesn't register high on the chocolate scale, as it only has one-quarter cup of cocoa. But by the time you add the glaze and encrust it in crushed homemade toffee, chocolate fans will be singing your praises.

Light Cocoa Cake

2½ cups unbleached all-purpose flour, preferably organic, plus more for the pan

¼ cup Dutch-processed cocoa powder

2½ teaspoons baking powder

½ teaspoon baking soda

½ teaspoon fine sea salt

½ cup sour cream

⅓ cup cold brewed espresso, or 1½ teaspoons instant espresso dissolved in ⅓ cup boiling water, cooled

16 tablespoons (2 sticks) unsalted butter, at room temperature, plus more for the pan

1½ cups granulated sugar

5 large eggs, at room temperature, beaten

1 teaspoon vanilla extract

⅔ cup semisweet chocolate chips

Chocolate Glaze

1¼ cups confectioners' sugar

2 tablespoons Dutch-processed cocoa powder

2 tablespoons cold brewed espresso, or ½ teaspoon instant espresso dissolved in 2 tablespoons boiling water, cooled

1½ cups crushed Creamy English Toffee (page 79, see Note)

- Position a rack in the lower third of the oven and preheat to 350°F. Lightly butter and flour a 10-inch tube (angel food cake) pan, tapping out the excess flour.

- To make the cake, sift together the flour, cocoa powder, baking powder, baking soda, and salt. Whisk together the sour cream and espresso to combine. Beat the butter and sugar in a large bowl with an electric mixer at high speed until the mixture is light and fluffy, about 3 minutes. Gradually beat in the beaten eggs, stopping to scrape down the sides of the bowl as needed. Beat in the vanilla. Reduce the mixer speed to low. Starting with the flour mixture, add three equal portions of the flour mixture alternating with two equal additions of the sour cream mixture. After each addition, scrape down the sides of the bowl and increase the mixer speed to high for a few seconds. When the batter is smooth, increase the speed to high and beat for 30 seconds. Fold in the chocolate chips. Spread the batter evenly in the pan and smooth the top.

- Bake until a wooden skewer inserted deep in the cake comes out clean, 50 to 60 minutes.

  Transfer to a wire cake rack and let stand for about 15 minutes. Run a thin knife around the inside of the cake and the tube to loosen the cake. Invert and unmold the cake onto the rack and let cool completely, bottom side up.

- Meanwhile, make the chocolate glaze. Sift the confectioners' sugar and cocoa together into a medium-size bowl. Gradually stir in the espresso to make a thick, pourable glaze. Pour and spread the glaze over the cake, letting the excess drip down the sides. Press the crushed toffee into the glaze. Let stand until the glaze firms, about 2 hours. (The cake can be stored, covered with a cake dome or plastic wrap, at room temperature for up to 2 days.) Transfer to a serving platter and serve at room temperature.

NOTE: To crush the toffee, place it in a zippered plastic bag and rap with a rolling pin or flat meat pounder.

Mai Tai Chiffon Cake

Makes 10 to 12 servings

• •

A CROSS BETWEEN a sponge cake (which has a butter-free batter based on separately whipped egg yolks and whites) and an angel food cake (also butter-free, made with whipped whites only), the recipe to chiffon cake was closely guarded since 1927 by its inventor, a caterer named Harry Baker. No one knew his formula until he sold it to Betty Crocker (a division of General Mills) in 1947. Baker's innovation was to add fat to the whipped egg batter in the form of vegetable oil. The chiffon cake lends itself to many flavor variations, but my favorite is this pineapple and rum version, two components of the heady Mai Tai cocktail. The combination of superfine sugar and pineapple juice concentrate in the batter make this the moistest, most tender chiffon cake you will ever eat.

Pineapple Chiffon Cake

2 cups unbleached all-purpose flour, preferably organic

1½ cups superfine sugar

2½ teaspoons baking powder

½ teaspoon fine sea salt

7 large eggs, separated

½ teaspoon cream of tartar

½ cup canola oil

¾ cup frozen pineapple juice concentrate, thawed

2 teaspoons vanilla extract

¼ cup dark rum

Mai Tai Glaze

2 cups confectioners' sugar, sifted

¼ cup frozen pineapple juice concentrate, thawed, as needed

Fresh mint, for garnish

• Position a rack in the bottom third of the oven and preheat to 325°F. Have an ungreased 10-inch tube (angel food cake) pan ready. Do not use a nonstick pan.

- To make the cake, sift together the flour, 1 cup of the sugar, the baking powder, and salt. Using an electric mixer at low speed, whip the egg whites and cream of tartar in a large bowl until foamy. Increase the mixer speed to high. Gradually add the remaining $1/2$ cup of sugar, and beat until the whites are stiff and shiny but not dry. In another large bowl, using the mixer at high speed, beat the yolks, vegetable oil, pineapple juice concentrate, and vanilla until the yolks are thick and pale yellow, about $3 1/2$ minutes. Add the flour mixture and beat at medium speed until the batter is well blended, scraping down the sides of the bowl often, about 2 minutes.

- Stir one-fourth of the whites into the batter. In three equal additions, fold in the remaining whites. Pour into the pan and smooth the top.

- Bake, without opening the door for at least 45 minutes, until the cake springs back when pressed, about 1 hour. Invert the cake pan upside down on a wire cake rack. (If the cake rises over the edge of the pan, let the inverted cake pan stand on its "feet" (or stick the tube in a wine bottle.) Let cool for 30 minutes. Stand the cake pan right side up. Poke a few discreet holes in the top of the cake. Drizzle the rum over the cake, and let cool completely in the pan on the cake rack.

- To make the Mai Tai glaze, sift the confectioners' sugar into a bowl. Whisk in enough of the pineapple juice to make a thick but pourable icing.

- Run a dinner knife around the inside of the pan and the tube. Invert and unmold the cake onto a serving platter. Spread the top of the cake with the glaze, letting the excess drip down the sides. Let stand until the icing sets. Garnish with the mint, slice, and serve. (The cake can be stored at room temperature, loosely covered with plastic wrap or a cake dome, for up to 3 days.)

TIP FROM A PRO

Never buy a nonstick tube cake pan. There are two categories of cake that require a tube pan, angel food and chiffon—neither of which has butter in the batter. Both require a tactile surface to cling to as their batters rise. If the pan surface is slick, the batters have nothing to grip, and won't rise as well.

Melt-in-Your-Mouth Chocolate Cake with Dulce de Leche

Makes 10 servings

• •

WHEN I WAS in Buenos Aires on a vacation, I met Lula Dana Smith, a friend of a friend who told me that I could not leave Argentina without tasting her special chocolate cake. When we met again, she produced her masterpiece, and I was not disappointed. A high proportion of cornstarch in the batter gives the single-layer cake an amazingly delicate, light crumb, one that literally melts in your mouth. The crowning glory of this cake is a generous topping of *dulce de leche*. For total decadence, add a scoop of vanilla ice cream.

2/3 cup unbleached all-purpose flour, preferably organic

2/3 cup cornstarch

3/4 teaspoon baking powder

1/2 teaspoon baking soda

1/4 teaspoon fine sea salt

1 1/3 cups granulated sugar

12 tablespoons unsalted butter (1 1/2 sticks), at room temperature

2 large eggs, at room temperature

1 teaspoon vanilla extract

3/4 cup whole milk

1 1/2 cups Dulce de Leche (page 221), for serving

- Position a rack in the center of the oven and preheat to 350°F. Butter and flour a 9-inch springform pan, and tap out the excess flour.

- Melt the chocolate in the top part of a double boiler over hot, not simmering water. Remove from the heat and let cool until tepid.

- Sift together the flour, cornstarch, baking powder, baking soda, and salt. Using an electric mixer at high speed, beat the sugar and butter in a large bowl until the mixture is light and fluffy, about 3 minutes. Gradually beat in the eggs, then beat in the melted chocolate and vanilla. Reduce the mixer speed to low. Starting with the flour mixture, add three equal additions of the flour, alternating with two equal additions of the milk, beating until smooth and scraping down the sides of the bowl after each addition. Spread the batter in the pan.

- Bake until a wooden toothpick inserted in the center of the cake comes out clean, 45 to 50 minutes. Let cool in the pan on a wire cake rack.

- Run a sharp knife around the inside of the pan to loosen the cake from the sides of the pan. Release the sides of the pan. Transfer the cake, keeping it on the pan bottom, to a serving platter. Spread the top of the cake with *dulce de leche*, allowing it to drizzle down the sides. Slice and serve.

Rich Cocoa Cake with Double-Chocolate Frosting

Makes 8 to 10 servings

. . . .

A MOIST, DARK chocolate layer cake, frosted with a smooth and silky frosting, is the holy grail of American baking. Superfine sugar is the sweetener of choice, as its tiny crystals work with the butter to make an especially tender crumb. Sifting the flour mixture three times aerates the dry ingredients and helps ensure a light cake—and makes it absolutely worth the minor additional time and effort required to do this.

2¼ cups unbleached all-purpose flour, preferably organic

¾ cup natural (not Dutch-processed) cocoa powder

2 teaspoons baking soda

½ teaspoon fine sea salt

12 tablespoons (1½ sticks) unsalted butter, at room temperature

1¾ cups superfine sugar

3 large eggs, at room temperature, beaten

2 teaspoons vanilla extract

1 cup whole or low-fat (not nonfat) plain yogurt

Double-Chocolate Frosting (page 98)

- Position a rack in the lower third of the oven and preheat to 350°F. Lightly butter two 9-inch (1½-inch-high) round cake pans. Line the bottoms of the pans with rounds of parchment or waxed paper. (No need to flour the pans in this recipe.)

- Sift the flour, cocoa powder, baking soda, and salt together onto a large sheet of waxed paper. Place the sieve over a large bowl. Lift up the waxed paper on both sides, slip the dry ingredients into the sieve, and sift them into the bowl. Place the sieve on the waxed paper, and sift the dry ingredients again onto the paper, then sift back into the bowl. Repeat once again for a total of three siftings.

- Using an electric mixer at high speed, beat the butter and sugar in a medium-size bowl until creamy, about 2 minutes. Over the course of the next 2 minutes, gradually pour in the eggs, scraping down the bowl as needed. Beat in the vanilla.

- Reduce the mixer speed to low. Starting with the flour mixture, add three equal portions of the flour mixture alternating with two equal additions of the yogurt, stopping to scrape down the sides of the bowl after each addition. Divide the batter evenly among the cake pans and smooth the tops.

- Bake, rotating the pans halfway through baking, until the cake just begins to shrink from the edges of the pan and a toothpick inserted in the center comes out clean, 30 to 35 minutes. Transfer to wire cake racks and let cool for about 10 minutes. Invert the cakes onto the racks and remove the paper. Turn the cakes right side up and let cool completely.

- To assemble the cake, using a long serrated knife, cut each cake layer horizontally in half. Brush away any stray crumbs from the cake layers. Place a dab of frosting in the center of a serving platter. Place a cake layer, rounded side down, on the platter. Slide strips of parchment or waxed paper under the cake layer to protect the platter from the frosting. Reserve about 1 1/4 cups of the frosting.

- Using a metal icing spatula, spread the top of the cake with about one-third of the remaining frosting. Top with a second layer, flat side up, and spread with another third of the frosting. Top with the third layer, flat side up, and spread with the remaining frosting. Top with the fourth layer, rounded side up. Taking care not to get crumbs into the frosting, spread a thin layer of frosting all over the cake. Refrigerate until the frosting is set, about 10 minutes. Spread the cake with the remaining frosting, creating swirls. Slip the paper strips out from under the cake. (The cake can be stored at room temperature, covered with a cake dome, for up to 2 days.)

TIP FROM A PRO

When making a batter or dough, have all the ingredients at the same ambient room temperature, ideally around 70°F. If the temperatures are disparate, cold eggs can curdle and too-warm butter can deflate, and your baked goods won't rise properly. As eggs must be stored in the refrigerator, take them out about an hour before using to let them lose their chill. Or place the uncracked eggs in a bowl of warm tap water, and let stand for 5 minutes to warm a bit.

Mint Julep Cake with Bourbon Buttercream

Makes 8 servings

• •

INSPIRED BY THE famous, lightly sweetened bourbon cocktail, this layer cake may inspire you to throw a Kentucky Derby party. The cake is a classic French genoise, which is leavened by the air beaten into the eggs, not by chemical leaveners. Unlike fat-rich American layer cakes, genoise has only a small amount of butter, so it is purposely dry and must be moistened with syrup. The light caramel flavor of cane syrup works beautifully with the bourbon. I like to serve this with a fresh orange and strawberry salad to balance the cake's richness.

Genoise

3 tablespoons unsalted butter,
   plus more for the pan

¾ cup unbleached all-purpose flour,
   preferably organic, plus more for
   the pan

1 tablespoon cornstarch

⅛ teaspoon fine sea salt

5 large eggs

½ cup granulated sugar

1 teaspoon vanilla extract

Mint Julep Syrup

½ cup light cane syrup (page 88,
   see Note)

3 tablespoons coarsely chopped
   fresh mint

¼ cup bourbon

Mint Garnish

8 small mint sprigs (with only
   2 leaves per sprig, or use 8 large
   mint leaves)

1 large egg white, or 1 tablespoon
   powdered egg whites mixed with
   2 tablespoons water

¼ cup granulated sugar

Bourbon Buttercream (page 100)

- Position a rack in the center of the oven and preheat to 350°F. Lightly butter a 9-inch springform pan. Line the bottom of the pan with a round of parchment or waxed paper. Lightly flour the pan and tap out the excess flour.

- To make the genoise, melt the butter in a small saucepan over medium-low heat until the milk solids are lightly browned. Pour into a medium-size bowl and set aside to cool slightly.

- Sift together the flour, cornstarch, and salt. Whisk the eggs and sugar in a large stainless-steel bowl or the work bowl of a standing heavy-duty electric mixer. Place over a saucepan of lightly simmering water over low heat—the water should not touch the bottom of the bowl. Whisk until the sugar is completely dissolved and the eggs are warm (rub a dab between your fingers to check). Beat with an electric mixer at high speed until the eggs are very light and fluffy and have tripled in volume—this will take about 5 minutes with a hand mixer, or 3 minutes with a standing mixer.

- Sift one-half of the flour mixture over the egg mixture, and fold it in with a rubber spatula. Repeat with the remaining flour mixture, leaving some streaks of flour visible. Scoop about 1 cup of the batter into the bowl of melted butter, add the vanilla, and fold together. Pour into the batter and fold together until smooth and combined. Spread in the pan and smooth the top.

- Bake until the cake is golden brown and the top springs back when pressed in the center, about 25 minutes. Let cool on a wire cake rack for 5 minutes. Run a sharp knife around the inside of the pan to loosen the cake. Remove the sides of the pan. Invert onto the cake rack, remove the cake bottom, and peel off the paper. Turn the cake right side up onto the rack and let cool completely. (The cake can be made up to 2 days ahead, cooled, wrapped in plastic wrap, and stored at room temperature.)

- Meanwhile, make the mint julep syrup. Bring the cane syrup, 1/4 cup of water, and the mint to a boil in a small saucepan over medium heat. Remove from the heat and let stand for 15 minutes to infuse the syrup with the mint. Strain through a wire sieve into a small bowl. Stir in the bourbon. Let cool completely. (The syrup can be made up to 1 day ahead, covered tightly, and stored at room temperature.)

- To make the mint garnish, rinse the mint sprigs and pat them completely dry with paper towels. Beat the egg white in a small bowl until foamy. Place the sugar in another small bowl. Using a small paintbrush, coat the mint sprigs with the beaten egg. Roll in the sugar to coat. Place on a wire cake rack to dry completely, at least 1 hour. (Use the mint garnish within 8 hours of making it.)

- Using a long serrated knife, cut the cake in half horizontally. Place a dab of buttercream in the center of an 8-inch cardboard cake round, a wide, flat plate, or a cake stand. Place the top cake layer on the round, rounded side down. Slip strips of waxed paper under the perimeter of the cake layer. Using a pastry brush, drizzle and brush the cake layer with half of the mint syrup. Spread with $1/2$ cup of the buttercream. Top with the second cake layer, cut side down, and drizzle and brush with the remaining syrup. Spread a thin layer of the buttercream over the top and sides of the cake. Refrigerate until the buttercream sets, about 10 minutes. Keep the remaining buttercream at room temperature.

- Transfer about $2/3$ cup of the reserved buttercream to a pastry bag fitted with a $1/2$-inch star tip (such as Ateco #825 or #865). Spread the remaining buttercream over the top and sides of the cake. Using the buttercream in the pastry bag, pipe 8 equally spaced stars around the perimeter of the cake, and top each with a sugared mint sprig. Slip the paper strips out from under the cake. (The cake can be made up, without the mint garnish, up to 1 day ahead, covered with a cake dome and refrigerated. Add the mint garnish just before serving.) Serve chilled or at room temperature.

NOTE: If cane syrup is unavailable, bring $1/2$ cup of water and $1/3$ cup of packed light brown sugar to a boil in a small saucepan over high heat, stirring to dissolve the sugar. Boil for 2 minutes. Let cool completely. Substitute $1/2$ cup of this syrup for the cane syrup.

Decorating Cakes

As a rule, I do not decorate cakes with festoons of flowers crafted from frosting. You can accomplish a lot in the decorating department with the right frosting and one pastry bag with a single pastry tip. Make the right choices, and you are home free. You can find the pastry bag and tip at kitchenware shops and online. Ateco is a well-distributed manufacturer.

First, the frosting. The Meringue Buttercream Frosting on page 99 is bound to become your go-to icing for layer cakes. It tastes of butter, unlike the terrible shortening-based stuff that is used at too many old-school bakeries (but none that I have ever been involved with), and it holds its shape when used to make rosettes, scallops, and other decorations. Use any of the variations, as befits the cake.

Next, the pastry bag. You want a 14-inch-long plastic-lined canvas bag (the length is clearly marked on the bag). There are disposable plastic bags, but I think they are wasteful and harder to control, so I don't use them at home, where it is not difficult to wash the canvas pastry bag with hot soapy water and air-dry it.

As for the pastry tip, unless you are doing complicated designs such as roses and leaves, you really only need one tip for your basic cake-decorating needs. The most versatile tip is a $1/2$-inch-wide open star tip, such as Ateco #825. For a somewhat more delicate design, you can get an open French star tip (Ateco #865).

To fill the pastry bag, insert the pastry tip through the small end of the bag, with the small end of the tip poking through the bag. (You may have to trim the end of the bag with scissors to enlarge the opening to fit the tip. You will not need a coupler, a plastic gadget that holds the tip in place.) Fold down the top of the bag a few inches to make a cuff. Stand the bag, tip end down, in a tall glass. This makes it easier to fill the bag with frosting. Do not fill the bag more than two-thirds full—you won't need more than $2/3$ cup to pipe eight average-size decorations. Remove the bag from the glass and twist the open end closed, forcing the frosting in the bag down toward the tip.

You are now ready to decorate. Practice on a large sheet of waxed or parchment paper or on a plate. You can scrape up your practice decorations with a metal spatula and reuse the frosting.

To make stars, hold the bag just above the surface of the frosted cake and use steady pressure, without turning the bag, to pipe out a star, then lift up quickly just as you stop squeezing, to finish the decoration.

For rosettes, hold the bag just above the surface of the frosted cake. Using steady pressure, squeeze the frosting out of the bag, turning the bag in a tight circle, and the extruded frosting will swirl on itself to make a rosette. Lift up the bag and stop squeezing the frosting to finish the rosette.

Banana Cake with Malt Chocolate Ganache

Makes 8 servings

· ·

BANANAS AND CHOCOLATE are a very popular couple, and they really strut their stuff in this cake. The bananas should be soft and ripe, with lots of brown spots, but not black-ripe. For a special Valentine's Day dessert, bake the cake batter in a 8- to 9-inch heart-shaped pan. And it is easy to make this in a vegan variation. The cake's moistness can be attributed to the agave syrup, working in tandem with the mashed bananas.

Banana Cake

- 1½ cups unbleached all-purpose flour, preferably organic
- ¾ teaspoon baking soda
- ½ teaspoon baking powder
- ½ teaspoon ground cinnamon
- ¼ teaspoon ground ginger
- ¼ teaspoon fine sea salt
- ¾ cup mashed very ripe bananas (2 medium-size bananas)
- 1 cup agave syrup
- ⅓ cup plus 2 tablespoons canola oil
- 1 teaspoon vanilla extract

Malt Chocolate Ganache

- ⅔ cup heavy cream
- 2 tablespoons malted milk powder (page 91, see Note)
- 1½ cups (9 ounces) bittersweet or milk chocolate chips

For Assembly

- 1 ripe banana
- 1 cup fresh raspberries, for garnish

- Position a rack in the center of the oven and preheat the oven to 350°F. Lightly butter and flour a 9-inch (2-inch-high) round cake pan, tapping out the excess flour.

- To make the cake, sift together the flour, baking soda, baking powder, cinnamon, ginger, and salt into a medium-size bowl. Make a well in the center of the dry ingredients.

- In another medium-size bowl, using an electric mixer at medium speed, beat the bananas till very smooth. Beat in the agave syrup, oil, and vanilla until well combined. Pour into the dry ingredients. With the mixer at medium speed, beat until smooth, scraping down the sides of the bowl with a rubber spatula as necessary. Pour the batter into the pan and smooth the top.

- Bake until a wooden toothpick inserted in the center of the cake comes out clean, about 25 minutes. Let the cake cool on a wire cake rack for 20 minutes. Gently loosen the sides of the cake by running a metal spatula around the inside of the pan. Place the wire rack over the cake and invert. Tap the pan to loosen and remove. Turn the cake right side up and let cool completely.

- To make the ganache, bring the heavy cream to a simmer. Remove from the heat, add malted milk powder, and whisk until dissolved. Add the chocolate and let stand until the chocolate is softened. Whisk until the chocolate is smooth. Transfer to a small bowl. Let stand at room temperature, stirring occasionally, until it cools and is thick and spreadable, about 3 hours. Do not refrigerate.

- To assemble the cake, using a long serrated knife cut the cake horizontally into 2 layers, leveling the top if necessary. Place a dab of the ganache into the center of a serving plate. Place the bottom cake layer on the plate. Spread about one-third of the ganache over the bottom layer, banking it a little thicker around the perimeter of the cake layer. Thinly slice the ripe banana and arrange it around the frosted layer. Top with the second cake layer and press lightly. Frost the top and sides of the cake with the remaining ganache and outline the perimeter of the cake with the fresh raspberries. (The cake can be refrigerated, covered loosely in plastic wrap or a cake dome, for 1 day. Remove the cake from the refrigerator at least 1 hour before serving.)

MIX IT UP

Vegan Banana Cake: In the ganache, omit the malted milk powder. Substitute soy milk for the heavy cream. Use vegan semisweet chocolate chips instead of milk chocolate.

NOTE: It can be a bit of challenge locating malted milk powder at the supermarket. First look in the section with instant milk powder, and if it's not there, it might be with the instant flavorings for stirring into milk. If you can't find plain malted milk powder, use a chocolate-flavored malted milk flavoring, such as Ovaltine.

Burnt Sugar Almond Cake

Makes 12 servings

· ·

THIS EXTRAORDINARY CAKE uses two quick caramelizing techniques to transform the taste of sugar: First, a simple caramel syrup is made to flavor the cake and its icing. The almond crunch is really a kind of toffee, and its ever-so-slightly tannic crispiness cuts nicely through the richness of the icing. Refrigerate any extra caramel syrup and drizzle it, warmed, over ice cream.

Caramel Syrup

½ cup granulated sugar

½ cup boiling water

Caramel Cake

2½ cups unbleached all-purpose flour, preferably organic

2½ teaspoons baking powder

¼ teaspoon fine sea salt

8 tablespoons (1 stick) unsalted butter, at room temperature

1½ cups granulated sugar

2 large eggs, at room temperature, beaten

1 cup whole milk

1 teaspoon vanilla extract

3 tablespoons Carmel Syrup, cooled

Almond Crunch

1½ tablespoons butter

3 tablespoons granulated sugar

¾ cup slivered blanched almonds

Caramel Frosting

2 cups confectioners' sugar

4 tablespoons (½ stick) unsalted butter, at room temperature

1 teaspoon vanilla extract

1½ tablespoons Caramel Syrup, cooled

3 tablespoons whole milk, as needed

- To make the caramel syrup, bring the sugar and 2 tablespoons cold water to a boil in a small, heavy saucepan over high heat, stirring until the sugar dissolves. Cook without stirring until the sugar turns amber and it gives off a whiff of smoke. Carefully and slowly, stir in the boiling water (it will steam and sputter). Boil, stirring often to dissolve any solidified caramel, until it reduces to ½ cup. Let cool completely.

- To make the cake, position a rack in the center of the oven and preheat the oven to 350°. Butter and flour two 9-inch (1½-inch-high) round cake pans, tapping out the excess flour.

- Sift together the flour, baking powder, and salt. Using an electric mixer at high speed, beat the butter in a large bowl until creamy, about 1 minute. Gradually beat in the sugar and beat until the mixture is light and fluffy, about 2 minutes. Gradually beat in the eggs. Reduce the mixer speed to low. Starting with the flour mixture, add three equal additions of the flour, alternating with two equal additions of the milk, beating until smooth and scraping down the sides of the bowl after each addition. Beat in 3 tablespoons of cooled caramel and the vanilla. Divide the batter between the pans and smooth the tops.

- Bake until a toothpick inserted in the center comes out clean, about 25 minutes. Transfer to wire cake racks and let cool for 20 minutes. One at a time, gently loosen the sides of the cake by running a metal spatula around the inside of the pan. Place the rack over the cake and invert. Tap the pan to loosen and remove. Turn the cake right side up and let cool completely.

- To make the almond crunch, line a rimmed baking sheet with parchment paper or a silicone baking mat. Melt the butter and sugar in a heavy duty skillet over medium heat, stirring often. Stir in the almonds. Cook, stirring constantly, reducing the heat if the mixture begins to smoke, until the nuts turn a deep, golden brown, about 6 minutes. Immediately scrape the mixture onto the prepared baking pan and spread thinly. Let cool completely. Break up the crunch into pieces. (The crunch can be prepared up to 1 day ahead, stored in an airtight container at room temperature.)

- To make the frosting, using an electric mixer at low speed, mix the confectioners' sugar, butter, and vanilla until crumbly. Add the cooled caramel, then beat in enough of the milk to make a smooth, spreadable frosting.

- Brush away any stray crumbs from the cake layers. Place a cake layer, flat side down, on a serving platter. Slide strips of parchment or waxed paper under the cake layer to protect the platter from the frosting. Using a metal icing spatula, spread the top of the cake with about $1/2$ cup of the frosting. Top with the second layer and press gently. Taking care not to get crumbs into the frosting, spread a thin layer of frosting all over the cake. Refrigerate for a few minutes to set the frosting. Spread the cake with the remaining frosting. Press the almond crunch over the top and against the sides of the cake. Drizzle a little of the reserved caramel over the top. Slip the paper strips out from under the cake. (The cake can be stored at room temperature, covered with a cake dome, for up to 2 days. If making the cake ahead of time, decorate with the almond crunch just before serving.)

Lemon Cupcakes with Mascarpone Cream and Raspberries

Makes 12 cupcakes

• •

THE HONEYLIKE FLAVOR of agave goes beautifully with citrus flavors, and it's used here to sweeten these lemon cupcakes. Mascarpone has a lemony tartness, too, so the combination is perfect. Use any kind of berries you like to top the cupcakes—blueberries are also good.

Lemon Cupcakes

1¾ cups unbleached all-purpose flour, preferably organic

1½ teaspoons baking powder

½ teaspoon baking soda

¼ teaspoon fine sea salt

10 tablespoons (1¼ sticks) unsalted butter, at room temperature

¾ cup agave syrup

2 large eggs, at room temperature, beaten

½ teaspoon vanilla extract

½ cup whole milk

Grated zest of 1 large lemon

Mascarpone Cream

8 ounces mascarpone, at room temperature

3 tablespoons agave syrup

2½ tablespoons fresh lemon juice

Zest of 1 lemon, removed in thin strips with a lemon zester (see Note)

1 cup fresh raspberries

• Position an oven rack in the bottom third of the oven and preheat the oven to 350°F. Line twelve muffin cups with paper liners.

• To make the cupcakes, sift together the flour, baking powder, baking soda, and salt. Using an electric mixer at high speed, beat the butter in a large bowl until smooth, about 1 minute. Mix in the agave syrup (don't worry if the mixture curdles). Gradually beat in the eggs, which will help the butter mixture emulsify. Beat in the vanilla. Reduce the mixer speed to low. Starting with the flour mixture, add three equal additions of the flour, alternating with **two** equal additions of the milk, increasing the speed to high for a few **sec**onds and beating until smooth after each addition. Be sure to scrape **the** sides of the bowl often during mixing. When the batter is smooth, return the mixer speed to high and whip the batter for about 20 seconds. Stir in the lemon zest. Divide the batter evenly among the muffin cups.

- Bake until a cupcake bounces back when pressed gently with a finger, 25 to 30 minutes. Let cool on a wire cake rack for a few minutes. Remove the cupcakes from the pan, transfer to the rack, and let cool completely.

- To make the mascarpone cream, put the mascarpone in a small bowl. Whisk in the agave syrup and lemon juice. Refrigerate until the cream is firm enough to spread, about 30 minutes. If the cream has separated, whisk well to recombine.

- Spread the cupcakes with the mascarpone cream. Garnish with freshly grated lemon zest and the raspberries. Store at room temperature until ready to serve. These cupcakes are best served the day they are made.

NOTE: Most serious cooks have a rasp-type zester, which removes citrus zest in very small shreds for flavoring food. However, the old-fashioned lemon zester, with three or four small holes to remove the zest in thin strips for garnishing, is also useful. If you don't have the latter, remove the zest from the lemon with a vegetable peeler, and cut it into very thin strips with a large knife.

Muscovado Cheesecake with Graham Cracker Cornmeal Crust

Makes 10 to 12 servings

●●●●●●●●●●●●●●●●●●●●●●●●●●●●●●

ZINGERMAN'S DELICATESSEN is not just the pride of Ann Arbor, Michigan—it is one of the best specialty food shops in the country. By coincidence, their pastry manager, Charlie Frank, and I come from the same town not far from Zingerman's. It was this hometown connection that helped me score the recipe for this excellent cheesecake. The rich taste of molasses infuses the cake from muscovado-sweetened filling and topping to the graham cracker crust, which has the unusual addition of crunchy cornmeal. (I've included a brown sugar option, should you not have muscovado on hand.)

Graham Cracker Cornmeal Crust

3/4 cup graham cracker crumbs

1/2 cup yellow cornmeal

3 tablespoons granulated sugar

6 tablespoons (3/4 stick) unsalted
   butter, melted

Pinch of fine sea salt

Filling

1 pound cream cheese, at room
   temperature

4 tablespoons (1/2 stick) unsalted
   butter, at room temperature

1 cup muscovado sugar, packed, or
   1 cup dark brown sugar, packed

3 large eggs

1/2 cup sour cream

1 1/2 tablespoons mild or robust
   molasses (increase to 3 tablespoons
   if using dark brown sugar)

1 1/2 teaspoons vanilla extract

Topping

2/3 cup sour cream

2 tablespoons muscovado sugar

1/2 teaspoon vanilla extract

- Position a rack in the center of the oven and preheat to 350°F. Butter a 9-inch springform pan. Wrap the bottom and sides with a double layer of aluminum foil.

- To make the crust, combine the graham cracker crumbs, cornmeal, granulated sugar, melted butter, and salt in a food processor fitted with the metal chopping blade. Pulse until the mixture is well combined. Transfer to the pan and press firmly and evenly into the bottom and 1 inch up the sides. Bake until the edges are lightly browned, about 15 minutes. Transfer to a wire cake rack and lower the oven temperature to 300°F.

- Using the flat blade of a stand mixer set on low to medium speed and whip the cream cheese and butter till smooth, stopping to scrape the sides and bottom of the bowl. Add the muscovado sugar, stop and scrape, then add the eggs one at a time. Finally, add the sour cream, molasses and vanilla. To ensure even mixing, stop and scrape as you go and do not mix on a high speed or you will add air to the mixture.

- Place the cheesecake in a roasting pan. Add enough hot tap water to the roasting pan to come about 1 inch up the sides of the springform pan. Transfer to the oven. Bake until the edges of the filling are lightly risen and the center barely jiggles when the pan is nudged, about 1 hour. Remove the cheesecake from the hot water. Run a thin sharp knife around the inside of the pan to loosen the cheesecake from the sides (this helps the cheesecake contract during cooling without cracking.)

- Meanwhile, prepare the topping. Whisk the sour cream, muscovado sugar, and vanilla in a small bowl. Spread the sour cream mixture over the baked cheesecake and return to the oven. Turn the oven off and leave the oven door barely ajar. Cool the cheesecake in the oven for 1 hour. Transfer to a wire cake rack and let cool completely.

- Remove the sides of the cake pan. Cover the cake loosely with plastic wrap and refrigerate until well chilled, at least 6 hours or up to 2 days. To serve, cut into wedges with a very sharp thin knife dipped into hot water and dried before making each slice. Serve chilled.

TIP FROM A PRO

One important tip about making cheesecake: Do not beat the cream cheese mixture at high speed, or you will add too much air to the batter. This makes the filling rise in the oven and then deflate and is one cause of cracked cheesecakes.

Double-Chocolate Frosting

Makes about 2½ cups frosting,
enough for one 9-inch four-layer cake

....

A COMBINATION OF melted chocolate and cocoa gives this frosting a deep, dark flavor that will take you right back to the best cakes of your childhood. Confectioners' sugar has an amazing ability to fluff into creamy and infinitely spreadable frosting. Soon after the cake is frosted, however, the sugar firms up, locking in flavor and holding those whimsical swirls in place with a slight crunch. Then, on the first bite, it melts away, revealing all the delectable richness of the chocolate, cream, and butter.

8 ounces unsweetened chocolate, chopped

7 tablespoons (½ stick plus 3 tablespoons) unsalted butter, at room temperature

2¼ cups confectioners' sugar

3 tablespoons Dutch-processed or natural cocoa powder (see Note)

¾ cup heavy cream

2 teaspoons vanilla extract

Scant ⅛ teaspoon fine sea salt

- Melt the chocolate and butter together in the top part of a double boiler set over hot, not boiling, water, stirring occasionally. Transfer to a medium-size bowl and let cool slightly.

- Sift together the confectioners' sugar and cocoa. Add the cream, vanilla, and salt to the melted chocolate mixture. Using an electric mixer at low speed, beat the mixture until combined. Gradually mix in the confectioners' sugar mixture, mixing until the frosting is smooth. Increase the mixer speed to medium and beat briefly until the frosting is fluffy. Use immediately.

NOTE: Because there are no chemical leaveners in this frosting, you don't have to worry about what kind of cocoa to use. Dutch-processed cocoa will give the brown frosting a reddish tinge; natural cocoa will have a slightly deeper color.

Meringue Buttercream Frosting

Makes about 3½ cups frosting,
enough for one 9-inch double-layer cake

∙∙∙∙∙∙∙∙∙∙∙∙∙∙∙∙∙∙∙∙∙∙∙∙∙∙∙

IVORY-HUED MERINGUE buttercream frosting is quite different from the typical American icing made with confectioners' sugar. Created by the Swiss meringue technique (see box on page 100), it is lighter in both color and texture, and it isn't as sweet. A standing electric mixer is really required here, as the various steps are hard to juggle with a handheld mixer. *The* classic buttercream, it deserves to be in every baker's repertoire and is easy to make in various flavors.

1 cup superfine sugar

4 large egg whites

28 tablespoons (3½ sticks) unsalted butter, at room
    temperature, cut into 1-tablespoon pieces

2 teaspoons vanilla extract

- Whisk the sugar, egg whites, and 2 tablespoons of water in the work bowl of a standing heavy-duty electric mixer, just to combine. Place over a saucepan of gently simmering water—the bottom of the bowl should not touch the water. Stir gently with the whisk (do not incorporate air at this point) until the sugar is completely dissolved and the mixture feels very hot to the touch.

- Attach the bowl to the mixer and affix the whisk attachment. Beat at low speed until the mixture is foamy. Increase the speed to high and beat until the meringue forms stiff, shiny peaks. Reduce the mixer speed to medium-low and beat until the meringue is cool, about 10 minutes.

- One tablespoon at a time, beat the butter into the meringue. Beat until the frosting is smooth and fluffy. Beat in the vanilla. Use immediately.

MIX IT UP

Bourbon Buttercream: Beat 2 tablespoons of bourbon into the finished buttercream.

Chocolate Buttercream: Melt 4 ounces of unsweetened chocolate and let cool until tepid. Beat the melted chocolate into the finished buttercream. This makes a pale brown frosting with a delicate chocolate flavor.

Citrus Buttercream: Beat the grated zest of two oranges or three lemons into the finished buttercream.

Meringues

A HAPPY MARRIAGE of whipped egg whites and sugar, meringue is one of the most versatile tools of the baker's trade. It can be baked on its own into confection-like cookies (or cookielike confections), or used as a topping for pies and tarts. It can even be transformed into a light buttercream frosting.

Meringue is another example of chemistry in cooking. When the egg whites are beaten, the proteins unfold, allowing air to be incorporated. Sugar helps coagulate the proteins, and the liquid whites become semisolid.

There are three kinds of meringues:

French meringue is the one that most home bakers are familiar with. Egg whites are whipped to the soft-peak stage, sugar is slowly added, and the meringue is beaten until stiff, shiny peaks form. As the meringue is raw, it is baked before eating.

Italian meringue is created by beating hot syrup into the egg whites. This makes a tender meringue that is cooked by the heat of the syrup. Italian meringue is usually only seared by a heat source (a kitchen torch or a broiler) to brown and set the outside, leaving the inside soft.

Swiss meringue is the result of heating the whites and sugar until the mixture is hot, then beating until cool and fluffy. It can be baked to make an especially crisp meringue, or used as the base of buttercream frosting.

Pies, Tarts, and Cobblers

5

*J*UST AS A PIE can be filled with slices of fruit, or lemon curd, or chocolate mousse, many different pastry doughs can be used to make crusts for baked goods. And just as I believe that one should choose the right sweetener for the job, I also feel that you should use a specific dough for your dessert. Therefore, each of these desserts comes with its own dough. Some pastry crusts are sweeter than others, the better to set off a less sweet filling. Some are purposely unsweetened to avoid competition with a sugary filling. Some pastries benefit from the rich flavor and crisp texture imparted by butter; others get their flakiness from shortening.

The choice of fat affects the ultimate tenderness of the crust. Again, understanding a little about how the ingredients work together will help you in the kitchen. Moisture strengthens the gluten in flour, as does handling the dough, which is why pastry recipes warn against overworking dough. However, because butter already contains moisture, as soon as you cut it into flour to make pastry, it begins to strengthen the gluten. Shortenings (and lard, which I do not cook with because of the strong flavor it gives dough) are almost 100 percent fat without any moisture, so the affect on gluten is minimized, and they make especially tender doughs. I much prefer trans fat–free shortening for my baking, however, it is made with tropical fats that are harder than hydrogenated vegetable fats, and the pastry can be quite crisp. To counter this, I add a little vegetable oil to my shortening-based doughs—a trick you might like to employ.

101

Meyer Lemon Shaker Pie

Makes 8 servings

· ·

THE **O**HIO **AND** Kentucky members of the Shaker religious group were fine cooks who knew about the various properties of sugar (they were famous for their preserves). This unusual lemon pie has a marmalade-like filling of very thin lemon slices macerated with sugar, which tenderizes the peel and makes it less bitter. The Shakers probably got the lemons in travels south along the river ways, and perhaps they preserved sliced lemons in sugar on the trip back. Regardless of its history, it is a winning dessert and sure to start a conversation. It is never better than when made with fragrant Meyer lemons, although regular supermarket lemons work well, too.

Filling

3 lemons, preferably Meyer

2 cups granulated sugar

4 large eggs

Pinch of fine sea salt

Double-Crust Pie Dough

2 cups unbleached all-purpose flour, preferably organic

1/4 cup granulated sugar

1/4 teaspoon fine sea salt

1 cup (2 sticks) unsalted butter, chilled, cut into 1/2-inch pieces

1/3 cup plus 1 tablespoon ice water, as needed

- Make the filling at least 18 hours before baking the pie. Using a serrated knife, cut the lemons as thinly as possible into rounds, removing the seeds as you go. Transfer to a nonreactive bowl and toss with the sugar. Cover and let stand at room temperature, stirring occasionally, at least 18 and up to 24 hours. Do not refrigerate the filling. The lemon juices and sugar will create a thick lemon syrup.

- To make the pie dough, mix the flour, sugar, and salt in a large bowl. Add the butter. Using a pastry blender, cut the butter into the flour until the mixture resembles coarse bread crumbs with some pea-size pieces of butter. Gradually stir in enough of the water for the dough to clump together. Gather up the dough and divide into two portions, one slightly larger than the other. Press each half into a thick disk, wrap in plastic wrap, and refrigerate until chilled but not hard, 1 to 2 hours.

- Drain the filling in a colander set over a large bowl. Measure out 1/2 cup of the lemon syrup. Discard the remaining syrup or refrigerate it in an airtight container for up to 1 month. (It is great stirred into hot or iced tea.) Whisk the eggs in a large bowl, then whisk in the syrup until combined. Add the drained lemon slices and mix gently.

- Position a rack in the lower third of the oven and preheat to 425°F.

- On a lightly floured work surface, roll out the larger portion of dough into a 1/8-inch-thick round. Transfer to a 9-inch pie dish, trimming the dough to a 1/2-inch overhang around the edges of the dish. Spread the lemon mixture in the dish. Roll out the remaining dough into a 1/8-inch-thick round, and center over filling. Pinch the edges of the dough layers together, and flute the edges. Cut a few slits in the top crust.

- Place the pie on a rimmed baking sheet. Bake for 20 minutes. Lower the oven temperature to 375°F and bake until the top is golden brown and a knife inserted through a slit into the filling comes out relatively clean, 25 to 30 minutes more. Let cool completely on a wire cake rack, at least 3 hours. Cut into wedges and serve at room temperature. (The pie can be stored, covered, and refrigerated, for up to 2 days. Remove from the refrigerator 1 hour before serving.)

Lemon Curd Pie with Brown Sugar Meringue

Makes enough for a 9½-inch tart shell

• •

THIS IS A slightly nontraditional take on a beloved dessert. The lemon curd filling is worth making on its own for slathering on muffins and scones. The Italian-style meringue (see page 100) imparts a rich, smooth, and luxurious texture. I often use light brown sugar in the meringue to cut through the tart richness of the lemon curd and add an element of contrast. You will need a hand mixer for the curd, but a heavy-duty standing mixer works best for the meringue.

Tart Shell

1¼ cups unbleached all-purpose flour, preferably organic

¼ teaspoon salt

8 tablespoons cold unsalted butter, cut into bits

¼ cup ice water

⅛ teaspoon cider vinegar

Lemon Curd

4 large eggs

1 cup granulated or superfine sugar

Grated zest of 1 lemon

⅔ cup freshly squeezed lemon juice

4 tablespoons (½ stick) unsalted butter, at room temperature, cut into 8 pieces

Brown Sugar Meringue

4 egg whites

⅛ teaspoon cream of tartar

1 cup light brown sugar, packed

• To make the tart dough, mix the flour and salt together in a large bowl. Add the butter. Using a pastry blender, cut the butter into the flour until the mixture resembles coarse bread crumbs with some pea-size pieces of butter. Mix the ice water and vinegar together. Gradually stir in enough of the water to the flour mixture for the dough to clump together. Do not overmix. Shape into a thick disk and wrap in plastic wrap. Refrigerate for at least 1 hour or up to 2 days.

- Place the chilled dough on a work surface and whack it a few times with a rolling pin to make the dough more malleable. Unwrap the dough and place on a lightly floured work surface. Dust the top of the dough with flour. Roll the dough into a round about 11 inches wide and 1/8 inch thick. Fold in half and transfer to a 9-inch tart pan with a removable bottom. Unfold the dough, letting the excess dough hang over the edges. Press the dough firmly into the corners of the pan. Fold over the excess dough so the fold is flush with the top of the pan. Press the sides of the dough against the pan so it rises about 1/8 inch above the top of the pan (this allows for shrinkage during baking). Refrigerate for 15 minutes.

- Preheat the oven to 350°F. Line the tart shell with parchment paper and fill with pie weights (or raw rice or beans), being sure the weights are pressed up against the sides of the pan. Bake for about 15 minutes, until the visible top of the crust looks set. Lift off the paper and weights. Continue baking the crust until it is golden brown, about 10 minutes more. Transfer to a wire rack and let cool completely.

- To make the lemon curd, combine the eggs and sugar in the top part of a double boiler or a heatproof bowl that fits snugly in a medium-size saucepan. Beat with a handheld electric mixer at high speed until the mixture is light and fluffy, about 3 minutes. Beat in the lemon zest and juice. Bring a small quantity of water to a simmer in the base section of the double boiler. Place the top of the double boiler over its base, being sure that the bottom of the insert does not touch the water. Beat with the mixer until the curd is thick and smooth (it will bubble up, but don't worry), about 8 minutes.

- Remove the insert from the base of the double boiler. Beat in the butter, one piece at a time, until it is fully incorporated. Strain through a wire sieve into a bowl. Press plastic wrap directly on the surface of the curd and poke a few holes in the wrap to allow steam to escape. Let cool until tepid. Refrigerate until chilled, about 2 hours.

- To make the meringue, place the egg whites and cream of tartar in a heavy-duty standing electric mixer fitted with the whisk attachment.

Combine the brown sugar and 1/2 cup water in a small, heavy saucepan. Bring to a boil over high heat, stirring to dissolve the sugar. Attach a candy thermometer to the pan and cook without stirring, brushing down any crystals that form on the inside of the pan with a pastry brush dipped in cold water, until the syrup reaches 240°F. At this point, start whisking the egg whites at low speed. When the sugar reaches 245°F (soft-ball stage), turn off the heat and remove the thermometer from the sugar. Increase the mixer speed to high. When soft peaks form, with the mixer still running, pour the syrup into the egg whites in a thin stream, taking care to avoid the whisk. When steam starts to come off the whites, add the sugar more quickly. When all sugar has been added, continue whipping the whites until they are stiff and glossy. The meringue should still be warm.

- To assemble the tart, spread the chilled lemon curd in the cooled tart shell, smoothing the top. Quickly spread the warm meringue on top of the filling, shaping it with a rubber spatula to form a high, smooth dome, being sure that the meringue touches the crust. Take care not to let the meringue touch the pan, or it may be difficult to remove the tart. With the back of a soup spoon, make decorative waves, working quickly because as the meringue cools it will become stiff and difficult to shape.

- Position the broiler rack about 8 inches from the source of heat and preheat the broiler. Place the pie on the rack and broil, turning the pie every 15 seconds or so, until the meringue is evenly browned. Remove the sides of the pan. Cut with a sharp knife dipped into hot water between slices. The pie is best served the day it is made.

Treacle Tart with Brown Sugar–Walnut Crust

Makes 8 servings

• •

TRADITIONAL RECIPES for this beloved British tart calls for golden syrup instead of the darker, thick-as-tar treacle. (I made one with treacle and it was too bitter, even for a molasses lover like me.) The walnut crust and ground walnut filling add another layer of flavor. If you are a fan of salty caramel, serve with a sprinkling of flaky sea salt, such as *fleur de sel* or Maldon, to accentuate the taste and cut the richness.

Walnut Crust

¾ cup (3 ounces) walnuts, toasted (see page 129)

¼ cup light muscovado or brown sugar, packed

1 cup unbleached all-purpose flour, preferably organic

⅛ teaspoon ground cinnamon

¼ teaspoon fine sea salt

8 tablespoons (1 stick) unsalted, cut into ½-inch pieces, chilled

1 large egg, beaten

½ teaspoon vanilla extract

Filling

1 lemon

1 cup golden syrup

3 tablespoons unbleached all-purpose flour, preferably organic

1 teaspoon ground ginger

Brown Sugar Whipped Cream (page 120) for serving

• To make the crust, pulse the walnuts and 2 tablespoons of the brown sugar in a food processor fitted with the metal chopping blade until the nuts are finely chopped but not oily. Measure out and reserve ½ cup of the walnut mixture for the filling. Leave the remaining walnut mixture in the food processor.

- Add the flour, remaining 2 tablespoons of brown sugar, the cinnamon, and the salt to the food processor and pulse briefly to combine. Add the butter and pulse until the mixture resembles coarse crumbs. Mix together the egg and vanilla in a small bowl. With the machine running, add the egg mixture through the feed tube and process just until the dough comes together. Do not overprocess. Shape the dough into a thick disk and wrap in plastic wrap. Refrigerate until chilled, at least 2 and up to 12 hours.

- Roll out the dough on a well-floured work surface into a 1/8-inch-thick round. Fit into a 9 1/2-inch tart pan and trim the dough flush with the edge of the pan. Line the dough with parchment paper. Refrigerate while preheating the oven.

- Position a rack in the bottom third of the oven and preheat to 375°F. Top the parchment paper–covered dough with aluminum pie weights or dried beans. Place the pan on a baking sheet. Bake until the edges of the dough are lightly browned, about 15 minutes. Remove the baking sheet with the pan from the oven. Remove the paper with the weights. Lower the oven temperature to 350°F.

- To make the filling, grate the zest from the lemon and squeeze 1 tablespoon of lemon juice. Heat the golden syrup in a small saucepan over low heat, just until it is more fluid. Mix the reserved walnut mixture with the flour, and stir into the saucepan, along with the lemon zest and juice, and the ginger. Pour into the tart shell. Return to the oven and bake until the filling is browned and bubbling, 25 to 30 minutes. Transfer to a wire cake rack and let cool. Cut into wedges and serve. (The tart can be stored, covered, and refrigerated, for up to 3 days. Remove from the refrigerator 1 hour before serving.)

TIP FROM A PRO

One of the challenges of baking a tart or pie is to ensure that the bottom crust is nice and crisp, even while the filling is moist. The best way to accomplish this balance is to bake the pastry on an oven rack positioned on the bottom third of the oven, where it is relatively close to a heating element and will brown more quickly from the additional heat. The opposite is true when you want to brown the top of a pastry—place it in the upper third of the oven where it will have radiant heat from the top element.

Dairy-Free Pumpkin Pie

Makes 8 servings

. . . .

I HAVE A number of friends who are lactose-intolerant, and I have made a specialty of dairy-free baking. I have served this soy milk–based pumpkin pie at Thanksgiving dinners without mentioning its dairy-free provenance, and everyone, milk lover or not, gobbles it up. (The sign of a really good "healthful" recipe is when no one can tell the difference from the traditional version.) It can be made with half-and-half if you like, but I actually prefer the natural sweetness of soy milk in the filling. And brown sugar really pumps up the squash flavor. If dairy products aren't an issue, serve it with whipped cream.

Tender Pie Dough

1 1/2 cups all purpose flour

1/2 teaspoon fine sea salt

6 tablespoons nonhydrogenated vegetable shortening

3 tablespoons vegetable oil

4 tablespoons ice water, as needed

Pumpkin Filling

2 cups canned solid-pack pumpkin

1 1/2 cups soy milk (or half-and-half, for a non-dairy-free pie)

2/3 cup dark brown sugar, packed

1/3 cup granulated sugar

1 teaspoon ground cinnamon

3/4 teaspoon ground ginger

1/4 teaspoon ground allspice

1/4 teaspoon freshly grated nutmeg

2 large eggs, beaten

- To make the dough, mix together the flour and salt in a medium-size bowl. Add the shortening and oil. Using a pastry blender, cut the shortening and oil into the flour until the mixture resembles coarse crumbs. Stirring with a fork, gradually add the ice water 1 tablespoon at a time, until the dough is moist enough to hold together when pinched between your thumb and forefinger. You may need more or less ice water to moisten the dough, and the dough need not form into a ball. Gather the dough into a thick disk and wrap in plastic wrap. Refrigerate for at least 1 and up to 12 hours.

- Position a rack in the center of the oven and preheat to 425°F.

- Roll out the dough on a lightly floured work surface into a 13-inch round about 1/8 inch thick. Fit into a 9-inch pie pan. Trim the dough to a 1/2-inch overhang. Fold the edge of the dough under and flute the edges. Pierce the dough in a few places with a fork. Refrigerate while making the filling.

- Combine the pumpkin, soy milk, brown and granulated sugars, cinnamon, ginger, allspice, and nutmeg in a blender and process till smooth. (You may have to do this in batches.) In a large bowl, whisk the eggs. Add the pumpkin mixture and whisk to combine. Pour into the crust. Place the pan on a baking sheet.

- Bake for 15 minutes. Lower the oven to 350°F. Bake just until the filling is puffed but the very center still trembles when the pan is gently shaken, 40 to 50 minutes more. (Do not test by inserting a knife to see if it comes out clean, as this small cut could grow into a large crack as the pie cools and contracts.) Transfer to a wire cake rack and let cool completely. (The pie can be made 2 days ahead, covered, and refrigerated.)

TIP FROM A PRO

Don't try to stir the brown sugar into the filling—it must be processed in a blender to dissolve. In fact, brown sugar often has large lumps that, although moist, may not break up in a batter that will be prepared with a mixer. In that case, sieve the sugar before adding to the batter. This will break up the lumps and give the sugar a lighter texture that dissolves readily. Set a coarse-meshed wire sieve over a bowl. Pack and measure the required amount of brown sugar, then use your fingers to rub the brown sugar through the sieve.

Deep-Dish All-Apple Kuchen

Makes 12 servings

· ·

IN THE GERMAN baking tradition, *Küchen* refers to just about any kind of cake or pastry, but in German-American communities, *kuchen* means a rectangular fruit dessert made with pastry dough—yes, a pie, but not a round one. It is also easy to transport, and a splendid choice to take to a tailgate party or potluck.

The apple juice concentrate and fresh apples really work hand in hand here, melding together in a way that captures the pure flavor of apples. Because the apple and lemon juice have a tart edge, it is best to use a sweet apple such as Golden Delicious or Fuji.

Deep-Dish Kuchen Dough

3 cups unbleached all-purpose flour, preferably organic

1½ teaspoons fine sea salt

1 cup (2 sticks) unsalted butter, cut in ½-inch pieces, chilled

¾ cup ice water, as needed

Apple Filling

8 Golden Delicious or Fuji apples (3½ pounds), peeled, cored, and sliced

3 tablespoons fresh lemon juice

1½ cups frozen apple juice concentrate, thawed

⅔ cup cornstarch

2 teaspoons ground cinnamon

- To make the dough, mix together the flour and salt in a large bowl. Add the butter. Using a pastry blender, cut in the butter until the mixture resembles coarse crumbs. Stirring with a fork, gradually add the ice water 1 tablespoon at a time, until the dough is moist enough to hold together when pinched between your thumb and forefinger. You may need more or less ice water to moisten the dough, and the dough need not form into a ball. Gather up the dough and press it together. Divide the dough into one-third and two-thirds portions and shape into rectangles. Wrap each in plastic wrap and refrigerate for at least 2 and up to 12 hours.

- To make the filling, toss the apples with the lemon juice. In another bowl, whisk the thawed apple juice concentrate, cornstarch, and cinnamon.

- Position a rack in the upper third of the oven and preheat to 325°F.

- Roll the larger portion of dough on a lightly floured surface to a 15 by 18-inch rectangle about $1/8$ inch thick. Transfer to a 9 by 13-inch baking dish. Spread the apples as evenly as possible in the crust, and drizzle with the apple juice mixture. Roll the remaining portion of dough into a 10 by 14-inch rectangle and place it on top of the apples. Tuck the edges of the top crust down the sides and pinch the edges of the top and bottom crust together. Cut several slits in the crust to allow steam to escape.

- Bake until the crust is golden brown and the apple juices are bubbling through the slits in the crust, about 2 hours. Transfer to a wire cake rack and let cool. Serve warm or cooled to room temperature. (The kuchen can be stored at room temperature for up to 3 days.)

TIPS FROM A PRO

For the best apple desserts, take a trip to your local farmers' market, and ask the orchard proprietors for recommendations. Often, they have unfamiliar varieties just waiting to be discovered. The apples should have a good tart-sweet balance, and hold their shape after baking. Reliable common apples perfect for apple pie include Jonathan, Jonagold, Pippin, Empire, Rome Beauty, and Mutsu. Granny Smiths are only okay for pies, as they turn gray when cooked. On the East Coast, Golden Delicious apples are a good choice, but they don't seem to travel too well. Some apples are quite tart (California's Gravenstein, for example), so you have the choice of adding more sugar to taste or just going with the natural tang. Many bakers like to mix firm apples with varieties that will break down into sauce during cooking, such as McIntosh or Cortland. This is just as valid as a filling with stacked layers of relatively intact apples. Use whatever apples you like, as experimenting and noting the results are part of the fun of baking.

Clockwise from center:
dark muscovado, panela, organic cane sugar,
palm sugar, demerara, light muscavado, turbinado

Clockwise from right:
yacón, molasses, cane syrup, honey, dark corn syrup

Inset: Wild Berry Pancakes (page 42)
Pumpkin Waffles with Muscovado Syrup (page 44)

Lemon Curd Pie with Brown Sugar Meringue (page 104)

Left to right:
Dulce de Leche Sandwich Cookies (page 150)
Semolina-Citrus Turbinados (page 142)
Black-and-White Chocolate Drops (page 130)

Sticky Toffee Pudding
(page 168)

Thai Sticky Black Rice and Mangoes (page 170)

Raspberry Sorbet Cream (page 214) with Semolina-Citrus Turbinados (page 142)

Smoky Pumpkin Seed Brittle (page 186)

Hazelnut-Espresso-Caramel Tart

Makes 8 to 10 very rich servings

. . . .

WHEN YOU NEED a showstopper dessert for a special dinner party or other celebration, consider this multifaceted tart, with flavor layered upon flavor, and a symphony of contrasting textures. When making the espresso-caramel syrup, you want to be sure to let the caramel get good and dark—the resulting bitter edge will serve to cut through the sweetness. Undercooked, pale caramel just doesn't have much flavor.

Tart Dough

1¼ cups unbleached all-purpose flour, preferably organic

¼ teaspoon fine sea salt

1 cup (2 sticks) unsalted butter, cut into ½-inch pieces, chilled

4 tablespoons ice water, as needed

⅛ teaspoon cider vinegar

1½ cups (6 ounces) hazelnuts

Espresso-Caramel Syrup

½ cup granulated sugar

¼ cup hot freshly brewed espresso, or 1 tablespoon instant espresso dissolved in ¼ cup boiling water

Hazelnut Pastry Cream

2 tablespoons whole milk

2 tablespoons cornstarch

2 cups heavy cream

1 large egg plus 1 large egg yolk

⅓ cup plus 1 tablespoon granulated sugar

Zest of ¼ lemon, removed with a vegetable peeler, cut into strips

4 tablespoons (½ stick) unsalted butter, cut into ½-inch pieces

1 teaspoon vanilla extract

Bittersweet Chocolate Glaze

5 ounces bittersweet chocolate, chopped coarsely

6 tablespoons unsalted butter, cut into ½-inch pieces

1 tablespoon light corn syrup

- To make the tart dough, whisk the flour and salt together in a medium-size bowl. Add the butter. Using a pastry blender, cut in the butter until the mixture resembles coarse crumbs. Mix together the ice water and vinegar. Using a fork, stir enough of the ice water mixture into the flour mixture for the dough to begin to come together into a ball. If the dough is too dry, add more ice water, 1 teaspoon at a time. Do not overmix. Shape into a thick disk and wrap in plastic wrap. Refrigerate until chilled, at least 1 hour and up to 2 hours. (The dough is easiest to roll out if it is chilled, but not hard.)

- Unwrap the dough and place on a lightly floured work surface. Roll out the dough into 14-inch round about ⅛ inch thick. Transfer the dough to a 9-inch tart pan, being sure that the dough fits snugly in the corners of the pan. Allow the excess to hang over the edges and fold this under to align with the rim of the pan, creating a double thickness at the sides of the pan. Press the sides in firmly so the dough edge rises about ⅛ inch above the edge of the pan, as it will shrink while baking. Line the dough with aluminum foil. Refrigerate for 30 minutes.

- Position a rack in the lower third of the oven and preheat to 350°F. Top the aluminum foil–covered dough with aluminum pie weights or dried beans. Place the pan on a baking sheet. Bake until the edges of the dough are lightly browned, about 15 minutes. Remove the baking sheet with the pan from the oven. Remove the foil with the weights. Return the sheet and pan to the oven and bake until the crust is golden brown, 10 to 15 minutes more. Transfer to a wire cake rack and let cool completely.

- While the oven is still hot, toast the hazelnuts. Spread the hazelnuts on a rimmed baking sheet. Bake in a preheated 350°F oven, stirring occasionally, until the skins are cracked and the nut is lightly toasted, about 10 minutes. Transfer to a clean kitchen towel and let cool for a few minutes. Rub the nuts in the towel to remove as much of the skin as possible—a few clinging skins won't hurt. You will use ½ cup of the hazelnuts in the pastry cream, and the remainder to garnish the tart.

- To make the espresso-caramel syrup, combine the sugar and 2 tablespoons of water in a heavy-bottomed, small saucepan. Bring to a boil over high heat, stirring constantly until the sugar dissolves. Stop stirring and boil, occasionally swirling the pan by its handle and brushing down any crystals that form on the sides of the pan with a pastry brush dipped in cold water, until the mixture turns dark caramel brown (you may see a wisp of smoke), about 5 minutes. Use your nose as well as your eyes here, and detect a sharp, toasted aroma before you deem the caramel finished. Remove the pan from the heat. Carefully—it will bubble up—stir in the espresso until combined. If the caramel solidifies, return the saucepan to low heat and stir until it dissolves. Pour into a glass measuring cup and let cool completely.

- To make the pastry cream, pour the milk into a heavy-bottomed medium-size saucepan. Sprinkle in the cornstarch and whisk to dissolve. Whisk together the cream, egg, egg yolk, and 1/3 cup of sugar in a medium-size bowl, then whisk into the milk mixture. Add the lemon zest and the butter. Cook over medium-low heat, stirring constantly, until the mixture comes to full boil. Remove from the heat and stir in the vanilla. Strain through a wire sieve into a bowl and discard the lemon zest and press a piece of plastic wrap directly on the surface of the pastry cream. Pierce a few slits in the plastic and let cool.

- Just before assembling the tart, make the chocolate glaze. Melt the chocolate and butter in the top part of a double boiler over hot, not simmering, water, stirring occasionally. Remove from the heat and stir in the corn syrup.

- To assemble the tart, finish the pastry cream. Pulse 1/2 cup of the toasted hazelnuts with 1 tablespoon of sugar in a food processor fitted with the metal chopping blade until very finely chopped but not oily. Add to the cooled pastry cream. Add 1/2 cup of the chocolate glaze and 1/4 cup of the espresso-caramel syrup (reserve the remaining caramel for later use) and fold everything together to combine. Do not whisk the cooled pastry cream, or it may thin out.

- Immediately spread the pastry cream in the cooled tart shell. Drizzle the remaining chocolate glaze in a freeform, decorative pattern on top. If you wish, spread the glaze evenly in a very thin layer that reaches the crust. Arrange the remaining hazelnuts around the edge of the tart, placing a few in a jumble in the center. Refrigerate until the glaze sets, at least 1 hour. (The tart can be made and refrigerated, up to 1 day ahead.) Remove from the refrigerator 1 hour before serving. Cut into wedges and serve.

Apple and Rhubarb Cobbler with Semolina Biscuit Crunch

Makes 6 to 8 servings

• •

Even when I don't think that I have anything on hand to make dessert, I can pull together a cobbler from fruit in the kitchen. This version combines sweet apples with tart rhubarb, but you can substitute raspberries for the latter's tang, or just add another apple: the idea is to have about 8 cups of fruit, sweetened accordingly, so don't hesitate to be creative and resourceful. I've made hundreds of cobbler toppings, but this is the easiest, as it requires neither cutting in butter nor rolling out. A combination of sweeteners—honey to complement the apples, superfine sugar for a tender topping, and turbinado for a crunchy topping—gives this simple dish an unexpected complexity.

Filling

2 tablespoons unsalted butter, plus more for the dish

4 Golden Delicious apples, peeled, cored, and sliced

1 cup (1/4-inch dice) rhubarb, 1 cup fresh or frozen raspberries, or an extra apple

1/2 cup honey

2 tablespoons fresh lemon juice

1 1/2 teaspoons cornstarch

Topping

1 1/2 cups unbleached all-purpose flour, preferably organic

3/4 cup finely milled semolina or cornmeal

1/4 cup superfine sugar

1 tablespoon baking powder

1/2 teaspoon fine sea salt

1 1/3 cups heavy cream

5 tablespoons (1/2 stick plus 1 tablespoon) unsalted butter, melted

1/2 cup turbinado sugar

Brown Sugar Whipped Cream (page 120) for serving

- Position a rack in the center of the oven and preheat to 350°F. Lightly butter a 9 by 13-inch baking dish.

- To make the filling, melt the butter in a large skillet over medium heat. Add the apples, rhubarb, honey, and lemon juice. Cook, stirring occasionally, until the apples are barely tender, about 5 minutes. Dissolve the cornstarch in 1/4 cup of cold water, stir into the skillet, and bring to a boil. Transfer to the prepared baking dish.

- Meanwhile, to make the topping, whisk together the flour, semolina or cornmeal, superfine sugar, baking powder, and salt. Add the cream and stir just until combined (the dough will be somewhat rough). Scatter the topping over the fruit mixture. Drizzle with the melted butter and sprinkle with the turbinado sugar.

- Bake until the topping is golden brown and the juices in the center are bubbling, about 30 minutes. Let cool until warm. Spoon into bowls, top with the whipped cream, and serve.

Peach Cobbler with Cornmeal Crust

Makes 6 to 8 servings

• •

THE SWEET QUALITY in cornmeal makes this topping the perfect foil for height-of-summer peaches when they are at their juiciest. Demerara sugar makes a crisp, slightly firmer topping than one made with the typical granulated sugar, keeping the cobbler from becoming soggy. When you spoon it up and it mixes with the fruit juices and cream, the contrast of crunchy, tender, and creamy is the epitome of simple, delicious, only-at-home cooking.

Filling

2 pounds ripe, juicy peaches

1 tablespoon unbleached all-purpose flour, preferably organic

1 tablespoon demerara or turbinado sugar

1 tablespoon fresh lemon juice

Cornmeal Topping

Softened butter, for the dish

1 cup unbleached all-purpose flour, preferably organic

1 cup stone-ground yellow cornmeal

2/3 cup demerara or turbinado sugar

2 teaspoons baking powder

1/2 teaspoon baking soda

1/2 teaspoon fine sea salt

1 cup low-fat buttermilk

4 tablespoons (1/2 stick) unsalted butter, melted and cooled until tepid

1 large egg, beaten

Heavy cream, for serving

- Position a rack in the upper third of the oven and preheat to 375°F. Lightly butter a 9 by 13-inch baking dish.

- For the filling, bring a large saucepan of water to a boil over high heat. A few at a time, add the peaches and cook until the skin loosens, which can be anywhere from 30 to 60 seconds, depending on the ripeness of the peaches. (If the peaches are underripe, the skin will not loosen no matter how long you cook them, and you will have to resort to a vegetable peeler to remove the skin.) Using a slotted spoon, transfer the peaches to a bowl of ice water. Let stand until cool.

- Peel and pit the peaches, then cut them into $1/4$-inch-thick wedges. Transfer to a bowl, add the flour, sugar, and lemon juice, and toss well. Spread in the dish.

- For the topping, whisk together the flour, cornmeal, sugar, baking powder, baking soda, and salt. Make a well in the center and pour in the buttermilk, melted butter, and egg. Whisk just until combined and pour over the peaches.

- Bake until the topping springs back when pressed in the center and the peach juices are bubbling, 45 to 50 minutes. Let cool briefly. Spoon into dishes and serve, with a pitcher of cream passed on the side for pouring over the cobbler.

TIPS FROM A PRO

It is important to buy peaches from a reliable source. Again, start at the farmers' market, where peaches are likely to have been tree ripened. This is a key phrase, as once peaches are picked, they may soften, but they won't truly ripen or get any sweeter. A ripe peach, ready for eating or cooking, will yield to gentle pressure (hold the peach in the palm of your hand, and don't use your fingers, which are sure to cause bruises). But the best determining factor is aroma—a deep whiff should smell peachy sweet.

Brown Sugar Whipped Cream

Makes about 2 cups whipped cream

● ●

WHIPPED CREAM complements many desserts—cobblers and pies are especially happy when topped with a big dollop. This slightly pumped-up version, made with brown sugar for extra depth of flavor, elevates any dessert a notch or two. As the brown sugar may not dissolve in the chilled cream, it is necessary to heat, dissolve, and cool it in a small amount of the cream before whipping.

> 1 cup heavy cream
> 3 tablespoons of your favorite brown sugar, such as
>   muscovado, demerara, or grated *panela*
> 1 teaspoon vanilla extract

- Combine 1/4 cup of the heavy cream and all of the brown sugar in a small saucepan. Heat over low heat, stirring until the sugar is dissolved. Transfer to a medium-size bowl nestled in a larger bowl of ice water. Let stand until the cream and the bowl are chilled.

- Add the remaining 3/4 cup of cream and the vanilla. Using a handheld electric mixer at high speed, beat the cream until soft peaks form. Refrigerate until ready to use.

TIPS FROM A PRO

Although an electric mixer makes short work of beating heavy cream to fluffy peaks, there may be times when the mixer isn't handy. (My hand mixer, more appropriate for small amounts than a standing mixer, hides in a deep, dark corner of the bottom drawer in my cabinet, where it is usually hard to get to when I want it, and amounts of cream less than 1 1/2 cups don't whip well in the standing mixer on my kitchen counter.) In that case, use a whisk. A bulbous-shaped balloon whisk, with many thin wires, will incorporate more air than an elongated saucier's whisk with thick wires. While the cream and brown sugar are chilling in the ice water, place the whisk in the freezer so it can chill, too. With the cream, bowl, and whisk all ice cold, your cream will whip up in no time. And remember rotary beaters? They do a fine job, too.

6

Cookies

*I*F, LIKE ME, you like to keep the cookie jar full, this chapter will help to keep yours overflowing. Baking cookies can be a matter of mood. Do you feel like sandwich cookies, where the creamy filling does as much to satisfy your craving as the cookies themselves? Moist and chewy bar cookies? Frosted cookies? Cookies packed with nuts, fruits, or both? Chocolate cookies or ones scented with cinnamon? Do you have the time to chill the dough, then roll out and decorate the cookies with an artistic touch? Or do you need to quickly satisfy your cookie craving?

In the commercial bakeries I have worked in, cookies are always top sellers. A professional baker doesn't have time to fool around with cookies with burned bottoms, or buttering and flouring pan after pan. We need to work quickly, with reliable results. For the best cookies, equip yourself with top-notch pans and nonstick liners.

Be sure to use a high-quality cookie sheet. A thin, flimsy cookie sheet absorbs heat unevenly, and creates hot spots that make the cookie bottoms burn. Every professional baker that I know prefers a heavy-gauge aluminum *half-sheet pan*, which measures about 13 by 18 inches, for their baking. (A full-sheet pan is 18 by 26 inches and is the size that fits into huge professional ovens used at commercial food manufacturers, but the half-sheet is the largest pan that will fit into most home ovens.) Not only will this pan hold a large amount of cookies, its sturdy construction makes it utterly dependable. It won't buckle or warp easily, and its dull surface absorbs oven heat at a steady level. If you are baking a lot of cookies, one pan after the other, it helps to have three or four pans so the pans can cool down between batches. (Never put cookie dough on a hot pan, or the dough will warm and throw off the estimated baking time.) Buy half-sheet pans at kitchenware or restaurant supply stores.

Many cookies recipes, especially in older cookbooks and periodicals, call for greased and floured baking sheets to keep the cookies from sticking. It is much easier to line the cookie sheet with baking parchment paper, one kitchen essential that I cannot live without. Rolls of parchment paper are sold at grocery stores and kitchenware shops, but these tend to curl up when unrolled—grease the pan with a little butter to get the curled paper to adhere and lay flat. Look for boxes of flat parchment paper sheets at restaurant supply stores. They come in a large quantity, but they can be shared with friends who are also bakers.

Silicone baking mats are another alternative to greasing baking sheets. They are pricey but can be used many (some say a thousand) times before replacing. Be sure to wash the baking mats immediately after use with soap and water, or butter residue will built up and turn rancid, giving the cookies an off flavor.

Maple-Pine Nut Shortbread

Makes 16 wedges

• •

EVERYONE IN MY family loves this crisp, nutty shortbread. As it is made from only a few ingredients, allowing the sweetness to come to the forefront, shortbread is a fine medium for showing off the characteristics of different sugars. You will be able to taste the rounded flavor of maple sugar in every bite.

2 cups unbleached all-purpose flour, preferably organic

¾ cup plus 3 tablespoons maple sugar

1 teaspoon fine sea salt

1 cup pine nuts

16 tablespoons (2 sticks) unsalted butter, chilled, cut into ½-inch pieces, plus more for the pans

- Preheat the oven to 350°F. Lightly butter two 8-inch cake pans or pie pans.

- Combine the flour, ¾ cup sugar, salt, and ½ cup of the pine nuts in the bowl of a heavy-duty electric mixer fitted with the paddle attachment. At low speed, mix briefly to combine. Add the butter and mix with the mixer at medium speed until the mixture resembles coarse bread crumbs with some pea-size pieces of butter and holds together when a handful is squeezed, about 2 minutes.

- Place half of the dough in each pan, and press firmly and evenly in the pans. Sprinkle ¼ cup of the remaining pine nuts and 1½ tablespoons of the remaining sugar over each, and score each into eight equal wedges.

- Bake until the tops are golden brown, rotating the pans halfway through baking, 25 to 30 minutes. Transfer to a wire cake rack and cool for 5 minutes. Cut through the previously scored lines, and cool completely. Remove from the pans. (The shortbread can be stored in an airtight container at room temperature for up to 2 weeks.)

Muscovado and Rum Cookies

Makes about 3 dozen cookies

· ·

IF YOU LIKE moist, chewy cookies as much as I do, then you will be happy to add this recipe to your repertoire. (Not that I have anything against crisp, crunchy cookies!) Any time you bake with muscovado sugar, you get the double benefit of additional moisture and robust molasses flavor. A jigger of dark rum plays up the molasses flavor.

1 1/2 cups unbleached all-purpose flour,
    preferably organic

1/2 teaspoon baking soda

1/2 teaspoon fine sea salt

8 tablespoons (1 stick) unsalted butter,
    at room temperature

1/2 cup plus 1/3 cup dark or light
    muscovado sugar, packed

1/4 cup plus 3 tablespoons granulated
    sugar

1 large egg

2 tablespoons dark rum

- Sift together the flour, baking soda, and salt. Using an electric mixer at high speed, beat the butter, 1/2 cup of the muscovado sugar, and 1/4 cup of the granulated sugar in a large bowl until the mixture is light in color and texture, about 3 minutes. Add the egg, and beat well, then beat in the rum. Stir in the flour mixture until well mixed. Cover the bowl with plastic wrap and refrigerate until it firms up a bit, about 1 hour.

- Position racks in the center and upper third of the oven and preheat to 350°F. Line two baking sheets with parchment paper or silicone baking mats.

- Mix together the remaining ⅓ cup of muscovado sugar and 3 table-spoons of granulated sugar in a small bowl. Using a level tablespoon of dough for each cookie, roll the dough into balls. A few at a time, roll the balls in the sugar mixture to coat them. Place 2 inches apart on the baking sheets. Flatten the tops of the balls with the tines of a fork.

- Bake, switching the positions of the sheets from top to bottom and front to back halfway through baking, until the cookies are firm around the edges but the centers are slightly soft, about 10 minutes. Cool on the sheets for a few minutes, then transfer to wire cake racks and cool completely. (The cookies can be stored in an airtight container at room temperature for up to 1 week.)

Cinnamon-Cardamom Snickerdoodles

Makes about 3 dozen cookies

· ·

SNICKERDOODLES ARE an American cookie stalwart—they have been around for much longer than their chocolate chip cousins. They are always rolled in cinnamon sugar before baking to give them a crackled, crunchy glaze, but I like to literally spice things up with ground cardamom. The resulting aroma and flavor are incredible. The best snickerdoodles are crisp around the edges with a chewy center that may look a bit sunken.

2⅔ cups unbleached all-purpose flour, preferably organic

2 teaspoons cream of tartar

1 teaspoon baking soda

½ teaspoon fine sea salt

16 tablespoons (2 sticks) unsalted butter, at room temperature

1½ cups granulated sugar

2 large eggs, at room temperature

1½ teaspoons vanilla extract

Spiced Sugar

2 teaspoons ground cardamom seeds, from about 20 pods (page 127, see Note)

½ cup granulated sugar

2 teaspoons ground cinnamon

- Position oven racks in the center and top third of the oven and preheat to 375°F. Line two baking sheets with parchment paper or silicone baking mats.

- Sift together the flour, cream of tartar, baking soda, and salt. (This is important, to completely combine the cream of tartar and baking soda, and to break up any clumps of the latter.) Beat the butter and sugar in a medium-size bowl with an electric mixer at high speed until the mixture is light in color and texture, about 3 minutes. One at a time, beat in the eggs, then the vanilla. Reduce the speed to low. In four equal additions, add the flour mixture, beating the dough until it is smooth after each addition.

- To make the spiced sugar, combine the ground cardamom, sugar, and cinnamon in a small bowl.

- Using a level tablespoon of dough for each cookie, roll the dough into walnut-size balls. A few at a time, toss the balls in the spiced sugar to coat, and place about 2 inches apart on the cookie sheets. Sprinkle the top of each cookie with about $1/8$ teaspoon of the spiced sugar.

- Bake until the edges of the cookies are crisp and lightly browned, but the centers are still a bit soft, switching the positions of the sheets from top to bottom and front to back halfway through baking, about 10 minutes. Cool on the sheets for a few minutes, then carefully transfer to a wire cake rack to cool completely. (The cookies can be stored in an airtight container at room temperature for up to 5 days.)

NOTE: Cardamom seeds lose their flavor soon after grinding, so it is always best to grind your own, even if you find ground cardamom at a spice shop. Break open the green cardamom pods and grind the seeds in an electric spice grinder, mini food processor, or a mortar and pestle. Use immediately.

Lemon-Walnut Jumbles

Makes about 4 dozen cookies

• •

THE TART LEMON glaze accents the earthy, slightly tannic walnuts—these are simply a wonderful cookie jar filler. Muscovado sugar, which has so much character, makes them extraordinary.

1½ cups walnuts, toasted (page 129, see Note)

2½ cups unbleached all-purpose flour, preferably organic

1 teaspoon baking powder

½ teaspoon baking soda

½ teaspoon fine sea salt

12 tablespoons (1½ sticks) unsalted butter, at room temperature

2 cups light muscovado or light brown sugar, packed

1 large egg

3 tablespoons whole milk

Icing

2½ cups confectioners' sugar

4 tablespoons fresh lemon juice, as needed

• Position racks in the center and top third of the oven and preheat to 350°F.

• Coarsely chop 1 cup of the walnuts, reserving the remaining walnuts to decorate the cookies.

• Sift together the flour, baking powder, baking soda, and salt. Beat the butter and brown sugar in a large bowl with an electric mixer at high speed until the mixture is light in color and texture, about 3 minutes. Beat in the egg, and then the milk. Reduce the mixer speed to low. Add the flour mixture and mix just until smooth. Fold in the chopped walnuts.

- Line two baking sheets with parchment paper or silicone baking mats. Using about 1 tablespoon of dough for each cookie, roll the dough into oval mounds. Place about 1½ inches apart on the baking sheets.

- Bake, switching the positions of the sheets from top to bottom and front to back halfway through baking, until golden brown, 15 to 18 minutes. Cool on the sheets for a few minutes, then carefully transfer to a wire cake rack to cool completely.

- Sift the confectioners' sugar into a small bowl. A tablespoon at a time, whisk in enough of the lemon juice to make a glaze with the consistency of heavy cream. Do a test to gauge the icing's thickness. Spoon about 1 teaspoon of the glaze over a cookie. It should adhere but not run down the sides of the cookie in rivulets. If the glaze is too thick, thin it with more lemon juice. If too thin, add more confectioners' sugar. Glaze the cookies, topping them with the reserved walnuts. Let cool to set the icing. (The cookies can be stored in an airtight container at room temperature for up to 5 days.)

NOTE: To toast the walnuts, spread them on a baking sheet. Bake, stirring occasionally, until toasted and fragrant, about 10 minutes. Let cool completely.

TIP FROM A PRO

To chop walnuts for baking, you may not even need to use the cutting edge of the knife! Spread the nuts on the work surface. Place the flat side of a large chef's knife or cleaver over the nuts, and press hard on the knife, crushing the nuts beneath. Often, that's all the "chopping" the nuts need, and the resulting rough edges give the finished product a more interesting, crunchy texture. And even when you want finely chopped nuts, this initial crushing reduces the size of large nuts to make subsequent chopping easier (and keeps the nuts from jumping all over the work surface).

Black-and-White Chocolate Drops

Makes about 6 dozen cookies

· ·

A STUDY IN contrasts, these cookies will disappear from the cookie jar. They have everything that I look for in a chocolate snack: The earthiness of cocoa, a nice crunch, and a creamy component, here supplied by vanilla-scented white chocolate. Dutch-processed cocoa is required for the cookie's deep, dark color and mellow flavor.

2 cups unbleached all-purpose flour, preferably organic

¾ cup Dutch-processed cocoa powder

2½ cups turbinado sugar

½ teaspoon baking soda

½ teaspoon fine sea salt

4 large eggs, beaten

8 tablespoons (1 stick) unsalted butter, melted and cooled until tepid

2 tablespoons coffee-flavored liqueur, such as Kahlúa, or 2 teaspoons instant espresso dissolved in 2 tablespoons boiling water and cooled

1 teaspoon vanilla extract

White Chocolate Filling

½ cup heavy cream

5 ounces finely chopped white chocolate

- Whisk together the flour, cocoa powder, 1½ cups of turbinado sugar, baking soda, and salt in a large bowl. In a separate bowl, whisk the eggs briefly, then whisk in the melted butter, liqueur, and vanilla. Make a well in the center of the dry ingredients, pour in the egg mixture, and stir to mix well. Cover with plastic wrap and refrigerate until firm, at least 1 and up to 12 hours.

- Position racks in the center and upper third of the oven and preheat to 350°F. Line two baking sheets with parchment paper or silicone baking mats.

- Put the remaining cup of turbinado sugar in a wide bowl. Using a level tablespoon of dough for each cookie, roll the dough into balls. A few at a time, drop the balls into the sugar and coat them. Place 1 inch apart on the baking sheets. Using your thumb, make a deep indentation in the center of each ball.

- Bake until the cookies look set, about 12 minutes. If the indentations have lost their shape, use the end of a wooden spoon to reform them. Cool on the sheets for a few minutes, then transfer to wire cake racks to cool completely.

- To make the white chocolate filling, bring the cream just to a simmer in a small saucepan over medium heat. Remove from the heat and add the chocolate. Let stand until the chocolate softens, then whisk until smooth. Transfer to a small bowl. Place the bowl in a larger bowl of ice water and let stand, stirring occasionally, until spreadable, about 20 minutes.

- Transfer the filling to a small zippered plastic bag and squeeze the filling into one lower corner of the bag. Snip off the tip of the corner with scissors. Pipe a generous amount of the filling into the indentation of each cookie. Let stand until the filling is firm, at least 3 hours. (The cookies can be stored in an airtight container at room temperature for up to 3 days.)

MIX IT UP

Double-Chocolate Drops: Substitute bittersweet chocolate for the white chocolate in the filling.

ANZAC Biscuits

Makes 3 dozen cookies

• •

THESE DELECTABLE coconut and oat treats are the national cookie (I mean biscuit!) of both Australia and New Zealand. Theories abound as to their origin. Let's just say that the odd name is an acronym for Australia New Zealand Army Corps, and that they seem to have been popularized in the 1920s, perhaps to celebrate ANZAC's participation in World War I. They are so beloved that the name is protected by the governments to keep the recipe from being sullied, or from being referred to as anything other than ANZAC biscuits. (So don't call these "ANZAC cookies"!) A bit of golden syrup, which attracts moisture from the air, gives the cookies a long shelf life.

1 cup old-fashioned rolled oats

1 cup unbleached all-purpose flour,
    preferably organic

1 cup desiccated coconut

⅔ cup granulated sugar

8 tablespoons (1 stick) unsalted butter,
    cut up

2 tablespoons golden syrup

2 tablespoons boiling water

1 teaspoon baking soda

- Position racks in the center and upper third of the oven and preheat to 350°F. Line two baking sheets with parchment paper or silicone baking mats.

- Stir together the oats, flour, coconut, and sugar in a large bowl. Melt the butter in a medium-size saucepan over medium heat. Add the golden syrup. Stir together the boiling water and baking soda in a cup, then stir into the saucepan. Pour into the dry ingredients and mix until well blended.

- Using a heaping tablespoon for each, roll the dough into balls. Flatten the dough between your hands into $1\frac{1}{2}$-inch-diameter disks. Place the disks 1 inch apart on the baking sheets.

- Bake until the cookies turn a deep orange-brown, switching the positions of the sheets from top to bottom and front to back halfway through baking, about 15 minutes. Cool on the sheets for a few minutes, then carefully transfer to a wire cake rack to cool completely. (The cookies can be stored at room temperature in an airtight container for up to 2 weeks.)

Sand Dollar Cookies

Makes about 15 large cookies

. . . .

Inspired by a recipe from the late food writer Richard Sax, these delicate, buttery cookies require no mixing or equipment, just a little time to chill the dough. Like sand dollars found on the beach, they are thin and wispy at the edges. Decorated with sliced almonds, these perfectly shaped elongated ovals simulate the demarcations in real sand dollars. These are a great project for the budding young chefs in your family.

¾ cup plus 2 tablespoons unbleached all-purpose flour, preferably organic

2 tablespoons cornstarch

Pinch of fine sea salt

¼ cup light brown sugar, packed

8 tablespoons (1 stick) unsalted butter, cut into ½-inch pieces, chilled

1 teaspoon vanilla extract

For assembly

½ cup sliced almonds

1 tablespoon granulated sugar

½ teaspoon ground cinnamon

1 large egg white

- Whisk together the flour, cornstarch, and salt in a bowl. Toss the brown sugar and butter together in another bowl. Using a pastry blender, cut the ingredients together for about a minute until they are combined. Add the flour mixture, then the vanilla. Cut the ingredients together until the mixture resembles coarse crumbs and it holds together when a handful is squeezed in the palm of your hand.

- Gather up the dough into a ball. Place on a sheet of plastic wrap and shape into a log about 2½ inches in diameter. Wrap tightly in the plastic wrap and refrigerate for at least 1 and up to 12 hours.

- Position racks in the center and upper third of the oven and preheat to 375°F. Line two baking sheets with parchment paper or silicone baking mats.

- Spread the almonds on a plate to see them clearly, then pick out the most perfectly shaped slices for decorating the cookies. Mix the granulated sugar and cinnamon together in a small bowl. Place the egg white in another small bowl and beat with a fork until foamy.

- Slice the chilled dough into rounds about $1/4$ inch thick. Place them 1 inch apart on the baking sheets. Lightly brush the tops of the cookies with egg white. With the pointed ends of the sliced almonds inward, arrange five almond slices in a star pattern on each cookie, leaving the center empty. Sprinkle about $1/8$ teaspoon of the cinnamon-sugar in a small pile in the center of each cookie. Sprinkle any remaining cinnamon-sugar lightly and evenly over the entire surface of each cookie.

- Bake until the edges are golden brown, switching the positions of the sheets from top to bottom and front to back halfway through baking, about 10 minutes. Cool on the sheets for a few minutes, then carefully transfer to a wire cake rack to cool completely. (The cookies can be stored in an airtight container at room temperature for up to 5 days.)

Almond Crescents

Makes about 7 dozen cookies

· ·

You'll FIND THESE simple cookies throughout Europe, where they are especially popular as part of Christmas cookie platters, decorated with copious amounts of confectioners' sugar. (Note that this yields a large, holiday-size batch of cookies, so you may find it easiest to prepare the dough in a standing mixer.) My version uses golden baker's sugar in the dough and for coating the cookies, which gives them a very delicate crumb and a flavor boost. These are also wonderful with regular baker's (superfine) sugar or maple sugar.

2½ cups unbleached all-purpose flour, preferably organic

½ teaspoon baking powder

½ teaspoon fine sea salt

16 tablespoons (2 sticks) unsalted butter, at room temperature

2 teaspoons vanilla extract

1⅔ cups golden baker's or superfine sugar

1½ cups almond flour (page 137, see Note)

1 large egg, beaten

- Position oven racks in the center and top third of the oven and preheat to 350°F. Line two baking sheets with parchment paper or silicone baking mats.

- Sift together the flour, baking powder, and salt. Mix the butter in the bowl of a standing heavy-duty mixer fitted with the paddle attachment at high speed until the butter is smooth, about 1 minute. Beat in the vanilla, then ⅔ cup of the sugar. Reduce the mixer speed to low. Add the ground almonds, then the flour mixture. Add the beaten egg and mix just until the dough comes together.

- Place the remaining 1 cup of sugar in a wide bowl. For each cookie, pinch off a 1-inch piece of dough and roll into a small log. Bend the ends toward each other to form a crescent moon. Roll in the reserved sugar and place 1 inch apart on the cookie sheets.

- Bake until the cookies are golden brown, switching the positions of the sheets from top to bottom and front to back halfway through baking, 18 to 20 minutes. Cool on the sheets for a few minutes, then carefully transfer to a wire cake rack to cool completely. (The cookies can be stored at room temperature in an airtight container for up to 1 week.)

NOTE: Almond flour (also called almond meal), which is just very finely ground almonds, can be found at natural food stores and many supermarkets. Depending on where you buy it, it can be quite reasonable or very expensive, so shop around. You can make your own in a pinch, but because it is chopped and not ground, the texture will be a bit rougher than almond flour and the cookies will have a more rustic crunch. Combine $1\frac{1}{2}$ cups of sliced natural almonds with $\frac{1}{4}$ cup of the flour from the recipe in a food processor fitted with the metal blade. Process until the almonds are very finely chopped into a powder, at least 30 seconds. (The flour acts as a buffer and keeps the nuts from turning into butter.)

PBJ Cookies

Makes about 6 dozen cookies

· ·

THE ADDITION OF whole wheat flour to peanut butter cookie batter does not adversely affect the color and, in fact, accentuates the earthy, nutty taste. Here are a few baker's tricks for making them: Cornstarch helps lighten the flour, and shortening keeps the cookies tender. You can substitute butter for the all or part of the shortening, if you wish, but the cookies will be crisp. Fill them with preserves, or use a few different kinds for variety. This makes a large batch, but the cookies are small—and if you're like me, you may find yourself eating them by the handful.

1¾ cups whole wheat flour

¼ cup cornstarch

1 teaspoon baking powder

½ teaspoon baking soda

½ teaspoon fine sea salt

¾ cup nonhydrogenated shortening, or 12 tablespoons (1½ sticks) unsalted butter at room temperature, or a combination of shortening and butter

1½ cups dark brown or muscovado sugar, packed

3 tablespoons whole milk or soy milk

2 tablespoons canola oil

1 cup creamy peanut butter

1 teaspoon vanilla extract

¾ cup strawberry, or your favorite, preserves

- Position oven racks in the center and top third of the oven and preheat to 350°F. Line two baking sheets with parchment paper or silicone baking mats.

- Mix together the whole wheat flour, cornstarch, baking powder, baking soda, and salt. Using an electric mixer at high speed, beat the shortening in a large bowl until smooth. Gradually beat in the brown sugar, then the milk and oil, beating well after the addition of each. Add the peanut butter and vanilla and beat, scraping the sides of the bowl often, until the mixture is paler, about 2 minutes. Reduce the mixer speed to low. Add the flour mixture and mix just until combined.

- Using a level tablespoon of dough for each cookie, roll the dough into balls. Place 1 inch apart on the baking sheets. Using your thumb, make a deep indentation in the center of each ball. If the preserves have large chunks of fruit, whirl in a food processor fitted with the metal chopping blade until the fruit is very finely chopped. Transfer the preserves to a small zippered plastic bag and squeeze the preserves into one lower corner of the bag. Snip off the tip of the corner with scissors. Pipe the preserves into the indentations in the cookies, about $1/2$ teaspoon per cookie.

- Bake until the cookies are lightly browned around the edges, switching the positions of the sheets from top to bottom and front to back halfway through baking, 12 to 15 minutes. Cool on the sheets for a few minutes, then carefully transfer to a wire cake rack to cool completely. (The cookies can be stored in an airtight container at room temperature for up to 5 days.)

Whole Wheat Ginger Cookies

Makes about 3½ dozen cookies

. . . .

WHEN I WAS a private chef in England, these crisp little cookies were my employer's kid's favorites. But when I made them in the United States, I discovered that British wholemeal (whole wheat) flour is both lighter and grainier than ours. I adjusted by using a combination of whole wheat and unbleached flours, and by adding wheat germ. Those alterations give these cookies a hearty whole-grain flavor, accented by equally robust dark sugar. The dough is best made in a food processor, which blends the ingredients and cuts the ginger into very fine pieces at the same time. Be sure to allow time for the dough to chill.

1 cup unbleached all-purpose flour, preferably organic

1 cup whole wheat flour

1⅔ cups dark, grainy sugar, such as turbinado, demerara, or raw sugar

3 tablespoons wheat germ or rolled quinoa

1 teaspoon baking powder

½ teaspoon freshly grated nutmeg

¼ teaspoon fine sea salt

8 tablespoons (1 stick) unsalted butter, cut into ½-inch pieces, chilled

½ cup sliced crystallized ginger

½ cup heavy cream, as needed

- Combine the all-purpose and whole wheat flours, ⅔ cup of the sugar, and the wheat germ, baking powder, nutmeg, and salt in a food processor fitted with the metal chopping blade. Pulse a couple of times to combine. With the machine running, add a few butter pieces at a time through the feed tube, and process until the mixture looks sandy. Add all of the ginger at once. Gradually add the cream, and process, adding more cream if needed, until the mixture comes together into a stiff dough. (To make the dough by hand, finely chop the ginger. Combine the flours, ⅔ cup of the sugar, and the wheat germ, baking powder, nutmeg, and salt in a medium-size bowl. Add the butter. Using a pastry blender, cut the butter into the dry ingredients until the mixture looks sandy. Add the ginger. Gradually stir in enough of the cream to make a stiff dough. You may have to work in the last of the cream with your hands. Transfer to a very lightly floured work surface and knead briefly.)

- Divide the dough in half. Place each half on a piece of plastic wrap, form into a 9-inch-long log about $1^{1}/2$ inches in diameter, and wrap in the plastic. Refrigerate until chilled and firm, at least 2 hours and up to 2 days.

- Position racks in the center and upper third of the oven and preheat to 350°F. Line two baking sheets with parchment paper or silicone baking mats.

- Place the remaining sugar in a small bowl. Slice the dough into $^{1}/3$-inch thick disks. Roll the edges of each in the sugar, pressing in the sugar to help it adhere, and place 1 inch apart on the baking sheets. Bake, switching the position of the racks from top to bottom and front to back halfway through baking, until the cookies are dark golden brown, about 14 minutes. Cool on the sheets for a few minutes, then transfer to wire cake racks and cool completely. (The cookies can be stored in an airtight container at room temperature for up to 1 week.)

Semolina-Citrus Turbinados

Makes about 5 dozen cookies

. . . .

WITH THEIR FRAGRANT citrus scent and delicate flavor, these refrigerator sugar cookies are perhaps at their best nibbled when sipping a cup of Earl Grey tea. Semolina, the gritty yellow durum wheat product used to make pasta, is also used in Italian recipes to give texture to baked goods. By processing the orange zest and coarse turbinado sugar together, two things are accomplished. First, the sugar absorbs the zest's aromatic oils for extra citrus impact. And the turbinado is chopped into smaller grains, so the cookies have a tender crumb with full sugar flavor.

1 cup turbinado sugar

Grated zest from 1 large orange

1 cup unbleached all-purpose flour, preferably organic

¾ cup semolina

¼ teaspoon baking powder

½ teaspoon fine sea salt

12 tablespoons (1½ sticks) unsalted butter, chilled, cut into ½-inch cubes

2 tablespoons fresh lemon juice

1 large egg

Orange Glaze

2 ounces full-fat cream cheese, at room temperature

2 tablespoons fresh orange juice

1½ cups confectioners' sugar, sifted

Grated zest of 1 large orange

- Combine the sugar and orange zest in a food processor fitted with the metal chopping blade and pulse a few times. Add the flour, semolina, baking powder, and salt, and pulse about 10 times to combine. Add the butter and pulse until the mixture resembles fine bread crumbs, about 15 pulses. Whisk together the lemon juice and egg. With the machine running, take about 10 seconds to add the juice mixture. Process, stopping to scrape down the sides of the bowl if necessary, just until the dough begins to form a ball, 10 to 15 seconds longer.

- Turn out the dough and any crumbs onto a lightly floured work surface. Gently knead until the dough holds together. Divide in half, and shape each into a $1\frac{1}{2}$-inch-diameter log about 10 inches long. Wrap each in plastic wrap and refrigerate until firm, about 2 hours.

- Position oven racks in the center and top third of the oven and preheat to 350°F. Line two baking sheets with parchment paper or silicone baking mats.

- Slice the chilled dough into $\frac{1}{4}$-inch-thick rounds. Place about $1\frac{1}{2}$ inches apart on the baking sheets. Bake, switching the positions of the sheets from top to bottom and front to back halfway through baking, until the edges of the cookies are golden brown, about 14 minutes. Cool on the sheets for a few minutes, then carefully transfer to a wire cake rack to cool completely.

- To make the glaze, using an electric mixer at high speed, beat the cream cheese in a medium-size bowl until smooth. Reduce the mixer speed to low. Gradually beat in the orange juice. Add enough confectioners' sugar to make a glaze with the consistency of heavy cream. Stir in the orange zest.

- Spoon about 1 teaspoon of glaze on each cookie and spread with a small metal spatula. Let stand until the glaze is set and dry, about 1 hour. (The cookies can be stored in an airtight container at room temperature for up to 5 days.)

TIP FROM A PRO

When grating the zest from citrus, work directly over the bowl that holds the other ingredients for the batter or dough. This way, you are sure to catch every minuscule drop of the flavorful, aromatic citrus oil.

Fig and Chocolate Bars

Makes 32 small bars

• •

DURING A RECENT visit to a local pastry shop, I nibbled on the store's fig bar followed by a taste of their chocolate truffle and had a revelation: Figs and chocolate are made for each other! I immediately set to work to come up with my own interpretation of this unexpected pairing. The resulting bars are not too sweet, and deliciously chewy, thanks to brown sugar in the dough. Try the apricot or cherry variations, too.

Ganache

1/2 cup heavy cream

1 cup (6 ounces) semisweet chocolate chips

3 tablespoons orange-flavored liqueur, such as Grand Marnier

1 tablespoon unsalted butter, at room temperature

Dough

1 cup unbleached all-purpose flour, preferably organic

1/2 teaspoon baking powder

1/2 teaspoon fine sea salt

3 cups old-fashioned rolled oats

12 tablespoons (1 1/2 sticks) unsalted butter, at room temperature, plus more for the pan

1 cup light brown sugar, packed

1 egg

1 teaspoon vanilla extract

2 1/4 cups finely chopped dried figs

• Position a rack in the center of the oven and preheat to 350°F. Lightly butter a 9 by 13-inch baking pan.

• To make the ganache, bring the cream to a simmer in a medium-size saucepan over low heat. Remove from the heat and add the chocolate chips. Let stand until the chips soften, about 3 minutes. Stir until the chocolate is melted. Add the liqueur and butter, and stir until the butter melts. Let cool, stirring occasionally, until tepid and pourable, about 20 minutes.

- Whisk together the flour, baking powder, and salt in a bowl. Mix in 2 cups of the rolled oats.

  Beat the butter and brown sugar in a medium-size bowl with an electric mixer at high speed until the mixture is light in color and texture, about 3 minutes. Beat in the egg, then the vanilla. Reduce the mixer speed to low. Add the flour mixture and mix just until the dough barely comes together—it should not be absolutely smooth.

- Press three-quarters of the dough evenly over the bottom of the baking pan. Sprinkle the chopped figs into the pan. Pour the ganache over the figs and use a metal spatula to spread it as evenly as possible.

- Combine the remaining dough with the remaining 1 cup of oats in a medium-size bowl, and work together with your fingers until crumbly. Scatter the streusel over the chocolate and figs.

- Bake until the streusel is golden brown, 30 to 35 minutes. Let cool in the pan on a wire cake rack. Cut evenly into thirty-two bars. (The bars can be stored in an airtight container at room temperature for up to 3 days.)

MIX IT UP

Apricot and Bittersweet Chocolate Bars: Omit the semisweet chocolate chips and substitute 2¼ cups of chopped dried apricots for the figs and 6 ounces of finely chopped bittersweet chocolate (60 to 70 percent cacao content).

Cherry and White Chocolate Bars: Omit the swemisweet chocolate chips and substitute 2½ cups dried cherries for the figs and 6 ounces white chocolate chips. If the white chocolate chips are stubborn and don't melt, place the saucepan in a skillet of hot water and let stand until they cooperate.

Shoofly Pecan Bars

Makes 24 bars

· ·

PECAN PIE IS an old-fashioned favorite, but for many of today's bakers (and eaters), it has fallen out of favor because traditional recipes are cloying with an excess of corn syrup. My version, which transforms the pie into pecan bars, adds molasses, brown sugar, and brewed coffee for a less sweet filling.

Crust

1¾ cups unbleached all-purpose flour, preferably organic

3 tablespoons granulated sugar

¼ teaspoon fine sea salt

8 tablespoons (1 stick) butter, cold and cut into bits, plus more for the pan

4 tablespoons cold whole milk, as needed

1 large egg, beaten

Filling

⅔ cup unbleached all-purpose flour, preferably organic

½ cup light brown or muscovado sugar, packed

2 tablespoons unsalted butter, cut into ½-inch pieces, chilled

¾ cup mild or robust molasses

¾ cup light corn syrup

1 cup brewed hot coffee, or 2 teaspoons instant coffee dissolved in 1 cup boiling water

1 teaspoon baking soda

2 large eggs, beaten

1½ teaspoons vanilla extract

Pinch of fine sea salt

1½ cups (6 ounces) coarsely chopped pecans

• Position a rack in the upper third of the oven and preheat to 375°F. Lightly butter a 9 by 13-inch baking pan.

- To make the crust, whisk the flour, sugar, and salt together in a medium-size bowl. Add the butter. Using a pastry blender, cut in the butter until the mixture resembles coarse crumbs. Add the milk, a tablespoon at a time, just until the dough holds together when a handful is squeezed in the palm of your hand. Pat the dough firmly and evenly into the pan. Brush lightly with the beaten egg. This prevents the filling from running through any holes or cracks in the crust while baking. Bake until the crust is beginning to brown, about 15 minutes. Remove from the oven and cool slightly.

- Meanwhile, make the filling. Stir the flour, brown sugar, and butter together until the texture is sandy. Set aside. In another bowl, whisk together the molasses and corn syrup. Add the hot coffee and baking soda (the mixture will foam up), and whisk until combined. Add the beaten eggs, vanilla, and salt, and whisk well.

- Sprinkle the flour mixture over the baked crust. Pour the molasses mixture evenly on top, and sprinkle with the pecans. Bake for 10 minutes. Lower the oven temperature to 350°F, and continue baking until the center is set when the pan is shaken gently, about 25 minutes.

- Transfer to a wire cake rack and cool completely. Cut into twenty-four bars. (The bars can be refrigerated in an airtight container for up to 3 days. Serve at room temperature.)

Apple-Oatmeal Triangles (Flapjacks)

Makes 8 wedge-shaped cookies

• •

To an American, flapjacks are pancakes, but to the British, a flapjack is a chewy oat bar with toffee notes. In the British Isles, they are often made with treacle or golden syrup—my version combines brown sugar and golden syrup for a more complex flavor and adds an apple layer. Honey is a perfectly acceptable substitute if golden syrup is hard to find. Many people will appreciate the fact that these cookies are gluten-free and whole-grain.

2 large cooking apples, such as Granny Smith, peeled, cored, and diced

2 tablespoons peeled and grated fresh ginger

1 tablespoon fresh lemon juice

8 tablespoons (1 stick) unsalted butter, plus more for the pan

$1/2$ cup light brown sugar, packed

3 tablespoons golden syrup or honey

$2 1/2$ cups old-fashioned rolled oats

$1/2$ cup sliced natural almonds

$1/2$ teaspoon ground cinnamon

$1/4$ teaspoon fine sea salt

• Position a rack in the center of the oven and preheat to 375°F. Butter a 9-inch round cake pan.

• Combine the apples, ginger, lemon juice, and 3 tablespoons of water in a small saucepan. Bring to a simmer over medium heat. Lower the heat to low and simmer, stirring occasionally, adding a little more water if the mixture seems dry, until the apples are very tender, about 10 minutes, or until soft. Mash the apples and set aside.

• Warm the butter, brown sugar, and golden syrup in a medium-size saucepan over low heat, just until the butter is melted. Do not let the mixture come to a boil. Add the oats, almonds, cinnamon, and salt, and stir well. Press half the oat mixture in the cake pan. Spread the apple puree evenly over the top and cover with the remaining oat mixture.

- Bake until the top is golden brown, about 30 minutes. Remove from the oven and mark into wedges while still warm. (This will make it easier to cut and serve later.) Transfer to a wire cake rack and cool completely. Slice through the marks to cut the flapjacks into wedges and serve directly from the pan. (The flapjacks can be stored at room temperature, covered, for up to 3 days.)

Dulce de Leche Sandwich Cookies

Makes about 2½ dozen cookies

· ·

HERE IS ANOTHER Argentinean recipe that caught my attention when I was in Buenos Aires, where they are called *alfajores*. These crumbly-crisp cookies sandwiched with *dulce de leche* are springing up at some American bakeries and on Latino-influenced restaurant menus. They are best when made with homemade *dulce de leche*, but when I need to take a shortcut, they are awfully delicious with a good store-bought brand, too. Cornstarch gives these cookies their divine melt-in-your-mouth quality.

1½ cups cornstarch

½ cup unbleached all-purpose flour, preferably organic

1 teaspoon baking powder

¼ teaspoon fine sea salt

8 tablespoons (1 stick) unsalted butter, at room temperature

1 cup granulated sugar

1 large egg plus 2 large egg yolks

1 teaspoon vanilla extract

Grated zest of 1 large lemon

1¼ cups Dulce de Leche, page 221, or use store-bought *dulce de leche*

- Position oven racks in the lower and upper third of the oven and preheat to 350°F. Line two baking sheets with parchment paper or silicone baking mats.

- Sift together the cornstarch, flour, baking powder, and salt. Using an electric mixer at high speed, beat the butter in a medium-size bowl until smooth, about 1 minute. Gradually beat in the sugar over the course of 2 minutes. Beat in the egg, then the yolks, one at a time. Add the vanilla and lemon zest. Scrape down the sides of the bowl with a rubber spatula.

- Reduce the mixer speed to low. Beat in the cornstarch mixture in four equal additions, mixing thoroughly after each addition. Using a teaspoon of dough for each cookie, drop the dough onto the cookie sheets, leaving 1 inch between each cookie, as they will spread.

- Bake until the cookies are set (they will remain light in color), switching the positions of the sheets from top to bottom and front to back halfway through baking, about 15 minutes. Cool on the sheets for a few minutes, then carefully transfer to a wire cake rack to cool completely.

- Using about 2 teaspoons of *dulce de leche*, sandwich the flat sides of two cookies together. (The cookies can stored at room temperature in an airtight container for up to 3 days.)

Dulce de Leche

I HAVE PROVIDED my recipe for homemade dulce de leche, the gooey and luscious caramelized milk sauce, on page 221. You will also come across jars of *dulce de leche* in the Latino foods sections of many supermarkets, or it might even be stocked with the caramel sauce near the ice-cream toppings. If you shop at Latino grocery stores, it may be labeled under another name, depending on the nationality of the clientele. The Mexican version of *dulce de leche*, *cajeta*, is darker and more deeply flavored than its Argentinean cousin. You may also find Colombian *arequipe* (sometimes with figs) or Peruvian *manjar blanco* (not as intensely caramelized as either of the other countries' versions). They are also available online at Latino grocers, at such sites as www.amigofoods.com. Some standard supermarkets carry French *confiture de lait* in their jams and jellies aisle, which is meant to be spread on crusty bread, but it is just as wonderful as a stand-in for *dulce de leche*.

Oatmeal-Almond Cremes

Makes 2 dozen cookies

· ·

ANYONE WHO HAS ever licked the filling from sandwich cookies knows this is one of the best ways to satisfy any number of primal cravings. Sandwich cookies are just fun to eat, and to make. The filling for these orange-flavored treats has a base of almond butter, which really elevates matters in terms of flavor and sophistication. Orange is not a subtle flavoring, so to match it in strength, I use brown, and not white sugar, which also gives the cookies their tenderness.

2 cups old-fashioned rolled oats

1¼ cups light brown sugar, packed

1 cup unbleached all-purpose flour, preferably organic

½ teaspoon baking soda

½ teaspoon fine sea salt

8 tablespoons (1 stick) unsalted butter, at room temperature

2 large eggs, beaten

2 teaspoons vanilla extract

3 tablespoons whole milk

Filling

¾ cup almond butter

4 tablespoons (½ stick) unsalted butter, at room temperature

1 cup confectioners' sugar

Grated zest of 1 large orange

½ teaspoon ground cinnamon

½ teaspoon vanilla extract

⅛ teaspoon fine sea salt

- Position oven racks in the center and top third of the oven and preheat to 350°F. Line two baking sheets with parchment paper or silicone baking mats.

- Pulse the oats and ¼ cup of the brown sugar in a food processor fitted with the metal chopping blade, until the oats are flourlike. Add the flour, baking soda, and salt, and pulse to combine.

- Using an electric mixer at high speed, beat the butter and remaining cup of brown sugar in a large bowl until the mixture is light in color and texture, about 3 minutes. Gradually beat in the eggs, beating well, then the vanilla. Stir in the flour mixture until mixed, then stir in the milk. Drop teaspoons of the dough on the cookie sheets, spacing them 2 inches apart (these cookies spread quite a bit during baking).

- Bake, switching the positions of the sheets from top to bottom and front to back halfway through baking, until the edges of the cookies are lightly browned, 10 to 12 minutes. Cool on the sheets for a few minutes, then carefully transfer to a wire cake rack to cool completely.

- To make the filling, using an electric mixer at high speed, beat the almond butter and butter in a medium-size bowl until combined. Reduce the mixer speed to low and gradually beat in the confectioners' sugar. Beat in the orange zest, cinnamon, vanilla, and salt.

- Using about 2 teaspoons of the filling, sandwich the flat sides of two cookies together. (The cookies can stored at room temperature in an airtight container for up to 3 days.)

Almond-Sucanat Biscotti

Makes about 32 biscotti

· ·

As Sucanat's grainy texture never completely dissolves in a dough, it works best in baked goods where a crunchy texture is desirable. Biscotti are a perfect showcase for the natural sugar's mild sweetness and roasted flavor. I've supplied a basic almond recipe with a few ideas for some variations. This is a somewhat dense dough, most easily made in a standing mixer.

1½ cups (6 ounces) slivered almonds

1 cup Sucanat

2 cups unbleached all-purpose flour,
    preferably organic

1½ teaspoons baking powder

3 large eggs, beaten

1½ teaspoons vanilla extract

- Position racks in the center and upper third of the oven and preheat to 350°F. Spread the almonds on a baking sheet. Bake, stirring occasionally, until lightly browned, about 12 minutes. Cool completely.

- Combine ½ cup of toasted almonds with ½ cup of Sucanat in a food processor fitted with the metal chopping blade. Pulse until the almonds are very finely chopped, but not a powder. Transfer to the bowl of a standing heavy-duty mixer, and add the remaining ½ cup of sugar. Whisk together the flour and baking powder, and add to the bowl. Affix the paddle attachment, and mix at low speed to combine. Add the eggs and vanilla, and mix just until the mixture forms a stiff dough. Mix in the remaining 1 cup of almonds.

- Line a baking sheet with parchment paper or a silicone baking mat. Transfer the dough to a lightly floured work surface. Divide the dough in half. Shape each half into a log about 9 inches long and 2 inches in diameter. Place the logs on the baking sheet, spacing them as far apart as possible. Bake in the center of the oven until the logs are golden and set, but still somewhat soft to the touch, 25 to 30 minutes. Remove from the oven, but leave the oven on. Transfer the baking sheet to a wire cake rack. Cool the logs on the baking sheet for 10 minutes.

- Transfer the logs to a cutting board. Using a serrated knife and a light touch, cut the logs on a slight diagonal into $1/2$-inch-thick slices. Line a second baking sheet with parchment paper or silicone baking mats. Arrange the slices, $1/2$ inch apart and cut sides down, on the baking sheets. Bake, switching the positions of the baking sheets from top to bottom and front to back halfway through baking, until the biscotti are golden and crisp, about 20 minutes. Cool completely on the baking sheet. (The biscotti can be stored in an airtight container at room temperature for up to 2 weeks.)

MIX IT UP

Orange-Sucanat Biscotti: Add the grated zest of one large orange to the ground almond mixture and pulse briefly to distribute the zest.

Spiced Sucanat Biscotti: Add $1/2$ teaspoon each of ground cinnamon, ground ginger, and ground allspice to the flour mixture.

Espresso-Sucanat Biscotti: Add 2 teaspoons of instant espresso to the almond and sugar mixture in the food processor before chopping the almonds.

7

Spoon Desserts

*H*ERE IS A collection of smooth, silky puddings, custards, and other desserts that you eat with a spoon, scraping the sides of the bowl to be sure to get every last lick. As sugar comes from all over the world, so do these desserts. Black rice and mango pudding from Thailand, French crème brûlée, Mexican sweet potato pudding, and Hawaiian coconut squares may all be soft in texture, but that's about the only thing they have in common.

Actually, there is one preparation technique that many puddings share: cooking in a water bath (also known by the French term, *bain-marie*). Custard-type puddings usually include eggs, whose proteins swell and absorb liquid when heated and give the dessert its semisolid consistency. Sugar is an imperative ingredient in custard, here, as it helps coagulate the eggs. If the eggs are overheated, the swelled proteins will expand too much, and break, releasing the liquid back into the custard and making it wet and soggy. Placing the custard cups in a pan filled with water insulates the cups and helps keep the custard from overheating.

To pull off getting a pan of custards into the oven, all you need is a fairly steady hand. Put the custard cups or ramekins in a larger pan that will hold them comfortably without crowding. Cover the pan with aluminum foil, crimp the foil around the edges of the pan, but leave one corner open. Pull out the oven rack by a few inches, and put the pan on the rack with the open corner facing you. Pour in just enough hot tap water to come about 1/2 inch up the sides of the cups. The water does not have to be boiling, as it only insulates the custards and does not have to be hot enough to cook them. Don't overfill the pan—1/2 inch is enough to get the job done. Now crimp the open corner closed and slide the rack with the pan into place.

You will see custard recipes that do not cover the pan with foil. There are also recipes where the water is left out altogether, and the custards are allowed to slowly set in an oven with lower than usual temperature (300°F or so). Although both methods make acceptable custard, I strongly believe that the foil-covered method is the best. The foil traps the steam in the pan, gently cooking the custard from above and giving the eggs a creamy consistency.

The road to a perfectly cooked custard can easily lead, though, to over-cooking. First of all, be very careful when removing the foil. Lots of hot steam will be released, so avert your face. The knife test is the most reliable method for doneness (a dinner knife inserted into the custard will come out clean), but this can create a slit that will only widen as the custard cools and contracts. So, make the slit as inconspicuous as possible. Better yet, learn to evaluate the custard's doneness by eye—it should look set around the outside, even if it is a little wiggly in the very center. The custard will continue to cook outside of the oven from the residual heat, and the center will eventually set throughout.

Crème de Café

. . . .

THIS COFFEE CUSTARD is like eating a creamy yet solidified latte. A coarse-crystal second-stage sugar, such as demerara or turbinado, is perfect here, as the caramel undertone accentuates the lush taste of coffee. Although any brewed coffee will do, dark roasted beans give the richest flavor.

¹/₂ cup plus 1 tablespoon granulated sugar

1¹/₂ cups whole milk

¹/₂ cup demerara or turbinado sugar

10 whole coffee beans, preferably French roast

1 vanilla bean, or 1 teaspoon vanilla extract

¹/₂ cup strong brewed coffee, preferably dark roast

5 large egg yolks

1 teaspoon cornstarch

- Position a rack in the center of the oven and preheat to 350°F. Have four 6-ounce (³/₄-cup) ramekins ready.

- Combine ¹/₂ cup of the granulated sugar and 2 tablespoons of water in a small saucepan. Cook over high heat, stirring just until the sugar dissolves. Stop stirring and cook, occasionally swirling the pan by its handle and washing down any sugar crystals that form on the side of the pan with a pastry brush dipped in cold water, until the syrup becomes a dark amber caramel. Pour equal amounts of the caramel into the ramekins. Immediately tilt each ramekin to coat it on the bottom and up the sides (as much as possible) with the caramel.

- Bring the milk, demerara sugar, coffee beans, and vanilla bean to a boil in a medium-size saucepan over medium heat. Stir in the brewed coffee. Remove from the heat and let stand for 20 minutes. Strain through a wire sieve into a bowl. Using the tip of a knife, scrape the vanilla seeds from the bean into the milk mixture. (If using vanilla extract, stir it into the strained milk mixture.)

- Whisk the egg yolks in a medium-size bowl until they are pale yellow, about 1 minute. Combine the cornstarch and remaining tablespoon of granulated sugar in a small bowl, and whisk into the eggs. Gradually whisk in the warm milk mixture. Strain the custard into a container with a spout (a 1-quart glass measuring cup works well). Divide among the caramel-lined ramekins. Arrange the ramekins in a roasting pan. Cover the pan with aluminum foil and crimp the foil around the edges of the pan, leaving one corner open. Slide out the oven rack by a few inches. Place the pan with the custards on the rack with the open corner facing you. Carefully pour in enough hot tap water to come about $1/2$ inch up the sides of the ramekins. Crimp the open corner closed. Slide the rack with the pan back into the oven.

- Bake until a knife inserted at the edge of a custard comes out clean, about 30 minutes. (The centers will seem unset, but they will firm as they cool.) Remove the ramekins from the water. Let cool to room temperature. Cover each custard with plastic wrap and refrigerate until chilled, at least 4 hours. (The custards can be refrigerated for up to 2 days.)

- To serve, one at a time, use your thumbs to gently press the custard around its perimeter to loosen it from the ramekin. Invert the ramekin onto a dessert plate. Holding the ramekin and plate together, shake them to unmold the custard. Lift up and remove the ramekin, letting the caramel pour over the custard. Serve chilled.

TIPS FROM A PRO

You've worked carefully to create a silky-smooth custard, but getting it out of its container can be a challenge. The obvious solution is to run a knife around the inside of the ramekin, but it can slice into the custard and make a sloppy presentation. It is better to loosen the custard by pressing around its perimeter with your thumbs. Don't press too hard—you just want to break the seal.

Mexican Sweet Potato Pudding

Makes 6 servings

• •

ALTHOUGH YAMS and sweet potatoes are entirely different tubers, the former commonly found only in tropical regions, most Americans use the terms interchangeably. No matter what you call them, their inherently sweet flavor and bright orange color are expected at the holiday table, and while this pudding is a favorite Mexican dessert, you might want to consider serving it alongside your roast turkey or ham. Or, use it as a much lighter substitute for pumpkin or sweet potato pie. For this recipe, you want one of the familiar orange-fleshed varieties (such as Louisiana, garnet, or jewel), and not the scaly-skinned Latino yam (usually called *ñame*) or the true sweet potato, with a pale ivory flesh (and sometimes labeled *boniato*).

3 orange-fleshed sweet potatoes, such as Louisiana, garnet, or jewel yams (1½ pounds)

4 tablespoons dark rum

1 teaspoon vanilla extract

½ teaspoon nutmeg, preferably freshly grated

⅓ cup golden raisins

¾ cup grated *panela* or dark brown sugar, packed

1 cup heavy cream

½ recipe Brown Sugar Whipped Cream (page 120), for serving (optional)

• Position a rack in the center of the oven and preheat to 375°F.

• Place the sweet potatoes on a baking sheet and bake until tender when pierced with a knife, about 1 hour. Let cool until easy to handle, then peel and let cool completely. Cut the sweet potatoes into large chunks.

• Puree the sweet potatoes with 2 tablespoons of the rum, and the vanilla and nutmeg in a food processor fitted with the metal chopping blade. Transfer to a large bowl. Combine the raisins and the remaining 2 tablespoons of rum in a small bowl and set aside until ready to serve the pudding.

- Bring the *panela* and $1/3$ cup of water to a boil in a small saucepan. Boil until it reads 225°F on a candy thermometer, about 5 minutes. Stir into the sweet potato mixture.

- Using an electric mixer set at high speed, whip the cream until soft peaks form. Fold one-quarter of the whipped cream into the sweet potato mixture, followed by the remaining whipped cream. Cover and refrigerate until chilled, at least 2 and up to 12 hours.

- Spoon into small teacups or ramekins. Sprinkle with the raisins and their rum and a dollop of whipped cream. Serve chilled.

Earl Grey Palm Custards

Makes 6 servings

. . . .

I'D LIKE TO have my friend, cookbook author David Lebovitz's, job. He lives in Paris, where he works on his books and gives tours of the city's best chocolate shops. I've adapted these custards from one of his recipes. Fragrant with bergamot-scented Earl Grey tea, they're sweetened with full-flavored palm sugar. For an added treat, try the black-bottom variation.

1 cup heavy cream

3 tablespoons Earl Grey tea leaves

1 cup whole (not low-fat) coconut milk

1/2 cup palm sugar, crushed, if necessary

6 large egg yolks

- Position a rack in the center of the oven and preheat to 350°F.

- Bring the cream just to a simmer in a small saucepan over medium-low heat. Remove from the heat and add the tea leaves. Cover and let steep for 15 minutes. Strain through a wire sieve into a medium-size bowl. Return to the saucepan. Add the coconut milk and palm sugar, and cook over low heat, stirring constantly, until the sugar is completely melted. Remove from the heat.

- Whisk the yolks in a medium-size bowl until they are pale and thickened, about 1 minute. Gradually whisk in the hot coconut milk mixture. Strain through a wire sieve into a container with a spout (a 1-quart glass measuring cup works well). Divide among four 6-ounce (3/4-cup) ramekins. Arrange the ramekins in a roasting pan. Cover the pan with aluminum foil and crimp the foil around the edges of the pan, leaving one corner open. Slide out the oven rack by a few inches. Place the pan with the custards on the rack with the open corner facing you. Carefully pour in enough hot tap water to come about $\frac{1}{2}$ inch up the sides of the ramekins. Crimp the open corner closed. Slide the rack with the pan back into the oven.

- Bake until a knife inserted at the edge of a custard comes out clean, about 30 minutes. (The centers will seem unset, but they will firm as they cool.) Remove the ramekins from the water. Let cool to room temperature. Cover each custard with plastic wrap and refrigerate until chilled, at least 2 hours. (The custards can refrigerated for up to 2 days.) Serve chilled.

MIX IT UP

Black-Bottom Tea Custards: Bring $\frac{1}{3}$ cup of heavy cream to a simmer in a small saucepan. Remove from the heat and add 3 ounces of finely chopped bittersweet chocolate. Let stand until the chocolate softens, about 3 minutes. Whisk until smooth. Divide among the ramekins. Freeze until the chocolate is firm, about 1 hour. Fill the ramekins with the prepared custard and bake.

Foolproof Crème Brûlée

Make 8 servings

• •

THERE SEEMS TO be a lot of mystery (if not downright hogwash) about making crème brûlée. In fact, it is one of the easiest desserts around—one reason why it is served at so many restaurants. To create the glassine top, forget what you may have heard about rubbing brown sugar through a sieve and equipping yourself with a blowtorch. All you need is turbinado sugar, with large crystals that melt and spread more quickly than other sugars, and a broiler.

2 cups heavy cream

1 cup milk

1/2 cup plus 3 tablespoons granulated
     sugar

6 large egg yolks

2 teaspoons vanilla extract

1/4 teaspoon fine sea salt

About 3 tablespoons turbinado sugar

- Position a rack in the center of the oven and preheat to 325°F.

- Bring the cream, milk, and 1/2 cup of the granulated sugar just to a simmer in a medium-size saucepan over medium-low heat, stirring often to dissolve the sugar. Remove from the heat. Whisk the egg yolks and remaining 3 tablespoons of granulated sugar until pale and thickened, about 1 minute. Gradually whisk in the hot cream mixture. Stir in the vanilla and salt. Strain into a container with a spout (a 1-quart glass measuring cup works well). Let stand for 10 minutes—this helps dissipate the bubbles formed by whisking.

- Divide the custard among eight 6-ounce (3/4-cup) ramekins. Arrange the ramekins in a roasting pan. Cover the pan with aluminum foil and crimp the foil around the edges of the pan, leaving one corner open. Slide out the oven rack by a few inches. Place the pan with the custards on the rack with the open corner facing you. Carefully pour in enough hot tap water to come about $\frac{1}{2}$ inch up the sides of the ramekins. Crimp the open corner closed. Slide the rack with the pan back into the oven.

- Bake until a knife inserted at the edge of a custard comes out clean, about 30 minutes. (The centers will seem unset, but they will firm as they cool.) Remove the ramekins from the water. Let cool to room temperature. Cover each custard with plastic wrap and refrigerate until well chilled, at least 2 hours. (The custards can be refrigerated for up to 2 days.)

- Position a broiler rack about 6 inches from the source of heat and preheat the broiler. Unwrap the custards. Sprinkle 1 heaping teaspoon of the turbinado sugar evenly over the surface of each custard. Arrange the custards on a baking sheet. Broil, keeping a close eye on the sugar topping, just until the sugar is melted and bubbling, anywhere from 1 to 4 minutes, depending on your broiler. Let stand at room temperature for a few minutes until the sugar hardens, then serve immediately. (The custards can be refrigerated for up to 2 hours, but no longer, or the topping will soften.)

Hawaiian Coconut Milk Pudding

Makes 8 servings

. . . .

IF YOU HAVE ever been to Hawaii, it is likely that you have come across *haupia*, a firm, sliceable coconut milk pudding that is ubiquitous at luaus. It is one of those desserts that can arouse controversy, usually on the subjects of whether or not one should add shredded coconut, use gelatin to give the squares a firmer jiggle, or serve the squares with garnishes like fruit or whipped cream. I am asking for trouble by suggesting part of the final option, as it does add a splash of color to what is otherwise a plain but tasty dessert. In Hawaii, it is always served cut into squares, but divide the pudding mixture among individual dessert bowls (do not fill to the brim, to leave room for the fruit), if you wish.

1/3 cup granulated sugar

3 cups canned coconut milk, well shaken

1/3 cup cornstarch

Diced fresh tropical fruit, such as pineapple, mango, papaya, and banana

- Lightly oil an 8-inch square glass baking dish. Whisk the coconut milk and sugar together in a small saucepan. Gradually whisk in the cornstarch, being sure that it dissolves. Cook over medium heat, whisking constantly and reaching into the corners of the saucepan with the tip of the whisk, until the mixture comes to full boil and thickens, about 8 minutes.

- Spread in the dish and let cool until tepid. Cover with plastic wrap and refrigerate until chilled and firm, at least 2 hours.

- Cut the pudding into 2-inch squares. Place two squares in each serving bowl, top with the fruit, and serve.

Sticky Toffee Pudding

Makes 6 servings

● ●

STICKY TOFFEE PUDDING has probably done more to elevate the status of British cooking than the collective celebrity of Nigella Lawson, Jamie Oliver, and Gordon Ramsay. Please note that, here, the word *pudding* is used in the British manner, denoting just about any dessert. Therefore, this isn't soft and creamy like tapioca pudding, but a warm date cake smothered with toffee sauce. It is never better than when the crowning toffee sauce is made with demerara sugar, which has a toffee note of its own to begin with. Although its history is disputed, sticky toffee pudding was not a staple in the United Kingdom until recently. It has a Dickensian feel to it and makes a wonderful finale to a grand Christmas dinner.

Toffee Sauce

2 cups heavy cream

1/2 cup demerara sugar

2 1/2 tablespoons golden syrup, or mild or robust molasses

Cake

1 cup chopped (1/2-inch dice) pitted dates, packed (about 6 ounces)

1 teaspoon baking soda

1 1/4 cups unbleached all-purpose flour, preferably organic

1 teaspoon baking powder

1/2 teaspoon fine sea salt

4 tablespoons (1/2 stick) unsalted butter, at room temperature, plus more for the dish

3/4 cup granulated sugar

2 large eggs, beaten

1 teaspoon vanilla extract

- Position an oven rack in the bottom third of the oven and preheat to 350°F. Butter an 8$\frac{1}{2}$-inch-diameter soufflé dish.

- To make the toffee sauce, bring the cream, sugar, and golden syrup to a boil in a medium-size saucepan, stirring often to melt the sugar. Lower the heat to medium-low, stirring constantly, until the sauce is thick enough to coat the spoon, about 5 minutes. Pour half the sauce into the soufflé dish, and freeze to set while you make the pudding. Reserve the remaining sauce at room temperature.

- To make the pudding, bring the dates and 1 cup plus 2 tablespoons of water to a boil in a medium-size saucepan over medium heat. Remove from the heat and stir in the baking soda (it will bubble up). Set aside to cool slightly.

- Sift the flour, baking powder, and salt together into a medium-size bowl. Using an electric mixer set at high speed, beat the butter and sugar in a second medium-size bowl until the mixture looks lighter in color, about 2 minutes. Gradually beat in the eggs, then the vanilla. (The mixture may look curdled.) Stir in half of the flour mixture. Stir in warm date mixture, followed by the remaining flour mixture, and mix just until blended. Pour the batter into the prepared pan.

- Bake until a toothpick inserted into the center of the cake comes out with moist crumbs attached, about 50 minutes. Transfer to a wire cake rack. (The cake and sauce can be made up to 1 day ahead, cooled, covered with plastic wrap, and refrigerated. If planning to make in advance, keep the cake in the soufflé dish. Before serving, preheat the oven to 300°F and reheat the toffee sauce in a saucepan over low heat, whisking often. Poke a few holes in the surface of the cake with a chopstick, and pour about half of the toffee sauce over the cake. Cover the cake with aluminum foil. Bake until the cake is heated through, about 30 minutes. Divide the remaining toffee sauce over each serving.) Let the cake stand about 15 minutes to cool until no longer piping hot.

- Reheat the toffee sauce over low heat, whisking often. Spoon the cake and its toffee into individual dessert bowls, then top with the toffee sauce. Serve immediately.

Thai Sticky Black Rice and Mangoes

Makes 6 to 8 servings

• •

THIS IS UNDOUBTEDLY one of the most dramatic looking desserts one can serve—glistening black rice with the striking contrast of orange mangoes. As delicious as this is, it is still interesting to note how quickly it took hold to become ensconced at Thai (and Asian fusion) restaurants all over America. Both black sticky rice and palm sugar are sold at Asian markets but, just in case, I've provided excellent if slightly less vivid substitutes.

1 cup Thai sticky black rice, jasmine, or long-grain rice

2/3 cup palm sugar (page 171, see Note), crushed if necessary

1 cup canned coconut milk, well shaken

Pinch of fine sea salt

1 tablespoon cornstarch

1 teaspoon vanilla extract

Canola oil, for molding the rice

2 ripe mangoes, peeled, pitted, and sliced thinly

2 tablespoons sesame seeds and/or sweetened coconut flakes, for garnish

• Put the rice in a medium-size bowl and add enough warm water to cover by 1 inch. Let stand for 1 hour, then drain in a large sieve.

• Bring 1¼ cups of water to a boil in a medium-size saucepan. Add the drained rice and 3 tablespoons of the palm sugar, and stir to dissolve the sugar. Lower the heat to low and cover. Simmer until the water has evaporated, 8 to 10 minutes. Remove from the heat and let stand, covered, letting the residual heat finish cooking the rice until it is tender, about 20 minutes.

• While the rice stands, bring the coconut milk, the remaining ½ cup of palm sugar, and the salt just to a boil in another saucepan, over medium heat, stirring to dissolve the sugar. Pour ⅓ cup of water into a small bowl, sprinkle with the cornstarch, and stir until dissolved. Gradually stir the cornstarch mixture into the simmering coconut milk and return to a full boil, stirring constantly. Remove the coconut sauce from the heat and stir in the vanilla.

- Fluff the rice with a fork and stir in about half of the coconut sauce, enough to coat and moisten the rice without being runny. Let the rice stand until the sauce is absorbed, about 20 minutes. Reserve the remaining sauce. (The rice can be prepared up to 6 hours ahead, stored at room temperature. Do not refrigerate, or the rice will harden.)

- To serve, pack the rice in a lightly oiled 1/2-cup measure and unmold in the center of a serving plate. Surround with mango slices, and spoon a tablespoon or so of the reserved coconut sauce over and around the rice. Repeat with the remaining rice, mangoes, and sauce. Sprinkle each with the sesame seeds and coconut, if using, and serve immediately.

NOTE: If you wish, mix 1/2 cup of light brown sugar, packed, and 3 tablespoons of maple syrup and use instead of the palm sugar.

Jaggery Rice Pudding

Makes 4 servings

• •

RICE PUDDING SEEMS to be a take-it-or-leave-it dessert. When I was a kid, I was definitely in the "leave it" camp, as I could tell that it was left-over rice boiled in milk and sugar. As an adult, I have learned what I consider the proper way to make rice pudding: fresh, with cardamom (add a 3-inch cinnamon stick, too, if you like), and without any milk. Serve this warm, and you will see what I mean.

1/2 cup medium-grain rice, such as
   Arborio

4 tablespoons (1/2 stick) unsalted
   butter

3/4 cup crushed jaggery

1/4 cup chopped cashews

1/2 teaspoon freshly ground cardamom
   (see page 127)

- Bring the rice and 2 cups of water to a boil in a medium-size saucepan over high heat. Lower the heat to low and cover. Cook for 15 minutes (the rice will not be quite tender at this point).

- While the rice is cooking, clarify the butter. Heat the butter in a small saucepan over medium heat until it is boiling with small brown specks. Remove from the heat. Skim off the foam from the surface, and carefully pour off clear yellow clarified butter into a small bowl, leaving the browned bits at the bottom of the pan. You should have 3 tablespoons of clarified butter. If necessary, add plain melted butter to make up the difference. Set aside in a warm place so the clarified butter stays melted.

- Stir 2$\frac{1}{2}$ tablespoons of the clarified butter and the jaggery into the rice. Cook until thickened and custardlike, stirring every 2 minutes or so, about 12 minutes.

- Heat the remaining 1$\frac{1}{2}$ teaspoons of clarified butter in a small skillet over medium-high heat. Add the cashews and cook, stirring often, until lightly toasted, about 2 to 3 minutes.

- Spoon the hot pudding into serving bowls, top with the cashews and ground cardamom, and serve hot.

Quick Butterscotch Pots de Crème

Makes 6 servings

. . . .

SILKY SMOOTH *pots de crème* (literally, French for "pots of cream") custards are made with just a few ingredients so the creaminess is accentuated. Just as there are egg/no-egg versions of ice cream and gelato custards, so, too, can pudding-style desserts be made with or without eggs. These butterscotch *pots de crème* come together in no time and need no baking, offering the home cook a last-minute pudding option. They get an extra creamy boost from Greek yogurt, which is thicker than the regular variety.

2 cups half-and-half

⅔ cup muscovado or dark brown
   sugar, packed

2 tablespoons cornstarch

¾ cup plain Greek yogurt or sour
   cream

1 teaspoon vanilla extract

Pinch of fine sea salt

- Combine the half-and-half and sugar in a medium-size saucepan. Sprinkle with the cornstarch and whisk to dissolve. Bring to a boil over medium heat, stirring almost constantly for 3 minutes, being sure to reach into the corners of the saucepan with the tip of the whisk.

- Whisk together the yogurt, vanilla, and salt in a medium-size bowl. In three equal additions, whisk in the half-and-half mixture. Divide among six 6-ounce (¾-cup) *pots de crème* cups or ramekins. Cover each with plastic wrap and refrigerate until chilled and set, at least 1 hour. (The *pots de crème* can be made up to 1 day ahead.)

Passion Fruit Soufflé

Makes 6 soufflés

••••••••••••••••••••••••••••

I INCLUDE THIS recipe in honor of the role that Hawaii played in supplying sugar to the West Coast. In Hawaii, the purple fruit that mainlanders call passion fruit is known as *lilikoi*, and it is beloved in many desserts, including these elegant soufflés—just the kind of thing one might order at a Maui resort. Ripe passion fruit is dimpled, not smooth. To get to the fabulously fragrant and exotic tasting pulp, cut each fruit in half and scoop it out. The seeds are edible, so don't strain them out. You will only get about 1 tablespoon of pulp from each fruit, so buy accordingly. Otherwise, look for yellow-orange frozen passion fruit pulp at Latino markets (where it may be labeled *maracuya*).

Softened butter, for the ramekins

1/2 cup unstrained passion fruit pulp (from about 10 fruit) or thawed frozen puree

3/4 cup granulated sugar, plus more for the ramekins

1 1/2 tablespoons fresh lime juice

4 large eggs, separated, plus 1 large egg white, at room temperature

- Position a rack in the center of the oven and preheat to 375°F. Butter the insides of six 6-ounce (3/4-cup) ramekins with the softened butter. Coat with the sugar, tapping out the excess sugar. Place the ramekins on a baking sheet.

- Whisk together the passion fruit pulp, 1/4 cup of the sugar, and the lime juice in a small bowl. Let stand for 10 minutes, then whisk again to dissolve the sugar. In another bowl, whisk the egg yolks until they are pale and thickened, about 1 minute. Whisk in half of the passion fruit mixture. Transfer the remaining passion fruit mixture to a small serving pitcher and set aside at room temperature.

- Using an electric mixer at low speed, beat the egg white in a medium-size bowl until foamy. Increase the mixer speed to high and beat until soft peaks form. One tablespoon at a time, beat in the remaining $1/2$ cup of sugar, just until the peaks are stiff and glossy. Using a large rubber spatula, stir one-third of the meringue into the passion fruit mixture to lighten it until almost, but not completely, incorporated. In two equal additions, gently fold in the remaining whites.

- Divide the mixture among the ramekins and smooth the tops. Run your forefinger along the inside edge of each ramekin to level the soufflé mixture so the soufflés will rise evenly.

- Bake until the soufflés are puffed and golden brown, 14 to 18 minutes. Using tongs, quickly but carefully transfer each ramekin to a plate. Serve immediately, allowing each guest to puncture the soufflé and pour in the passion fruit mixture from the pitcher. Writhe in ecstasy.

Candy

8

*O*F ALL THE ways that a cook can create something delectable from plain sugar, perhaps candy shows the transformation at its most magical. Most candies are made from the same handful of ingredients—such dairy products as butter and milk; chocolate; and often fruit, nuts, and/or coconut. It is how these ingredients are cooked and combined with sugar that makes candy.

Why is candy cooked to specific temperatures? As sugar syrup cooks, the liquid evaporates away and the temperature rises. The higher the temperature, the denser the syrup, and the firmer it will be when it cools. Different stages of syrup cooking have names that are based on the "cold-water test," which was used to establish the syrup's consistency before the arrival of thermometers in home kitchens. (A little of the hot syrup dropped into ice water will set into a soft ball, or what have you. See "Sugar Syrup Stages" on page 179 for details.)

A few rustic candies in this chapter don't require a candy thermometer; however, most are made from sugar syrup cooked to a specific temperature. Get a reliable candy thermometer. Styles include plaques, dials on stems, and digital thermometers. Buy whichever kind is easiest for you to read. One common problem with candy thermometers is that they must be submerged deep into the cooking syrup to obtain an accurate reading, as the sensor is often an inch or so from the bottom of the thermometer. If this happens, tilt the pan so the syrup collects in a deep pool around the bottom end of the thermometer, and this might help the accuracy. And double-check with the cold-water test.

When melting sugar into syrup, you will be warned not to stir after the sugar in the syrup has come to a boil. Stirring will encourage the sugar crystals to dissolve, but after that point, if you stir the syrup, it will want to attach itself to any foreign object, such as a spoon, and recrystallize. For this reason, a saucepan of cooking sugar syrup is swirled by the handle to combine the ingredients, and never stirred. When you make fudge and certain other candies, the syrup is deliberately stirred to encourage a specific amount of crystallization that gives the candy the desired texture. Some ingredients, such as corn syrup and butter, serve to discourage sugar crystallization in syrup, so that's why they are included in so many candy recipes.

A single grain of sugar can start a chain of recrystallization, so be sure to wash down any crystals that form on the sides of the saucepan with a pastry brush dipped in cold water. Really press the brush bristles against the crusty crystals so they dissolve.

One last word of advice: Do not try to make candy on a humid or rainy day. Sucrose (table sugar) that has been melted becomes an invert sugar (inverted into glucose and fructose). As invert sugar absorbs humidity from the atmosphere, your candy would never set up properly.

With these simple rules in mind, you are well on your way to make candies to fill up the candy dish. During the holidays, is there any food gift more welcome than a tin of homemade candy? Not at my house.

Sugar Syrup Stages

As SUGAR SYRUP cooks and liquid in the syrup evaporates, its density increases as the sugar concentration rises. At different stages of cooking, if the syrup is dropped into ice water, it will set into specific shapes, and these signify the texture of the finished candy. Even if a candy thermometer is used, it is a good idea to use the cold-water test as a second confirmation.

Note that you do not have to cook the syrup to a single temperature; there is a range of a few degrees within each stage. The higher the temperature, the more evaporation and the denser the syrup, but the mixture will still behave within the expectations of its category.

To do the cold-water test, set a glass with ice water near the stove. Be sure to remove the ice cubes from the water, as any syrup that was to fall on them would set too rapidly and behave inaccurately. Without stirring the syrup, quickly scoop up about 1/2 teaspoon of the hot syrup and pour it into the water. How the syrup sets up will indicate its approximate temperature. Let the syrup cool for a moment or two, then use your fingers to pick it up and evaluate the texture.

Candy temperatures are given for sea-level cooking. For every 500 feet above sea level, subtract 1°F.

Thread Stage

230° to 235°F
Sugar concentration: 80%

This temperature is not used often in candy making. The syrup forms a thin, liquid thread.

Soft-Ball Stage

235° to 240°F
Sugar concentration: 85%

Fudge, fondant (used as a candy filling and cake coating), and pralines are cooked to this temperature. The syrup forms a mass that sinks to the bottom of the water, and can be shaped into a flexible ball.

(continues)

Firm-Ball Stage

245° to 250°F
Sugar concentration: 87%

Caramels are cooked to the firm-ball stage. The syrup can be shaped into a firm but malleable ball.

Hard-Ball Stage

250° to 265°F
Sugar concentration: 92%

Divinity and marshmallows are two of the candies cooked to the hard-ball stage. When the syrup is removed from the water, it can be manipulated into a hard ball that doesn't yield easily to pressure.

Soft-Crack Stage

270° to 290°F
Sugar concentration: 95%

Butterscotch is an example of a candy that is cooked to the soft-crack stage. You can tell that the syrup is reaching soft-crack stage by its appearance, as the surface bubbles become small and thick as the syrup thickens. The syrup forms threads in the water that, when removed, remain flexible when bent.

Hard-Crack Stage

295° to 305°F
Sugar concentration: 99%

With virtually all of the water cooked out of the syrup, candies cooked to this stage will be very firm. Lollipops and the coating for candied apples are cooked to this stage. The syrup dripped into cold water will make threads that will be quite brittle when removed from the liquid. This is the highest temperature used in candy recipes.

Caramel

After 320°F, all liquid is evaporated, and the sugar concentration reaches 100 percent. After this point, the sugar begins to break down into different compounds, and it will eventually turn brown and become caramel. These compounds are what give caramel its unique taste, which is more complex than the strictly sweet sugar syrup. Caramel is made without a thermometer because it is easier to gauge this stage by look (deep amber, about the color of a copper penny) and smell (sharp, but not burned), and a thermometer just gets in the way.

Mumbai Caramels with Cashews and Coconut

Makes 1¼ pounds caramels

All across India you'll find this sweet treat, known as *burfi*. My version is quick to make and requires no special equipment or thermometers. Be sure to use cardamom seeds freshly ground in a spice grinder, as their aromatic flavor breaks down quickly. The finished caramels should be individually wrapped for the best storage—and they'll make a gorgeous gift from your kitchen, too. You can use waxed paper, but make them special with colored foil or cellophane, available at craft shops. (The online candy supply shop Sugarcraft, at www.sugarcraft.com, has an especially large variety.)

8 tablespoons (1 stick) unsalted butter

¾ cup (3 ounces) coarsely chopped cashews or pistachios

2 cups crushed jaggery, or 1½ cups light brown sugar, packed

2 cups desiccated or shredded coconut flakes

⅓ cup whole milk, heated above lukewarm

25 green cardamom pods, seeds removed and ground (1½ teaspoons ground cardamom)

½ teaspoon fine sea salt

- First, clarify the butter. Cook the butter in a medium-size saucepan over medium-high heat just until it boils and a layer of foam forms on the top. Remove from the heat. Let stand a few minutes. Skim off and discard the foam from the top. Pour the clear yellow melted butter into a glass measuring cup, leaving the milky solids behind in the pan. You should have ⅓ cup of clarified butter.

- Lightly brush an 8-inch square metal baking pan with some of the clarified butter.

- Heat 1 tablespoon of the clarified butter in a medium-size saucepan over medium heat. Add the cashews and cook, stirring often, until they are toasted, 2 to 3 minutes. Transfer the cashews to a plate.

- Return the pan to the stove and lower the heat to low. Add the jaggery and coconut. Cook, stirring constantly, until the sugar is melted (it will pull together into a mass) and the coconut is browned, about 4 minutes. Carefully stir in the milk and stir until the melted sugar dissolves and the mixture is smooth. Stir in the remaining clarified butter with the cashews, cardamom, and salt. Increase the heat to medium-high and cook, stirring constantly, until the mixture stiffens and pulls away from the sides of the pan, about 8 minutes. Spread the hot caramel in the baking pan.

- Let stand for 5 minutes. Using a buttered knife, score the caramels into sixty-four 1-inch squares. Cool completely. Cut through the scoring marks into individual pieces and remove from the pan. Wrap each piece in aluminum foil or waxed paper. Store in an airtight container for up to 1 week.

Karen's Spiced Cashew Suca-Nuts

Makes 2 cups nuts

· ·

IN THIS RECIPE from pastry chef Karen DeMasco, two sweeteners are used, as each has properties unique from the other. To create a simple syrup to coat the nuts, Karen uses granulated sugar, which melts easily. But to give her spicy candied cashews toasty flavor and a gentle crunch, she adds Sucanat, which will *not* dissolve. Serve a bowl of these with cocktails and watch them disappear—actually, they'll disappear regardless of the accompanying beverage.

¼ cup granulated sugar

Nonstick cooking spray, for the
    baking sheet

2 cups (8 ounces) unsalted cashews

⅓ cup Sucanat

2 teaspoons chile powder

1 teaspoon ground cumin

½ teaspoon kosher salt

Pinch of cayenne

- Make a simple syrup: Bring the sugar and ¼ cup of water to a boil in a small saucepan over high heat, stirring until the sugar dissolves. Boil, without stirring, for 2 minutes. Let cool completely.

- Position a rack in the center of the oven and preheat to 300°F. Lightly spray a baking sheet with the cooking spray.

- Place the cashews in a medium-size bowl, add 3 tablespoons of the simple syrup (discarding the remainder or save for another use), and toss to coat.

Mix the Sucanat, chile powder, cumin, salt, and cayenne in a small bowl, sprinkle over the nuts, and toss. Spread on the baking sheet.

- Bake, stirring every 7 minutes or so, until the nuts smell lightly toasted, about 25 minutes. Let cool completely. (The nuts can be stored in an airtight container at room temperature for up to 1 week.)

MIX IT UP

Sweet Spice Suca-Nuts: Omit the chile powder, cumin, and cayenne, and substitute 1 1/2 teaspoons of vanilla extract and 1 teaspoon of ground cinnamon.

Smoky Pumpkin Seed Brittle

Makes about 1½ pounds brittle

··

I FIND THE combination of sweet and spicy tantalizing, and this riff on peanut brittle tells the story in broad, flavorful strokes. The brittle gets its light texture from the chemical reaction between the alkaline baking soda and the acidic syrup—be sure to use a tall saucepan to allow room for the syrup to foam when the baking soda is added. *Pimentón de La Vera*, Spanish paprika made from oak-smoked peppers, provides the underlying smoky note. It is not as unusual as you might think—look for it labeled simply "smoked paprika" in the spice section of your supermarket, at specialty food stores, or online.

Vegetable oil, for the baking sheet

1½ cups granulated sugar

¾ cup light corn syrup

2 cups (8 ounces) raw green pumpkin
   seeds (*pepitas*)

1½ teaspoons smoked paprika
   (*pimentón de La Vera*) or chile
   powder

2 teaspoons kosher salt

1 tablespoon butter

1½ teaspoons baking soda, sifted

- Lightly yet thoroughly brush a baking sheet and a metal spatula with the vegetable oil.

- Stir together the sugar, 1 cup of water, and corn syrup in a tall, heavy-bottomed medium-size saucepan. Bring to a boil over low heat, stirring to help dissolve the sugar. Stop stirring, cover, and cook for 3 minutes.

Uncover and attach a candy thermometer and boil until the thermometer reads 260°F.

- Meanwhile, toss together the pumpkin seeds, smoked paprika, and salt in a small bowl. When the syrup reaches 260°F, add to the saucepan, along with the butter. Cook, stirring almost constantly, until the syrup reaches 295°F.

- Remove from the heat and carefully stir in the baking soda, which will make the syrup foam and sputter. Immediately pour the mixture onto the baking sheet, using your other hand to spread it as thinly as possible with the metal spatula as you pour. Cool for 5 minutes, then run the spatula under the candy to prevent sticking. Cool completely. Crack into bite-size pieces. (The brittle can be stored in an airtight container at room temperature for up to 1 week.)

Creamy Chocolate and Almond Toffee

Makes 1½ pounds toffee

. . . .

I'M LUCKY ENOUGH to have various friends and relatives who, come holiday season, turn up with a tin of delectable homemade toffee. But if it gets late in the season, and I haven't yet received any, I'll make this creamy, slowly melting version. The small amount of rum in the toffee isn't really a flavoring, but the alcohol does act as a fixative to heighten the flavors.

Nonstick cooking spray, for the pan

1¾ cups granulated sugar

1 cup heavy cream

⅛ teaspoon cream of tartar

8 tablespoons (1 stick) unsalted butter, cut into tablespoon-size chunks

2 tablespoons dark rum

6 ounces bittersweet chocolate, chopped finely

1 cup (4 ounces) coarsely chopped roasted salted almonds

- Line the bottom and sides of a 9 by 13-inch metal baking pan with aluminum foil. Spray the foil and a metal icing spatula with the cooking spray.

- Combine the sugar, cream, and cream of tartar in a heavy-bottomed, medium-size saucepan and bring to a boil over medium-high heat, stirring just until the sugar dissolves. Add the butter, stir until it melts, and cover. Cook for 3 minutes. Uncover and attach a candy thermometer.

Boil, washing down any sugar crystals that form on the sides of the pan with a pastry brush dipped in cold water, until the thermometer reads 270°F. Remove from the heat and stir in the rum.

- Pour the toffee mixture into the pan and let it spread naturally to fill the pan. Cool for 5 minutes. Sprinkle the chocolate over the top and let it stand until softened, about 3 minutes. Spread the chocolate evenly over the toffee. Sprinkle with the almonds. Let cool completely.

- Invert and unmold the toffee onto a cutting board, and peel off the foil. Cut or break the candy into chunks. (The toffee can be stored in an airtight container at room temperature for up to 2 weeks.)

Brown Sugar Meringue Kisses

Makes about 6½ dozen meringues

• •

CRISP ON THE outside, and slightly gooey within, meringues are a very useful addition to any home baker's repertoire. Meringue kisses can be a little on the innocuous side, but this version, with brown sugar, gives them a much bolder flavor. They can be served on their own, or as accompaniments to ice cream or sorbet.

4 large egg whites, at room
temperature

1 teaspoon vanilla extract

⅛ teaspoon fine sea salt

⅛ teaspoon cream of tartar

⅔ cup light brown sugar, packed,
ground to a powder in a food
processor

- Position racks in the upper and lower thirds of the oven and preheat to 200°F. Line two baking sheets with parchment paper or silicone baking mats.

- Beat the egg whites in a medium-size bowl with an electric mixer at low speed until the whites are foamy. Add the vanilla, salt, and cream of tartar, and increase the speed to high. Beat just until soft peaks form. Beat in the sugar, 1 tablespoon at a time, until stiff, shiny peaks form.

- If using parchment paper, use a dab of the meringue batter under the corners of the parchment to keep it in place. Fit a large pastry bag with a ½-inch-wide open star tip. Holding the end of the tip about ¼ inch above the baking sheet, pipe 1¼-inch-wide stars, 1 inch apart, onto the baking sheets.

- Bake, rotating the meringues from top to bottom and back to front halfway through baking until the meringues look set, about 1 hour and 15 minutes. Turn off the oven. If you like meringues slightly soft in the center, let them stand for 15 minutes in the oven. If you prefer dry and crisp meringues, leave them in the oven, without opening the oven door, for about 2 hours or overnight. Transfer the sheets to wire cooling racks and let cool completely. (The meringues can be stored in an airtight container at room temperature for up to 1 week.)

Cocoa-Almond Meringues

Makes about 3½ dozen meringues

• •

ANOTHER VARIATION on the meringue theme, these are wonderful served with vanilla ice cream or sorbet. Try them as a mix-in with ice cream and chocolate sauce for a grown-up sundae.

3½ ounces bittersweet chocolate, chopped

4 egg large whites, at room temperature

1 teaspoon vanilla extract

⅛ teaspoon cream of tartar

¾ cup superfine sugar

½ cup chopped almonds, toasted (see page 154)

2 tablespoons cocoa powder, either Dutch-processed (alkalized) or natural

• Melt the chocolate in the top part of a double boiler over hot, not simmering, water. Remove from the heat and let cool until tepid.

• Position racks in the upper and lower thirds of the oven and preheat to 200°F. Line two baking sheets with parchment paper or silicone baking mats.

• Beat the egg whites in a medium-size bowl with an electric mixer at low speed until the whites are foamy. Add the vanilla and cream of tartar, and increase the speed to high. Beat just until soft peaks form. Beat in the sugar, 1 tablespoon at a time, until stiff, shiny peaks form. Fold in the nuts, chocolate, and cocoa. The meringue will deflate a bit, but that's fine.

- If using parchment paper, use a dab of the meringue batter under the corners of the parchment to keep it in place. Drop the meringue by 1¼-inch-wide dollops, 1 inch apart, onto the baking sheets.

- Bake, rotating the meringues from top to bottom and back to front halfway through baking until the meringues look set, about 1 hour and 15 minutes. Turn off the oven. If you like meringues slightly soft in the center, let them stand for 15 minutes in the oven. If you prefer dry and crisp meringues, leave them in the oven, without opening the oven door, for about 2 hours or overnight. Transfer the sheets to wire cooling racks and let cool completely. (The meringues can be stored in an airtight container at room temperature for up to 1 week.)

MIX IT UP

Cocoa Meringue Kiss Sandwiches: Melt 4 ounces of coarsely chopped bittersweet chocolate in a heatproof bowl over hot, not simmering, water. Remove from the heat. Using the back of a spoon spread melted chocolate over the smooth side of a meringue kiss, and sandwich with a second kiss. Place on a waxed paper–lined baking sheet and let stand until the chocolate sets. Makes about 20 cookies.

Brown Sugar Divinity

Makes 4 dozen pieces

. . . .

Divinity, with its melt-in-your-mouth creaminess, highlighted with chunks of nuts (try it with pistachios sometime), is really a kind of meringue, with syrup beaten into the egg whites. A good dose of corn syrup keeps the meringue from drying out completely and contributes to its chewy texture.

1½ cups light brown sugar, packed

1 cup granulated sugar

½ cup light corn syrup

2 large egg whites

¼ teaspoon cream of tartar

1 teaspoon vanilla extract

1 cup (4 ounces) coarsely chopped
   roasted and salted almonds

- Line a baking sheet with parchment paper or a silicone baking mat.

- Combine the brown and granulated sugars, corn syrup, and ½ cup of water in a heavy-bottomed, medium-size saucepan. Bring to a boil over high heat, stirring just until the sugars dissolve. Cover and boil for 3 minutes. Uncover and attach a candy thermometer to the pan. Cook without stirring, brushing down any crystals that form on the sides of the pan with a pastry brush dipped in cold water, until the temperature reaches 255°F.

- While the syrup is boiling, using an electric mixer at low speed, beat the egg whites until foamy. Add the cream of tartar, increase the speed to high, and beat until stiff peaks form.

- If you wish, carefully pour the hot syrup into a glass measuring cup to make it easier to pour. With the mixer set at medium speed, beat the hot syrup in a steady stream into the whites. Beat until the divinity has thick-

ened and cooled, almost to room temperature. Beat in the vanilla, then
3/4 cup of the nuts.

- Using two teaspoons, drop the mixture to form 1-inch-round spoonfuls.
  Press a few almond chunks into the top of each candy. Let stand until set,
  about 2 hours. (The divinity can be stored between sheets of waxed or
  parchment paper in an airtight container at room temperature for up to
  1 week, or refrigerated for up to 2 weeks.)

Flowery Lemon Lollipops

Makes 15 lollipops

• •

Homemade lollipops are much easier to make than you might think. Here, colorful edible flower petals are encased in the clear candy, making them look almost like flowers in amber. Try other color and flavor combinations, but use ones that will make sense to the eye and palate. Citrusy lemon goes well with yellow, orange, or white blossoms (such as marigold, nasturtium, or basil flowers); you might want to pair purple Johnny-jump-ups with grape. These are pretty and feminine and would make a lovely favor at a bridal or wedding shower, wrapped in cellophane. Lollipop molds, sticks, candy flavoring oils, and cellophane candy bags are available at crafts shops, cake and candy supply stores, and online at www.sugarcraft.com. Be sure to use only edible flower petals that have never been sprayed with insecticides or other chemicals.

15 lollipop sticks

About 1 tablespoon marigold petals (available at specialty food stores, or use unsprayed petals from your garden)

1 cup granulated sugar

1/3 cup light corn syrup

1 teaspoon lemon candy flavoring

Yellow food coloring (optional)

• Use lollipop molds according to manufacturer's instructions. Alternatively, invert two large baking sheets and line the upended bottoms with parchment paper. Arrange the lollipop sticks around the outside edge of each baking sheet, placing them well apart, letting the bottom ends of the sticks hang over the edges of the baking sheet. Place a few petals at the top of each stick.

- Combine the sugar, corn syrup, and $1/3$ cup of water in a heavy-bottomed, medium-size saucepan. Attach a candy thermometer to the pan. Bring to a boil over medium-high heat, stirring until the sugar dissolves. Cook, without stirring, occasionally swirling the pan by the handle and washing down the crystals that appear on the sides of the pan with a pastry brush dipped in water, until the syrup reaches 295°F. Remove the pan from the heat and let cool to 280°F.

- Add the lemon flavoring and a drop or two of food coloring, if using. Swirl the pan by the handle to incorporate the flavoring (and coloring). Immediately pour pools of the hot syrup over the petals, being sure that the syrup encloses the top end of the lollipop stick. If the syrup becomes too cool to pour, reheat it over low heat, but do not stir.

- Let the lollipops stand until completely cooled and hardened. Lift from the parchment. (The lollipops can be stored, separated with waxed paper, in an airtight container for up to 3 days. If serving as a party favor, slip each lollipop in a small cellophane candy bag and tie closed with a ribbon.)

Cinnamon Candied Apples

Makes 6 apples

. . . .

GLEAMING WITH A glassy coating, candied apples require nerve to take the first bite. Once you've taken the plunge, the apple juices mingle with the candy to melt it a little, and eating becomes less nerve-racking. Use attractive apples, as the skin's pattern will be seen through the clear candy—the Pink Lady variety is striated and tasty, and a fine choice. Smallish apples work best, as they are easier to dip in the hot syrup.

6 wooden caramel apple sticks
   (page 199, see Note)

6 small to medium-size apples, washed
   and dried

2 cups (8 ounces) toasted and coarsely
   chopped walnuts (see page 129),
   optional

2½ cups granulated sugar

⅓ cup light corn syrup

1 teaspoon oil of cinnamon (page 199,
   see Note)

- Insert a wooden stick into each apple, from the bottom to top of the fruit, allowing the remaining stick to protrude from the base to serve as a handle. Line a baking sheet with parchment paper or a silicone baking mat. If using, put the walnuts in a medium-size bowl and place near the baking sheet.

- Bring the sugar, corn syrup, and 1 cup of water to a boil in a heavy-bottomed, medium-size saucepan over high heat, stirring just until the sugar dissolves. Attach a candy thermometer to the pan. Boil without stirring until the mixture reaches 295°F on the thermometer. Remove from the heat and let cool slightly.

- Add the oil of cinnamon and swirl the pan by its handle to combine. Tilt the pan slightly so the syrup collects in a deep pool on one side of the pan. One at a time, holding an apple by the stick, dip into the syrup, coating the fruit completely. If using the nuts quickly dip the apple in the walnuts to coat on the sides (but not the bottom, or the apple won't stand) and place, stick up, on the baking sheet. If the syrup cools and thickens too much to dip and coat the apples, return it to low heat until it is fluid again. You may have leftover syrup, but don't make less, or you won't have enough to submerge the apples. Let stand until the coating cools completely. The apples are best the day they are made. Do not refrigerate.

NOTE: Wooden craft sticks and oil of cinnamon (do not use cinnamon extract, which will evaporate and lose flavor from the high syrup temperature) are available at crafts and candy-making stores, and online from www.sugarcraft.com.

Chocolate–Demerara Fudge

Makes 1½ pounds fudge

• •

MAKING FUDGE is a simple exercise in melting crystallized sugar with chocolate, milk or cream, and corn syrup, then recrystallizing the sugar, accomplished by cooling and then beating the chocolate mixture. The combination of granulated and demerara sugar yields a fudge with bright flavor notes of caramel.

Vegetable oil, if using aluminum foil, for brushing

1 cup demerara sugar

1 cup granulated sugar

¾ cup half-and-half

¼ light corn syrup

¼ teaspoon salt

6 ounces bittersweet chocolate (with a cacao content of about 65%), chopped

2 ounces unsweetened chocolate, chopped

2 tablespoons unsalted butter

2 teaspoon vanilla extract

1 cup walnuts, toasted (see page 129) and chopped (optional)

- Line the sides and bottom of an 8-inch square baking pan with parchment or aluminum foil. If using foil, brush lightly with the oil.

- Combine the demerara and granulated sugar, half-and-half, corn syrup, and salt in a heavy, 3-quart saucepan. Cook over medium heat, stirring constantly, until boiling. Cover and boil without stirring for 3 minutes. Remove the pan from the heat, uncover, and add the bittersweet and unsweetened chocolates. Stir until the chocolates melt completely. Return the pan to medium-high heat and attach a candy thermometer to the pan. Cook, without stirring, until the thermometer reads 238°F. If sugar crystals form inside the pan, brush them down with a pastry brush dipped in warm water.

- Remove from the heat and let stand until cooled to 110°F. This will take over an hour. Transfer the chocolate mixture to the bowl of a heavy-duty standing mixer fitted with the paddle attachment. (Or, keep in the bowl and use a hand mixer with a strong motor for the next step.) Add the butter and vanilla and beat at medium speed until the fudge loses its gloss, 2 to 5 minutes. Mix in the nuts, if using. Turn out the fudge into the prepared pan and smooth the surface. Let cool at room temperature or in the refrigerator until firm, about 2 hours.

- Invert the pan onto a cutting board and peel off the parchment or foil. Cut the fudge into 1-inch squares. Store in an airtight container for 2 to 3 weeks.

Raw Cacao Truffles

Makes about 3 dozen truffles

....

THE RAW FOODS movement has spawned some exemplary culinary inventions with the dessert course yielding some of the most crowd-pleasing results. As many sweeteners are heated (and therefore not raw) during processing, it is a challenge to make a "raw" dessert. *Yacón* is the perfect sweetener for the proponents of this cuisine, since is not heated above 104°F. It has an earthy quality that goes well with raw cacao.

1¼ cups raw cacao nibs (page 203, see Note)

1½ cups raw almonds, sliced

Pinch of fine sea salt

⅓ cup "virgin" coconut oil (page 203, see Note)

6 tablespoons raw *yacón* syrup

1½ teaspoons pure vanilla extract

1 cup finely grated fresh coconut, for rolling truffles

• Grind the cacao nibs, almonds, and salt in the work bowl of a food processor for several minutes, until powdery. Remove and reserve 2 tablespoons of the mixture. Add the coconut oil to the processor bowl and continue to mix, slowly pouring the *yacón* syrup and vanilla through the feed tube. The mixture should pull together into a ball. Stop and scrape the sides as you go, to ensure even mixing.

• To form and roll the truffles: Toss the reserved cocoa and almonds with the cup of coconut and place in a small bowl. Scoop and roll the truffle mixture into walnut-size balls, about 1¼ inch in diameter. Roll and press the truffles in the bowl, pressing gently yet firmly to ensure they are evenly coated. Place the finished truffles on a platter or sheet pan and allow to sit for a few minutes. Store at room temperature in an airtight container for up to 5 days or freeze for up to 2 months and allow to warm to room temperature to serve.

NOTE: Raw cacao nibs are small chunks of coarsely chopped cacao beans—they are not sweetened or roasted. There are roasted cacao beans, too, so if you are making this recipe because you want to cook with raw foods, double-check the label. Coconut oil can be heated during processing, so again, look for a brand that clearly states that it has been processed without heat. It may be labeled "virgin" or "traditional-method." You can find both raw cacao nibs and coconut oil at www.wildernessfamilynaturals.com

Buenos Aires Dulce de Leche

Makes about 1¾ cups "thin" or
1¼ cups "thick" dulce de leche

• •

I EXPECTED TO enjoy a recent trip to Buenos Aires, but I didn't count on loving the local cuisine. My sweet tooth appreciated the Argentinean habit of topping almost every dessert with a thick layer of caramel-like *dulce de leche*. You can buy *dulce de leche* at Latino markets, but it is easy and fun to make your own. Depending on how long it is cooked, the sauce can be pourable (just right for ice cream) or spreadable (slather it on toast or croissants for a sweet breakfast). While I store the bulk of my homemade *dulce de leche* in the refrigerator, I keep a small container of it at room temperature (where it will not spoil for a day or so) to stir into tea or even snack on when no one is looking.

1 quart whole milk

1⅔ cups granulated sugar

½ teaspoon baking soda

1 vanilla bean, cut into ¾-inch
   lengths (page 222, see Note)

• Combine the milk and sugar in a tall, heavy-bottomed, medium-size saucepan. Bring to a simmer over medium heat, stirring often. Remove from the heat and carefully stir in the baking soda and vanilla (the mixture will bubble up). Return to medium-low heat.

• Cook, stirring every 10 minutes, until the mixture has reduced to a thick but pourable sauce (it will look like a vat of bubbling tar), 50 to 60 minutes. Remove from the heat. (For a thicker, spreadable *dulce de leche*, continue cooking, stirring every 5 minutes, until the sauce is very thick, about 20 minutes more. To check the consistency, drop ¼ teaspoon of the hot sauce into a glass of ice water—it should seize into a soft droplet.) Using kitchen tongs, remove the vanilla pieces.

- Let cool completely. The *dulce de leche* can be stored in an airtight container in the refrigerator for up to 3 weeks. To serve, scoop out the desired amount and reheat in a small saucepan or in a microwave oven until warm.

NOTE: Substitute vanilla extract for the vanilla bean, if you wish. Cook the *dulce de leche* to the desired thickness, then stir in 1 tablespoon of vanilla extract.

9

Frozen Desserts

*I*CE-COLD DESSERTS are delightful to our palates because ice creams, sorbets, and the like literally provide a shock to our system. We don't eat frigid food with regularity, and the element of surprise works hand-in-hand with the creamy texture and sweet flavor to make a frozen dessert a special treat.

There may be some pretty good ice cream at the supermarket (is there anyone who hasn't eaten a pint of their favorite flavor in one sitting?), but homemade ice cream is in a class by itself. You can be in control of what goes in it—the ripest, tastiest fruit in season, the perfect sweetener, the richest cream. Actually, when I make frozen desserts, I don't always reach for the heavy cream in the refrigerator; some of my favorites are made with soy milk products. These make ice "creams" with luscious body that are both lactose-free and have fewer calories.

Icy temperatures dull your taste buds. When making a base that will be frozen into an ice cream, sorbet, or granita, it must be very sweet to compensate for this phenomenon. So don't be surprised if a taste of the un-frozen base seems too sweet. More than being only a sweetener, sugar also works to discourage ice crystals from forming in frozen mixtures.

If you love to make desserts, and you don't have an ice-cream maker, I encourage you to invest in one. There are many types on the market, from inexpensive models with inserts that require overnight freezing to pricey machines with self-contained freezing systems. But not all frozen desserts require an ice-cream maker, and I have included some granitas and other iced goodies that you can make in your refrigerator's freezer compartment.

Panela Ice Cream with Cinnamon Caramel Sauce

Makes about 1 quart, 4 to 6 servings

• •

THIS MAKES THE perfect ending to a Mexican-themed dinner, but it is too delicious to reserve for an ethnic menu. Perhaps you like *dulce de leche* ice cream? Even though this isn't quite *dulce de leche*, the double dose of caramel in this homemade version is sure to become a new favorite. In fact, thanks to the *panela*'s sassy flavor, you may like it even more.

Panela Ice Cream

2 cups whole milk

⅔ cup crushed *panela* or dark brown sugar, packed

5 large egg yolks

1½ cups heavy cream

2 teaspoons vanilla extract

Cinnamon Caramel Sauce

½ cup grated *panela* or dark brown sugar, packed

½ teaspoon ground cinnamon, preferably freshly ground

1 cup heavy cream

3 tablespoons unsalted butter

⅛ teaspoon fine sea salt

• To make the ice cream, bring the milk and *panela* to a simmer over medium heat, stirring to dissolve the sugar. Do not boil, or the mixture could curdle.

• Whisk the egg yolks in a medium-size bowl and whisk until they are pale yellow and thickened. Whisk in the cream. Gradually whisk in the hot milk mixture, then return to the saucepan. Cook over medium-low heat, stirring constantly with a wooden spatula, until the custard is thick enough to coat the spoon (an instant-read thermometer inserted in the mixture should read 185°F). Strain through a wire sieve into a bowl and stir in the vanilla. Place a piece of plastic wrap directly on the surface of the custard, and pierce a few holes in the plastic. Let cool until tepid, then refrigerate until chilled, at least 4 and up to 24 hours. (Or, place the covered bowl of hot custard in a larger bowl of ice water and let stand, stirring occasionally, until chilled, about 1 hour.)

- To make the caramel, stir the *panela* and cinnamon together in a heavy-bottomed, medium-size saucepan. Whisk in the cream, then add the butter and salt. Cook over medium-low heat, stirring often, until the sugar and butter begin to melt. Increase the heat to medium and stir constantly until the caramel has thickened and turns a rich golden brown, about 7-minutes. Do not overcook or leave unattended, as it burns easily. Remove from the heat and let cool until tepid but still pourable.

- Freeze the custard in an ice-cream machine according to the manufacturer's directions. Transfer half of the ice cream into an airtight, freezer-safe container. Drizzle about 1/4 cup of the caramel into the ice cream, top with the remaining ice cream and another 1/4 cup of the caramel, and fold the ice cream and caramel together with a few strokes to create swirls. Freeze for at least 4 hours. (The ice cream can be frozen for up to 5 days.)

- To serve, warm the remaining caramel in a small saucepan over low heat. Scoop the ice cream into individual bowls, and top with the warm caramel.

Pomegranate Marble Ice Cream

Makes about 1 quart

. . . .

POMEGRANATE JUICE has so much going for it—a fruity tang, lots of vitamin C and antioxidant properties, and a gorgeous red-purple color. I use it here to make a sensational marbled ice cream. The corn syrup bonds with the granulated sugar to keep the pomegranate "marble" gooey and caramel-like. To ensure that its color isn't muted, use granulated sugar.

2 cups unsweetened pomegranate juice

1⅓ cups granulated sugar

2 tablespoons corn syrup

2 cups whole milk

1 cup heavy cream

6 large egg yolks

2 teaspoons vanilla extract

Natural red food coloring (optional)

- Bring the juice and ½ cup of the sugar to a boil in a wide, nonreactive medium-size saucepan over medium-high heat. Simmer until reduced to ¾ cup, about 20 minutes. (Measure frequently to be sure that you don't reduce the pomegranate syrup to less than ¾ cup, or the mixture will be too firm to flow smoothly.) Stir in the corn syrup and let cool completely.

- Combine the milk, cream, and remaining sugar, minus 2 tablespoons, in a medium-size saucepan and cook over medium heat, stirring just until the sugar dissolves. Meanwhile, whisk the egg yolks with the remaining 2 tablespoons of the sugar until the yolks are pale yellow and thickened. Whisk in about 1 cup of the hot milk mixture, then whisk the yolk mixture into the saucepan. Cook over medium-low heat, stirring constantly with a wooden spatula, until the custard is thick enough to coat the spoon (an instant-read thermometer inserted in the mixture should read

185°F). Strain through a wire sieve into a bowl. Stir in half of the cooled pomegranate syrup and the vanilla. Place a piece of plastic wrap directly on the surface of the mixture, and pierce a few holes in the plastic. Let cool until tepid, then refrigerate until chilled, at least 4 and up to 24 hours. (Or, place the covered bowl of hot custard in a larger bowl of ice water and let stand, stirring occasionally, until chilled, about 1 hour. The syrup may sink somewhat, so give the custard a good stir before freezing.)

• Freeze the pomegranate custard in an ice-cream machine according to the manufacturer's directions. Transfer half of the ice cream into an air-tight, freezer-safe container. Drizzle about half of the pomegranate syrup into the ice cream, top with the remaining ice cream and the remaining syrup, and fold the ice cream and syrup together with a few strokes to marbelize. Freeze for at least 4 hours. (The ice cream can be frozen for up to 5 days.)

NOTE: While the pomegranate syrup is a vivid color, the ice cream base may be a bit pale for some. A few drops of natural red food coloring will pump up the color. Stir it in along with the vanilla!

Strawberry-Balsamic Ice Cream

Makes about 1 quart

. . . .

It is not a very-well kept secret that strawberries and balsamic vinegar are made for each other, as the fruitiness of the former is complemented by the complex sweet-tartness of the latter. This ice cream takes the pairing one step further and tops fresh strawberry ice cream with a balsamic vinegar–brown sugar syrup. It is important to let the berries macerate in the syrup so the sugar can break down the cellulose and soften the berries, otherwise they will freeze into hard bits.

1 cup balsamic vinegar

$1/2$ cup light brown or muscovado
    sugar, packed

1 pint strawberries, hulled and
    chopped coarsely

$1 1/2$ cups whole milk

$1 1/2$ cups heavy cream

1 cup granulated sugar

5 large egg yolks

2 teaspoons vanilla extract

- Bring the vinegar and brown sugar to a boil in a nonreactive small saucepan over high heat, stirring to dissolve the sugar. Lower the heat to medium-low and cook at a brisk simmer until reduced to a scant 1 cup, about 15 minutes. (Do not inhale deeply near the mixture while it is boiling, as the steam can be irritating.) Pour into a bowl and let cool completely.

- Combine the berries and $1/3$ cup of the syrup in another bowl. Let stand at room temperature until the berries soften, stirring occasionally, at least

1 and up to 4 hours. Save the remaining syrup for another use (page 211, see Note).

- Combine the milk, cream, and $1/2$ cup of the granulated sugar in a medium-size saucepan. Cook over medium heat, stirring often, until the sugar is just melted. Meanwhile, whisk the egg yolks with the remaining $1/2$ cup of sugar until pale yellow and thickened. Whisk in about 1 cup of the hot milk mixture, then whisk the yolk mixture into the saucepan. Cook over medium-low heat, stirring constantly with a wooden spatula, until the custard is thick enough to coat the spoon (an instant-read thermometer inserted in the mixture should read 185°F). Strain through a wire sieve into a bowl. Stir in the vanilla. Place a piece of plastic wrap directly on the surface of the mixture, and pierce a few holes in the plastic. Let cool until tepid, then refrigerate until chilled, at least 4 and up to 24 hours. (Or, place the covered bowl of hot custard in a larger bowl of ice water and let stand, stirring occasionally, until chilled, about 1 hour.)

- Freeze the custard in an ice-cream machine according to the manufacturer's directions. Transfer half of the ice cream into an airtight, freezer-safe container. Top with half of the strawberries and their syrup. Repeat with the remaining ice cream, berries, and syrup, and fold together with a few strokes to marbelize. Freeze for at least 4 hours. (The ice cream can be frozen for up to 5 days.)

NOTE: The remaining balsamic syrup can be covered and refrigerated for up to 1 month. Serve it as an accompaniment to cheese, fruit, and nuts. Do not try to make a smaller amount of syrup, as it could scorch before it reduces to the proper viscosity.

Raspberry Sorbet Cream

Makes about 4 servings

• •

ONE OF THE simplest, and most luscious, desserts is summer berries, sweetened with honey, topped with cream. Why not transform the trio into a a cool, refreshing, and vividly hued frozen dessert? And you won't need an ice-cream maker. Honey does not freeze solid, helping create a creamy texture. One caveat—if the cream is held for much longer than 8 hours before serving, it will crystallize, so serve it within a few hours after combining the fruit puree and whipped cream.

3 cups fresh raspberries

1/2 cup mild honey, such as raspberry,
    blackberry, or tupelo

2 tablespoons fresh lemon juice

3/4 cup heavy cream

- Mix the raspberries and honey in a bowl. Let stand until the berries release some juices, about 1 hour. Transfer to a food processor fitted with the metal chopping blade, add the lemon juice, and puree. Pour into a metal bowl or pan, cover with plastic wrap, and freeze until solid, at least 6 and up to 18 hours.

- Break up the frozen mass with a spoon or fork and place in a food processor or blender. Process until smooth and creamy. Using an electric mixer at high speed, whip the cream in a chilled bowl until it holds soft peaks. Fold three-quarters of the frozen fruit mixture into the whipped cream. Freeze the remaining sorbet and cover the bowl of "sorbet cream" and freeze that until scoopable, at least 1 and up to 4 hours before serving. Divide the two mixtures evenly into clear tumblers or martini glasses, with a small scoop of the vivid red raspberry sorbet at the bottom and the pale "sorbet cream" on top. It is best served in the first few hours. After that it will crystallize and lose its creamy texture but still taste good and refreshing.

Chocolate-Soy Milk "Gelato"

Makes about 1 quart

. . . .

I HAD MY doubts about a non-dairy gelato, until I took my first bite. Because the soy milk and creamer are so lean, they don't get in the way of the chocolate, which really asserts itself. High-quality bittersweet chocolate (use one with a cacao content of 60 to 70 percent) and organic sugar gives this gelato superior flavor. Gelato, the infamously rich Italian ice cream, is never made with eggs, rather always with cream. Although this "gelato" does not contain dairy products, it is also eggless and thereby qualifies for its Italian name.

2 cups nondairy soy creamer

1/3 cup organic granulated sugar

3 tablespoons cornstarch

2 teaspoons vanilla extract

Pinch of fine sea salt

1 cup soy milk

7 ounces bittersweet chocolate, chopped

- Combine the soy creamer and sugar in a heavy-bottomed, medium-size saucepan. Sprinkle with the cornstarch and whisk to dissolve. Bring to a simmer over medium heat, stirring constantly with a wooden spatula. Lower the heat to low and simmer, stirring often, until lightly thickened, about 3 minutes. Remove from the heat and pour into a medium-size bowl. Stir in the vanilla and salt.

- Bring the soy milk to a low boil, remove from heat, and add the chocolate. Stir until smooth and blended and strain into the soy creamer mixture, stirring until combined. Let cool until tepid, then refrigerate until chilled, at least 4 and up to 24 hours. (Or, place the covered bowl of hot custard in a larger bowl of ice water and let stand, stirring occasionally, until chilled, about 1 hour.)

- Freeze the chocolate mixture in an ice-cream machine according to the manufacturer's directions. Transfer to an airtight, freezer-safe container. Freeze for at least 4 hours. (The gelato can be frozen for up to 5 days.)

Green Tea Ice "Cream"

Makes about 1 quart, 4 to 6 servings

● ●

POWDERED GREEN TEA (*matcha*) and soy milk pair beautifully, and authentically, to concoct a gently flavored ice milk. (Without any cream, I cannot truly call it ice *cream*.) Although you can make this with half-and-half, the smooth soy milk mellows the herbal notes of green tea so well that I suggest that you make it in the Japanese way. The delicate flavor of the green tea would be overpowered by caramel-flavored sweeteners, so granulated sugar, the most neutral sugar of all, is the best choice.

3 cups soy milk

2/3 cup granulated sugar

1½ to 2 tablespoons powdered
   green tea (*matcha*)

6 large egg yolks

¼ teaspoon fine sea salt

- Combine the soy milk and ⅓ cup of the sugar in a heavy-bottomed, medium-size saucepan, and bring to a simmer over low heat, stirring often. Put the green tea in a small bowl and whisk in a few tablespoons of the heated soy milk to make a paste. Whisk in a few more tablespoons to thin the paste, then pour into the saucepan and mix well.

- Whisk the yolks, the remaining ⅓ cup of sugar, and the salt in a medium-size bowl until they are pale yellow and thickened. Whisk in about ½ cup of the hot soy milk mixture, then whisk the egg mixture into the saucepan. Cook over medium-low heat, stirring constantly with a wooden spatula, until the green tea mixture is thick enough to coat the spoon (an instant-read thermometer inserted in the mixture should read 185°F). Strain through a wire sieve into a bowl. Place a piece of plastic wrap directly on the surface of the mixture, and pierce a few holes in the plastic. Let cool until tepid, then refrigerate until chilled, at least 4 and up to 24 hours. (Or, place the covered bowl of hot custard in a larger bowl of ice water and let stand, stirring occasionally, until chilled, about 1 hour.)

- Freeze the mixture in an ice-cream machine according to the manufacturer's directions. Transfer to an airtight, freezer-safe container. Freeze for at least 4 hours. (May be frozen for up to 5 days.)

Madeira Granita

Makes about 1 quart, 6 to 8 servings

••••••••••••••••••••••••••••

MADEIRA IS A fortified wine in the style of port or sherry and can be enjoyed as an aperitif or after dinner. Mixed with a simple sugar syrup that not only sweetens the wine but keeps it from freezing solid, it can be made into a sophisticated dessert for wine-lovers. As the wine itself has a note of dried fruit, brown sugar muddles the flavors, so keep the tastes clean with granulated sugar. Serve it with plain cookies, such as the Maple–Pine Nut Shortbread (page 123).

1 cup granulated sugar

1 cup Madeira

2 oranges

2 teaspoons fresh lemon juice

- Place an 8-inch square metal baking pan and a metal serving spoon in the freezer and freeze while preparing the granita mixture.

- Bring 2 cups of water and the sugar to a boil in a medium-size saucepan over high heat, stirring often until the sugar dissolves. Lower the heat to medium and cook at a brisk simmer for 3 minutes. Pour into a medium-size bowl set in a larger bowl of ice water and let stand until chilled, about 1 hour.

- Grate the zest from one of the oranges. Squeeze the juice from both oranges, and measure out $1/2$ cup. Stir the Madeira, orange juice and zest, and lemon juice into the chilled syrup.

- Pour the mixture into the chilled pan and leave the spoon in the pan. Freeze until ice crystals form around the edge of the mixture, about 1 hour, and stir well. Freeze until the edges are icy again, about 1 hour more. Stir again, and freeze until the mixture is slushy, about 1 hour longer. (The granita can be made up to 2 hours ahead, stirred every hour or so.) Scrape up the granita with the cold spoon and serve immediately in dessert bowls.

Mango-Pineapple Mojito Granita

Makes 6 servings

• •

THE INDISPUTABLE popularity of the mojito proves my point about people loving sweet things. For a very adult dessert, serve this tropical fruit granita, sweetened with fruity agave, topped with a heady mash of rum and mint leaves.

Mango-Pineapple Granita

¾ pound fresh mango, peeled, pitted, and cut in bite-size chunks

1½ cups unsweetened pineapple juice

1¼ cups agave syrup

¼ cup fresh lemon juice

Mojito Muddle

Approximately 36 mint leaves

2 tablespoons agave syrup

¼ cup fresh lime juice

½ cup silver rum

- To make the granita, place an 8-inch square metal baking pan and a metal serving spoon in the freezer and freeze while preparing the granita mixture.

- In batches, puree the mango, pineapple juice, agave syrup, and lemon juice in a blender until smooth, and pour into the chilled pan. Mix well, and leave the spoon in the pan. Freeze until ice crystals form around the edge of the mixture, about 1 hour, and stir well. Freeze until the edges are icy again, about 1 hour more. Stir again, and freeze until the mixture is slushy, about 1 hour longer. (The granita can be made up to 2 hours ahead, stirred every hour or so.)

- To make the mojito muddle, mash the mint and 1 tablespoon of the agave syrup in a small bowl with a pestle or a wooden spoon until the mint is broken up and releases its juices. Stir in the remaining syrup. Stir in the lime juice and rum. Taste and add more agave syrup, if desired.

- Divide the mojito muddle among six decorative cocktail glasses, such as martini glasses. Scrape up the granita with the cold spoon, add equal amounts to the glasses, and serve immediately.

Snowcapped Espresso Granita

Makes 6 to 8 servings

· ·

ALL OVER HAWAII, "shave ice" parlors (which serve what is known in parts of the mainland as *snow cones*) always offer the option of "snow-capping" your selection with a dollop of condensed milk. To my mind (and taste buds), it is much better to skip the canned stuff and add your own sweet cream topping to the icy cold flavors on hand. Espresso granita takes well to a snowcap.

> ¾ cup hot brewed espresso or
>   Italian-roast coffee
> ¾ cup demerara sugar
> 1 teaspoon vanilla extract
> ⅔ cup heavy cream

- Place an 8-inch square metal baking pan and a metal serving spoon in the freezer and freeze while preparing the granita mixture.

- Combine the hot coffee with ½ cup plus 2 tablespoons of the sugar in a medium-size bowl and stir until melted. Stir in 1½ cups of water and the vanilla. Pour the mixture into the chilled pan and leave the spoon in the pan. Freeze until ice crystals form around the edge of the mixture, about 1 hour, and stir well. Freeze until the edges are icy again, about 1 hour more. Stir again, and freeze until the mixture is slushy, about 1 hour longer. (The granita can be made up to 2 hours ahead, stirred every hour or so.)

- Meanwhile, heat the cream with the remaining 2 tablespoons of the sugar in a small saucepan over medium heat, stirring just until the sugar dissolves. Pour into a small pitcher and let cool completely.

- Scrape up the granita with the cold spoon, transfer to glass tumblers or dessert bowls, and top with a generous drizzle of the cream. Serve immediately.

Sugar Cone Ice-Cream Bowls

Makes about 1 dozen cups

· ·

I<small>T'S A LOT</small> of fun to make crispy brown cookie cups just like the ones in fancy ice-cream shops. The procedure calls for a bit of dexterity, as you need to shape hot fresh-baked cookies over custard cups while they are still pliable, but you will get the hang of it. You will need six 10-ounce (1¼ cup) custard cups or similarly sized bowls or cups without handles, to mold the cookie bowls.

4 tablespoons (½ stick) unsalted butter

¼ cup granulated sugar

3 tablespoons mild or robust molasses

½ cup unbleached all-purpose flour,
   preferably organic

½ teaspoon ground cinnamon

Pinch of fine sea salt

2 teaspoons dark rum

- Position a rack in the center of the oven and preheat to 325°F. Line two baking sheets with parchment paper or silicone baking mats.

- Combine the butter, sugar, and molasses in a small saucepan. Cook over medium heat, stirring often, until the butter is melted. Sift the flour, cinnamon, and salt together in a medium-size bowl. Add the melted butter mixture and rum, and stir just until mixed into a relatively thin batter.

- Since the cookies cool and firm up quickly, making them difficult to mold, it is best to bake them one sheet at a time. Turn six 10-ounce custard cups upside down on a work surface. For three cookie bowls, drop 3 heaping tablespoons of the batter onto a baking sheet, spacing them well apart. Using a small offset metal spatula or the back of a spoon, spread each portion of batter into a thin 3½-inch round. Bake until the cookies are lightly browned around the edges, about 12 minutes. Let the cookies cool on the sheet for a minute, then drape each over a custard cup, molding each warm cookie to the shape of the cup. Let cool until firm and crisp, about 5 minutes.

- Carefully remove the cookie bowls from the custard cups. Repeat with the remaining batter. (The cookie bowls can be stored in airtight containers—they are very delicate, so do not stack them—at room temperature for up to 5 days.)

10

Savory and Sweet Main Courses

*M*OST COOKS THINK of sugar and its relatives as single note foods: sweet, and nothing more. But smart cooks know that sweeteners have many roles in the kitchen, even in so-called savory dishes. I refer to the sweet-and-sour sauces in old school Chinese-American restaurants as well as dishes relatively new to our shores, such as the caramel-sauced recipes of Vietnam. The key is skillfully blending the sweetener with sour, spicy, bitter, and salty ingredients, to create a delicate balance.

The dishes in this chapter are international, but a few areas show up most often. Asian cooks in particular have learned how to juggle sugar with such salty condiments as soy or fish sauce and such sour liquids as yuzu or tamarind juice. Latino cooks also love to use sugar in recipes to temper the heat of chiles.

Sweetness, if not sugar itself, plays a frequent part in savory cooking. Some cooks incorrectly refer to the tasty brown, slightly sweet crust of cooked protein foods (meat, poultry, chicken, and even eggs) as being caramelized. Actually, sugar has nothing to do with it. This phenomenon is called the *Maillard reaction*, after the French scientist who discovered that certain foods will brown and taste sweet when heated past a certain point. It seems that the chemical composition of the browned crust is similar to, but not exactly, sucrose, which is why the food tastes sweet without the addition of any sweeteners. But the recipes in this chapter capitalize on the undisguised use of sweeteners to achieve the harmony of sweet and savory.

Chicken Satay

Makes 6 to 8 appetizer servings

• •

THIS GRILLED meat-on-a-stick started out as one of the great street foods, sold by vendors all over Thailand (not to mention other Southeast Asian countries). With plenty of spice in both the marinade and peanut dip, sugar helps round out the flavors. Grilling over coals adds smokiness, and that is the classic way to make satay. However, for a weeknight meal, I often just sauté the strips and serve them over steamed rice with the sauce spooned on top, and a cucumber and red onion salad dressed with rice vinegar and a sprinkle of grated palm sugar. If you grill, it helps to wear flameproof gloves to turn the skewers, as the heat can sometimes get a little intense.

Satay Marinade

1 teaspoon ground turmeric or mild curry powder

1 teaspoon ground coriander

1 teaspoon ground cumin

1 teaspoon fine sea salt

2 tablespoons canned coconut milk

1 tablespoon palm sugar, grated

1 tablespoon vegetable oil

1 tablespoon Asian fish sauce, such as *nam pla* or *nuoc mam*

1½ pounds boneless and skinless chicken breasts

Wooden skewers, soaked in water for at least 30 minutes, drained

Satay Sauce

1 tablespoon canola oil

1 teaspoon crushed red pepper flakes, or more to taste

1 teaspoon Thai red curry paste, or more to taste

1¼ cups canned coconut milk

¾ cup natural creamy peanut butter

2 tablespoons palm sugar, grated if necessary

2 tablespoons fresh lime juice

Lime wedges and fresh cilantro leaves, for garnish

- To make the marinade, whisk together the turmeric, coriander, cumin, and salt in a medium-size bowl. Add the coconut milk, palm sugar, oil, and fish sauce, and whisk to combine.

- Slice the chicken across the grain into $1/4$-inch-thick strips. Toss the chicken in the marinade. Cover and let stand for 20 minutes at room temperature, or refrigerate for up to 6 hours.

- To make the satay sauce, warm the oil over medium heat in a small skillet. Add the red pepper flakes and stir until fragrant, about 1 minute. Stir in the curry paste and coconut milk and bring to a simmer. Adjust the heat to medium-low and cook at a steady simmer until the milk's oil separates and rises to the surface, about 10 minutes. Lower the heat to low and whisk in the peanut butter, palm sugar, and lime juice. Whisk until slightly thickened. Remove from the heat. If the sauce is too thick, thin with a little coconut milk or water. Transfer to a serving bowl for dipping (or individual bowls, if you prefer), and let stand at room temperature for up to 2 hours.

- Build a medium-hot fire in an outdoor grill. Thread the chicken onto the drained skewers. Discard any leftover marinade. Lightly oil the grill grate. Place the chicken skewers on the grill and cover. Grill the chicken, turning once, until cooked through, about 3 minutes.

- Transfer to a platter and garnish with the lime wedges and cilantro. Serve immediately, with the satay sauce passed for dipping.

TIP FROM A PRO

Wooden skewers for grilling must be soaked in water for at least 30 minutes to hydrate them, or else they'll burn up when placed over the fire. So they are ready to go when you are, store soaked and drained skewers in a plastic bag in the freezer. They also seem to retain more water and burn less easily than skewers that are freshly soaked.

Chile-Rubbed Agave Chicken

Makes 4 servings

. . . .

AT OPPOSITE ENDS of the taste spectrum, hot and sweet can harmonize together very nicely. In this case, ancho chile already has a sweet note of its own that is accented by the agave syrup. This simple chicken dish will bring lots of bold flavor to table, especially when served with a side dish of roasted sweet potatoes.

3 tablespoons pure ground ancho chile

2 teaspoons ground cumin

1 teaspoon garlic powder

1/8 teaspoon cayenne

1 teaspoon fine sea salt

4 chicken breast halves, with skin and bone (about 10 ounces each)

1 1/2 tablespoons canola oil

1/2 cup chicken stock, preferably homemade, or use low-sodium broth

3 tablespoons agave syrup

Lime wedges, for garnish

- Mix together the ground chile, cumin, garlic powder, cayenne, and salt. Using a small paring knife, working with one breast at a time, cut the meat away from the bones in one piece, keeping the skin attached. Place a boned breast between two pieces of plastic wrap, and pound gently with a flat meat pounder until the breast is about 3/4 inch thick. Rub the chile mixture all over the breasts.

- Heat the oil in a large skillet over medium heat until the oil is hot but not smoking. Place the chicken in the skillet, skin side down. Cook until the underside is well browned, about 4 minutes. Turn and cook until the other side is browned, about 3 minutes longer. Add the stock and agave syrup, being careful that the liquid doesn't boil over. Lower the heat to medium-low and cover. Cook until the chicken feels firm when pressed in the center, about 3 minutes longer.

- Transfer the chicken to dinner plates and pour the juices on top. Serve immediately with the lime wedges.

Vietnamese Caramel Chicken

Makes 4 servings

· ·

A BELOVED DISH of Vietnamese cuisine, this sweet-salty-spicy sauce may have complex flavors, but it is very easy to make. In fact, consider it when you want something a little exotic for a weeknight supper. Caramelizing the palm sugar gives it a savory bitter note that allows it to mesh with the salty fish sauce. Do try to make this with palm sugar, which has a much more interesting flavor than supermarket brown sugar. Serve over hot jasmine rice with steamed sugar snap peas.

¾ cup palm sugar or light brown sugar, packed

1 cup chicken stock, preferably homemade or use low-sodium broth

3 tablespoons Asian fish sauce, such as *nam pla* or *nuoc mam*

2 tablespoons vegetable oil

4 chicken leg quarters, skinned

½ cup sliced shallots

2 tablespoons minced lemongrass (page 228, see Note)

1 tablespoon peeled and minced fresh ginger

3 garlic cloves, minced

1 small Thai or serrano chile, cut crosswise into thin rounds

Hot cooked jasmine rice, for serving

• Combine the palm sugar and 3 tablespoons of water in a small saucepan. Bring to a boil over medium-high heat, stirring until the sugar is melted. Cook without stirring, occasionally swirling the pan by the handle, until the sugar is very dark brown and smells lightly caramelized, 2 to 3 minutes. (The caramelization will be hard to determine by look, as the sugar is already dark, so just go by smell, taking care not to overcook and burn the sugar.) Remove from the heat. Carefully add the chicken stock and fish sauce (the caramel will bubble up and harden). Return to low heat and cook, stirring constantly, until the caramel melts, about 1 minute. Remove from the heat again.

- Heat the oil in a large Dutch oven over medium-high heat. In batches without crowding, add the chicken and cook, turning once or twice, until lightly browned, about 6 minutes. Transfer to a platter. Add the shallots, lemongrass, ginger, garlic, and chile, and cook just until the shallots wilt, about 1 minute. Stir in the caramel mixture. Return the chicken to the Dutch oven and cover.

- Cook until the chicken is tender and shows no sign of pink when pierced at the bone with the tip of a knife, 35 to 40 minutes. Serve the chicken and sauce spooned over the rice.

NOTE: Lemongrass gives many Asian dishes an ineffable citrus aroma and flavor. To prepare it, trim off the bottom end of the stalk, make a shallow incision down the side of the stalk, and peel off the tough outer layer. Cut off and discard the woody top where it meets the tender bottom portion. Mince the bottom portion.

Pineapple-Ginger Beef on Vegetable Soba Noodles

Makes 4 servings

• •

THIS SIMPLE AND full-flavored glaze is extremely versatile. Here, it adds a sweet sheen to grilled beef and is also used to flavor a soba noodle and vegetable stir-fry. Try it as a marinade for chicken, pork, or even tofu, but do not soak the food for longer than four hours, as the acids in the pineapple could begin to break down the proteins and make the end product mushy.

Pineapple-Ginger Sauce

1 1/2 cups pineapple juice

1/4 cup muscovado or light brown sugar, packed

3 tablespoons soy sauce

3 tablespoons peeled and shredded fresh ginger (use a box grater)

1/2 teaspoon crushed hot red pepper flakes

1 1/2 pounds flank steak

1/2 pound soba noodles

2 tablespoons Asian dark sesame oil

2 tablespoons soy sauce

Nonstick cooking spray, for the broiler rack

2 tablespoons peanut or vegetable oil

5 ounces snow peas, trimmed

2 carrots, cut on the diagonal into very thin slices

3 scallions, white and green parts, sliced thinly

Sesame seeds, for garnish

• To make the pineapple-ginger sauce, combine the pineapple juice, brown sugar, soy sauce, ginger, and red pepper in a stainless-steel or enameled cast-iron saucepan. Bring to a boil over high heat, stirring to dissolve the sugar. Lower the heat to medium. Cook at a brisk simmer, stirring occasionally, until reduced to 1 cup, about 15 minutes. Strain through a wire sieve into a small bowl, pressing hard on the solids. Let cool completely.

- Measure out and reserve half of the pineapple-ginger sauce. Pour the remaining sauce into a zippered plastic bag. Add the steak and close the bag. Refrigerate for at least 2 and up to 4 hours.

- Bring a large pot of lightly salted water to a boil over high heat. Add the soba noodles and cook until they are almost tender, about 4 minutes. Be careful not to overcook them—they should be a bit chewy, as they will be stir-fried. Drain and rinse under cold running water. Drain again, then toss with the sesame oil and soy sauce.

- Meanwhile, position the broiler pan about 6 inches from the source of heat and preheat the broiler. Lightly oil the broiler rack. Remove the steak from the marinade and discard the marinade.

- Broil the steak, turning once or twice, until it shows only a resistance when pressed in the center with a finger, about 7 minutes for medium-rare meat. Transfer to a carving board and let stand for 5 minutes.

- Meanwhile, heat a very large skillet or wok over high heat until very hot. Add the peanut oil and swirl to coat the skillet. Add the snow peas and carrots with 2 tablespoons of water and stir-fry until the vegetables are crisp-tender and the water has evaporated, about 1 minute. Stir in two of the scallions, then the noodles and reserved ginger sauce. Stir-fry until the noodles are hot, about 1 1/2 minutes.

- Divide equal amounts of the noodles among four deep bowls. Using a sharp knife held at a slight diagonal, cut the steak into thin slices. Top each serving with an equal amount of beef. Sprinkle with the reserved scallion and the sesame seeds. Serve immediately.

Asian-Style Braised Pork Belly

Makes 4 servings

• •

PORK BELLY IS from the same cut of pork that gives us bacon, but it isn't cured or smoked. It is a favorite of Chinese cooks who prize it for its luscious texture, even if it is quite fatty. During its long braise, the pork soaks up the flavors in the pot and becomes meltingly tender. Serve the pork and its deeply flavored sauce spooned over rice with a slightly bitter cooked green vegetable, such as broccoli rabe. This recipe was given to me by my friend, chef Nathan Smith.

2 teaspoons peanut or canola oil

1½ pounds pork belly, rind left intact, cut in 1-inch cubes

2 tablespoons chopped fresh cilantro stems

2 garlic cloves, chopped

Grated zest of 1 lime

½ teaspoon black peppercorns

2 cups chicken stock, preferably homemade, or use low-sodium broth

⅓ cup grated palm sugar, packed, or ¼ cup light brown sugar, packed

3 tablespoons Asian fish sauce, such as *nam pla* or *nuoc mam*

2 tablespoons ponzu (page 232, see Note)

Hot cooked rice, for serving

• Heat a Dutch oven or flameproof casserole over medium-high heat until the pot is hot. Pour in the oil and tilt to coat the inside of the pan. In batches without crowding, add the pork and cook, turning occasionally, and removing the excess fat as it is rendered, until nicely browned on all sides, 12 to 15 minutes.

• Meanwhile, process the cilantro stems, garlic, lime zest, and peppercorns into a fine paste in a blender or mini food processor. When the pork is well browned, use a slotted spoon to transfer it to a platter. Pour off all but 1 tablespoon of the fat. Lower the heat to medium-low, add the cilantro paste, and stir until fragrant, about 2 minutes.

- Return the pork belly to the pot along with the stock, 1 cup of water, and the palm sugar, fish sauce, and ponzu. Bring to a boil over high heat. Return the heat to medium-low and cover. Simmer until the pork is fork tender, about 1 hour. Remove from the heat and let stand for 5 minutes. Skim off and discard the fat from the surface of the cooking liquid. (Or, let the pork cool in the pot. Cover and refrigerate until the fat hardens, at least 8 hours, and scrape off the fat. Reheat over low heat.) Spoon the rice into bowls and top with the pork and its sauce. Serve hot.

NOTE: Ponzu is a tart Japanese seasoning made from citrus juice, mirin (sweetened rice wine), bonito flakes, and other ingredients and is available at Asian grocers and supermarkets with good international foods sections.

Seared Pork Tenderloin with Tequila Adobo

Makes 6 to 8 servings

• •

THIS RECIPE FOR pork tenderloin draws on many Latino influences, from Spain to the Caribbean. The *panela* serves not just to tame the slightly bitter tequila and sour lime juice but to glaze the pork. Allow at least twelve hours to marinate the pork before roasting. Rice and black beans are the perfect accompaniment (just cook them separately and stir them together), or tuck the sliced pork into hot tortillas. It is best to use a blender and not a food processor for this liquid marinade, as the liquid tends to seep through the hole for the stem in the processor.

Tequila-Lime Adobo

1 cup gold tequila

Scant 1 cup (6 ounces) grated *panela*,
    or ¾ cup brown sugar, packed,
    plus ¼ cup mild or robust molasses

⅓ cup freshly squeezed lime juice

4 garlic cloves

1½ tablespoons pure ground ancho chiles

1½ tablespoons sweet Spanish or
    Hungarian paprika

Grated zest from 1 large orange

1½ teaspoons ground cumin

½ teaspoon ground allspice

2 teaspoons fine sea salt

3 (12-ounce) pork tenderloins,
    trimmed

2 tablespoons olive oil

2 limes, cut into wedges,
    for garnish

• To make the adobo, at least 12 hours before cooking, combine the tequila, *panela*, lime juice, garlic, ground chiles, paprika, orange zest, cumin, allspice, and salt in a blender. Process until very smooth, about 1 minute. Transfer to a small stainless-steel or enameled cast-iron saucepan and bring just to a boil over medium heat. Lower the heat to low and simmer for 10 minutes to heighten the flavors. Pour into a large glass or ceramic bowl and cool completely.

- Measure and reserve 1/2 cup of the adobo. Submerge the pork in the remaining adobo. Cover and refrigerate, turning the pork occasionally in the adobo, for at least 12 and up to 24 hours.

- Position a rack in the center of the oven and preheat to 450°F. Remove the pork from the adobo and discard the marinade. Pat the pork dry with paper towels. Heat the oil in a large ovenproof skillet over high heat until the oil is hot but not smoking. Add the tenderloins and cook, turning occasionally, until seared on all sides, 2 to 3 minutes. Place the skillet with the pork in the oven and roast, until an instant-read thermometer inserted in the center of a tenderloin reads about 140°F for medium rare or 155°F for medium well, about 15 to 18 minutes.

- Transfer the pork to a carving board and let stand for 5 minutes. Cut crosswise into 1/2-inch-thick slices. Pour the fat out of the skillet and place the pan over medium heat. Add the reserved adobo and cook, scraping up the browned bits in the skillet with a wooden spatula. Arrange the slices on a platter. Pour the carving and pan juices on top, garnish with the lime wedges, and serve hot.

Pork Chops with Honey-Miso Glaze

Makes 4 servings

• •

RED MISO IS a thick paste of fermented soybeans or barley, and it is the main component in this easy marinade for roasted pork chops. Miso is no shrinking violet and is usually diluted to make a soup, but honey smooths out its intense flavor. The chops are roasted to start the cooking, and then finished under the broiler—if broiled throughout, the glaze will burn. All you really need is a salad with these sweet-salty chops.

1/3 cup red miso

2 tablespoons honey

2 tablespoons Dijon mustard

1 tablespoon grated fresh ginger (use the medium-size holes on a box grater)

1 tablespoon soy sauce

4 center-cut (1-inch-thick) loin pork chops

Nonstick cooking spray, for the broiler rack

• Whisk the miso, honey, mustard, ginger, and soy sauce in a 10 by 15-inch glass baking dish. Add the pork chops and turn to coat. Cover and let stand at room temperature for 30 minutes. (Or refrigerate for up to 4 hours, and remove from the refrigerator 30 minutes before roasting.)

• Position a rack in the top third of the oven and preheat to 400°F. Roast the pork chops in their baking dish for 10 minutes. Turn the chops and continue roasting for 10 minutes more. Remove from the oven.

• Position the broiler rack about 8 inches from the source of heat and preheat the broiler. Spray the broiler rack with the oil spray. Remove the chops from the baking dish and place on the broiler rack. Broil, turning occasionally, until the glaze is browned and the meat shows just the barest hint of pink when pierced at the bone, 5 to 10 minutes. Serve hot.

Tamarind-Glazed Mahimahi

Makes 4 servings

• •

TAMARIND IS ONE of the essential flavors of Asian cooking, and it makes appearances in Indian and Caribbean cuisines, too. Its tart, sticky, seeded pulp is encased in thick brown pods that must be removed to get to the pulp. You can either remove the pulp from the pods, or use a jarred tamarind concentrate. You will find both the raw and "convenience" forms of tamarind at Asian, Indian, and Latino markets. Palm sugar is the sweet bridge between the sour splash of tamarind and the fiery spice of Thai red chile paste. Although the glaze is a great foil for the meaty texture of mahimahi, try it with other firm-fleshed white fish, such as snapper or tilapia. You will want to serve this with rice or noodles, to soak up every drop of the pan juices.

Tamarind Glaze

6 tamarind pods, or 2 tablespoons tamarind concentrate

1/2 cup boiling water

1/4 cup Asian fish sauce, such as *nam pla* or *nuoc mam*

3 tablespoons grated palm sugar, packed, or granulated sugar

2 teaspoons peanut or canola oil

1/2 teaspoon Thai chile paste or crushed hot red chile flakes, or more to taste

Nonstick cooking spray, for the broiler rack

4 (7-ounce) mahimahi fillets

2 garlic cloves, minced

1 teaspoon fine sea salt

• To make the tamarind glaze, remove the tamarind shells. Discard any fibrous strands, and break or cut the pulp into pieces between the seeds. Place the pulp (or the tamarind concentrate) in a small, wide-bottomed bowl and cover with boiling water. Let stand for 5 minutes. Strain through a coarse-meshed wire sieve over a bowl, reserving the soaking liquid. Using a rubber spatula, work the soaked pulp through the sieve, scraping off all of the pulp from the underside, and discard the seeds and fibers. Stir in the fish sauce and palm sugar.

- Heat the oil in a large skillet over medium heat. Add the chile paste and stir until it smells sweet, about 1 minute. Stir in the tamarind mixture. Bring to a simmer, lower the heat to medium-low, and cook to blend the flavors, about 5 minutes. Pour into a bowl and cool completely. Taste and add more chile paste, if you wish.

- Position the broiler pan about 6 inches from the source of heat and pre-heat the broiler. Line the pan with aluminum foil to help with cleanup. Generously oil the broiler rack. Season the fish all over with the garlic and salt. Place the fish on the broiler rack and brush generously with the tamarind glaze.

- Broil for 4 minutes. Turn the fish and brush again with the glaze. Continue broiling until the fish is almost opaque when pierced with a knife tip, 3 to 4 minutes more. Transfer each fillet to a dinner plate, and top with the pan juices. Serve hot.

Panela-and-Spice-Cured Salmon

Makes 6 servings

．．．．．．．．．．．．．．．．．．．．．．．．．．．．

JOSE LUIS FLORES is a master of Latino-American flavors and has worked for Miami's Ola restaurants as both pastry chef and executive chef. He grew up in Mexico City, where his mother used *panela* as the household sweetener. But it is more than nostalgia that keeps him cooking with *panela*—its rich, caramel-like taste is incomparable. This panela-spice cure for salmon illustrates not only the Mexican sugar's unique flavor profile but Jose's inventiveness. It is the alcohol in the rum that helps the flavors to penetrate the fish.

Panela-Spice Cure

   1/2 pound *panela*

   2 (3-inch) cinnamon sticks

   2 whole star anise

   2 whole cloves

   1 1/2 teaspoons yellow mustard seeds

   1/2 cup dark rum

   6 (6-ounce) salmon fillets with skin

   1/4 cup canola or peanut oil

- Make the *panela*-spice cure at least 12 hours before cooking the salmon. Combine the *panela*, cinnamon sticks, star anise, cloves, mustard seeds, and 6 cups of water in a saucepan. Bring to a boil over high heat, stirring often, to help dissolve the *panela*. Lower the heat to low and simmer to blend the flavors, about 10 minutes. Pour into a bowl and let cool completely. Stir in the rum.

- Arrange the salmon fillets in a 10 by 15-inch glass baking dish. Pour in enough of the *panela*-spice cure to cover the salmon. Cover with plastic wrap. Refrigerate, occasionally turning the salmon in the liquid, for at least 12 and up to 24 hours, the longer the better, but no more than 24 hours.

- Heat a large nonstick skillet over medium-high heat. Pour in the oil and tilt to coat the inside of the skillet. Place the salmon fillets, skin side down, in the skillet. Cook until the undersides are golden brown and crispy, 3 to 4 minutes. Turn and cook until the other side is browned and the inside of the salmon looks opaque with a hint of rose in the center when tested with a knife tip, 2 to 3 minutes more.

- Transfer each salmon fillet to a dinner plate and serve hot.

Maple-Chile Salmon

Makes 4 servings

• •

MAPLE SYRUP LENDS sweet, woodsy notes to the salmon. Broil the salmon at least eight inches from the source of heat so it cooks relatively slowly, giving the maple-chile glaze a chance to reduce without burning. As the syrup caramelizes, the salmon takes on a wonderful, slightly smoky flavor. You can use your favorite chile here, as the maple will temper extremes from mild ancho to fiery habanero nicely.

½ cup maple syrup

¼ cup Dijon mustard

2 teaspoons pure ground ancho chile, or ½ teaspoon pure ground habanero chile

4 (6-ounce) salmon fillets with skin

Canola oil, for the salmon and the broiler rack

1 teaspoon fine sea salt

½ teaspoon freshly ground black pepper

• Mix the maple syrup, mustard, and ground chile in a small bowl. Lightly oil the salmon skin. Season the salmon with the salt and pepper. Spread about one-third of the maple mixture over the flesh side of the salmon and let stand for 20 minutes. Set the remaining maple mixture aside at room temperature.

• Position the broiler rack about 8 inches from the source of heat. Lightly oil the broiler rack. Place the salmon, skin side down, on the rack. Broil until the glaze looks set, about 5 minutes. Spread with about half of the remaining maple mixture, and broil until the glaze is beginning to brown, about 3 minutes more. Spread with the remaining maple mixture and broil until the glaze is shiny and the salmon is barely opaque when flaked, about 3 minutes more.

• Transfer each fillet to a dinner plate and serve hot.

Sorghum-Glazed Sweet Potatoes

Makes 6 servings

. . . .

As a side dish to holiday turkey or ham, you can't go wrong with these glazed sweet potatoes. Unless you are from the South and grew up with it, sorghum will probably be new to your table and will garner comments from your guests who are likely to peg it as molasses. For a large crowd, make a double batch, and bake the sweet potatoes on two baking sheets.

Nonstick cooking spray, for the dish

1 large orange

1/3 cup sorghum, molasses, or honey

3 tablespoons unsalted butter

2 1/2 pounds orange-fleshed sweet
    potatoes, such as Louisiana, garnet,
    or jewel yams, peeled and cut into
    1/2-inch chunks

- Position a rack in the upper third of the oven and preheat to 400°F. Lightly oil a 9 by 13-inch ovenproof serving dish.

- Grate the orange zest. Squeeze the orange juice; you should have about 1/3 cup. Bring the orange juice, sorghum, and butter to a boil in a small saucepan over medium heat, stirring often to melt and combine the butter. Remove from the heat and stir in the orange zest. Put the sweet potatoes in the dish, drizzle with the sorghum mixture, and toss to coat.

- Bake for 30 minutes. Stir and continue baking, stirring every 10 minutes or so, until the sweet potatoes are tender and lightly browned at the edges, 20 to 30 minutes more. Serve hot.

Gado Gado Salad

Makes 4 main course or 8 appetizer servings

. . . .

Here is one of the classic dishes of Indonesian cuisine: a vegetarian salad made hearty with a spicy peanut dressing. Serve it either as a main course for a summer lunch, or a buffet offering as a side dish to grilled meat. Palm sugar and dried shrimp paste work with the peanuts to create deep sweet and salty notes that are irresistible. Use more or less vegetables as you wish, but the ones below are the traditional mixture.

Gado Gado Dressing

1/2 cup peanut or canola oil

2 shallots, sliced thinly

2 dried *chiles de árbol* (page 243, see Note)

2 garlic cloves, crushed under a knife and peeled

1 1/2 cups coarsely chopped roasted peanuts

1 cup natural peanut butter

3 tablespoons grated palm sugar, firmly packed

3 tablespoons soy sauce

2 tablespoons fresh lime juice

2 teaspoons dried shrimp paste

3/4 pound green beans, trimmed

2 large carrots, peeled and sliced thinly

4 red-skinned, medium-size potatoes, about 1 pound, scrubbed but unpeeled

1 tablespoon peanut or canola oil

1 pound firm tofu, cut in 1 by 1/2-inch strips

1 small head napa cabbage, sliced thinly

1 seedless (English) cucumber, sliced thinly

2 cups mung bean sprouts

6 hard-boiled eggs, peeled and sliced

- To make the gado gado sauce, warm the oil in a small saucepan over medium heat. Add the shallots and lower the heat to low. Fry the shallots until they are tender but not browned (the oil should form bubbles around the shallots), adjusting the heat as needed, about 6 minutes. Using a slotted spoon, transfer the shallots to a small bowl and set aside.

Add the chiles to the shallot-infused oil and cook for $1\frac{1}{2}$ minutes, then add the garlic and cook for 30 more seconds. Using the slotted spoon, discard the garlic and chilies.

- Transfer the infused oil to the work bowl of a food processor fitted with a steel blade. Add $3/4$ cup of the peanuts, the peanut butter, palm sugar, soy sauce, lime juice, shrimp paste, and reserved shallots. With the machine running, add enough water to make a thick, pourable sauce, about $3/4$ cup. Pour into a bowl and let stand at room temperature until ready to serve. (If the sauce thickens upon standing, thin it with water.) Transfer the remaining $3/4$ cup of peanuts to a bowl, to serve with the salad.

- Bring a large pot of lightly salted water to a boil over high heat. Add the green beans and cook until they are bright green and crisp-tender, about 2 minutes. Using a slotted spoon, transfer them to ice water. Add the carrots to the boiling water and cook until they are bright orange and crisp-tender, about 2 minutes. Using the slotted spoon, add to the green beans. Let stand until cooled, then drain and pat dry.

- Bring another pot of lightly salted water to a boil over high heat. Add the potatoes and lower the heat to medium-low. Cover and simmer until the potatoes are tender when tested with a knife tip, about 30 minutes. Drain and rinse under cold running water until cool enough to handle. Cut the potatoes crosswise into 14-inch-thick rounds and cool completely.

- Heat the oil in a medium skillet over medium-high heat. Add the tofu and cook, turning occasionally, until the tofu is browned, about 5 minutes. Using a slotted spoon, transfer the tofu to paper towels to drain.

- To assemble the salad, arrange the cabbage and cucumber on a large serving platter. Top with the carrots and green beans, then the bean sprouts, sliced potatoes, hard-boiled eggs, and tofu. Sprinkle with the remaining $3/4$ cup of peanuts. Serve at once, with the dressing passed on the side.

NOTE: *Chiles de árbol* are small, narrow, dried red chiles with a fairly spicy flavor profile. A staple of Mexican cooking, they are also the preferred chile in Chinese cooking—they are likely to be the whole ones you'll find in your order of General Tso's chicken. Buy them at Latino and Asian markets.

Hempseed-Crusted Tofu with Agave-Mustard Sauce

Makes 4 servings

• •

I HAVE BEEN cooking with chef and cookbook author Akasha Richmond for years. Akasha's eponymous restaurant has an impeccable reputation among Hollywood's elite as the place to turn to for healthful and delicious meals. In this meatless meal, hempseed, which is highly nutritional and loaded with amino and essential fatty acids, is used to add crunch to tofu. Nectarlike agave, blended with whole-grain mustard, makes a simple sauce.

Agave-Mustard Sauce
½ cup whole-grain mustard

⅓ cup agave syrup

Pinch of hot red pepper flakes

Vegetable or olive oil cooking spray

1 pound extra-firm tofu, sliced into ½-inch-thick slices

3 tablespoons olive oil

2 tablespoons soy sauce

½ cup unbleached all-purpose flour, preferably organic

¼ teaspoon sweet paprika

1 teaspoon fine sea salt

½ teaspoon freshly ground black pepper

¾ cup hempseeds

¾ cup dried bread crumbs, preferably whole-grain

¼ teaspoon dried thyme

½ cup unflavored soy milk

Additional cooking spray and olive oil

- To make the agave-mustard sauce, whisk the mustard, agave, and red pepper flakes in a medium-size bowl. Set aside while preparing the tofu.

- Preheat the oven to 400°F. Line a baking sheet with parchment paper and spray with the cooking spray. Arrange the tofu on the baking sheet. Mix the 3 tablespoons of the olive oil and the soy sauce in a small bowl, and drizzle over the tofu. Bake until the tofu is glazed, about 15 minutes. Let cool until easy to handle.

- Mix the flour, $1/2$ teaspoon of the salt, the paprika, and $1/4$ teaspoon of the pepper in a shallow dish. In another dish, mix the hempseeds, bread crumbs, thyme, the remaining $1/2$ teaspoon of salt, and the remaining $1/4$ teaspoon of the pepper. Pour the soy milk into a third shallow dish. One at a time, dredge a tofu slice in the flour, shaking off the excess flour. Dip in the soy milk, letting the excess soy milk drip off. Coat on both sides with the bread-crumb mixture, and place on a baking sheet.

- Heat a 12-inch skillet over medium-high heat until it is hot. Pour in 1 tablespoon of oil and heat until shimmering. In batches, add the tofu and cook, turning once, until browned on both sides, about 3 minutes, adding more oil as needed. Transfer to paper towels to drain briefly. (The tofu can be cooked up to 2 hours ahead, removed from the paper towels and stored at room temperature. Reheat on a parchment-lined baking sheet in a 350°F oven for about 10 minutes.) Serve hot, with the agave-mustard sauce passed on the side.

Mail-Order Sources

Here are some of my favorite mail-order sources for the more unusual sugars and sweeteners. However, start your search at your local supermarket, natural food store, or ethnic markets, as the range of readily available sweeteners is rapidly increasing.

Big Tree Farms
c/o WorldPantry.com, Inc.
601 22nd Street
San Francisco, CA 94107
1-866-972-6879
www.bigtreefarms.com

Producers of a wonderful Balinese coconut palm sugar, available plain and with ginger or turmeric. You may be tempted by their unusual honeys, sea salts, and peppercorns, too.

India Tree
1421 Elliott Avenue West
Seattle, WA 98119
1-800-369-4848
www.indiatree.com

Here are high-quality muscovado, demerara, and golden baker's sugars from Mauritius, as well as castor (superfine) and extra-fine fondant (powdered) sugars. They cannot be ordered directly from the site, but a store locator lists online sources.

iShopIndian.com
10633 W. North Avenue
Wauwatosa, WI 53226
1-877-786-8876
www.ishopindian.com

A reliable source for jaggery and cooking spices, such as cardamom.

MexGrocer.com, LLC
4060 Morena Boulevard, Suite C
San Diego, CA 92117
1-858-276-0577
www.mexgrocer.com

A good place to find *piloncillo*, which is sold in the smaller cones called *panocha*.

Steen Syrup
Box 339
Abbeville, LA 70510
1-800-725-1654
www.steensyrup.com

The place for mail-order Southern-style pure cane syrup.

Wholesome Sweeteners
8016 Highway 90-A
Sugar Land, TX 77478
1-800-680-1896
www.wholesomesweeteners.com

One-stop shopping for a wide array of sugars and sweeteners, produced under organic and fair trade guidelines. You can shop online for blue agave nectar, all kinds of granulated sugars, powdered sugars, brown sugars, and turbinado.

Maui Brand Sugars
P.O. Box 266
Puunene, Maui, HI 96784
1-800-735-9348 and 1-808-877-2969
www.mauibrand.com and www.hcsugar.com

One of the last sugar producers on the Hawaiian Islands, they sell natural, raw, turbinado, and premium Maui gold sugars. You can visit their historic sugar museum, too.

Yacón Syrup
www.essentiallivingfoods.com

This syrup from Peru is great for fans of raw food. I recommend an online source, as it has not turned up in most retail natural foods stores yet.

Bibliography

Macinnis, Peter. *Bittersweet*. Australia: Allen and Unwin, 2002.

McGee, Harold. *On Food and Cooking*. New York: Scribner's, 2007.

Mintz, Sidney. *Sweetness and Power: The Place of Sugar in Modern History*. New York: Penguin, 1986.

Nearing, Helen, and Scott Nearing. *The Maple Sugar Book*. White River Junction, Vermont: Chelsea Green, 2000.

Niall, Mani. *Covered in Honey*. Emmaus, PA: Rodale Press, 2003.

Ransome, Hilda. *The Sacred Bee*. New York: Houghton Mifflin, 1937.

Tannahill, Reay. *Food in History*. New York: Crown, 1973.

Toussaint-Samat, Maguelonne. *History of Food*, translated by Anthea Bell. Oxford: Blackwell Publishers, 1992.

Trager, James. *The Food Chronology*. New York: Henry Holt, 1995.

Acknowledgments

Many people—colleagues, friends, and relatives—helped in the creation of *Sweet!*

My dear friend Akasha Richmond has been with me since the very beginning of my career. She taught me more than she can ever realize, and I will always be grateful for her friendship.

My top two testers are also my sisters, Diana and Karing. It was fun messing up the kitchen with them as grown-ups.

Many bakers have provided me with constant inspiration over the years, none more so than Alice Medrich and the late Richard Sax. It is as much fun to spend time with David Lebovitz as it is to read his wonderful cookbooks. Rick Rodgers, who has written a cookbook or two himself, worked very closely with me to sweeten the manuscript to a sugary sheen. Special thanks to the restaurant chefs who provided recipes to *Sweet!*: Jose Luis Flores of Ola Miami, pastry chef Karen DeMasco, and *charcutière* Nathan Smith. I also appreciate the work of Melissa De León at www.panamagourmet.com, an excellent site about Latino cuisines.

I learned a lot about the world of sugar from Pauline McKee, Karen Stevenson, and the fantastic team at Wholesome Sweeteners. Thank you from the bottom of my heart for all of your support

Lisa Ekus, my invaluable agent, amazes me with her determination. Many thanks also to her associate, Jane Falla.

Much appreciation to Sheri Giblin and Dan Becker, who captured the images so perfectly.

Finally, an especially deep-felt thank-you goes out to Matthew Lore at Da Capo, who supported this idea from the beginning and dedicated countless hours to help this book become as good as it could be. My gratitude to the entire Da Capo team, including Cisca Schreefel, Georgia A. Feldman, Trish Wilkinson, and copy editor Iris Bass.

Index